BRAIN INJURY AND AFTER: TOWARDS IMPROVED OUTCOME

BRAIN INJURY AND AFTER: TOWARDS IMPROVED OUTCOME

Edited by

F. D. Rose

University of East London, UK

and

D. A. Johnson

Astley Ainsley Hospital, Edinburgh, UK

JOHN WILEY & SONS

Chichester · New York · Brisbane · Toronto · Singapore

Other Wiley Editorial Offices

John Wiley & Sons, Inc., 605 Third Avenue,
New York, NY 10158-0012, USA

Jacaranda Wiley Ltd, 33 Park Road, Milton,
Queensland 4064, Australia

John Wiley & Sons (Canada) Ltd, 22 Worcester Road,
Rexdale, Ontario M9W 1L1, Canada

John Wiley & Sons (Asia) Pte Ltd, 2 Clementi Loop #02-01,
Jin Xing Distripark, Singapore 0512

Library of Congress Cataloging-in-Publication Data

Brain injury and after: towards improved outcome / edited by F. David
  Rose and David A. Johnson.
      p.   cm.
    Includes bibliographical references and index.
    ISBN 0-471-95276-1 (cased)
    1. Brain damage—Patients—Rehabilitation.   I. Rose, David (F.
  David)   II. Johnson, David A.
    [DNLM: 1. Brain Injuries—therapy.   WL: 354 B813 1996]
  RC 387.5.B723   1996
  617.4/81044—dc20
  DNLM/DLC
  for Library of Congress   95-34970
                                                      CIP

British Library Cataloguing in Publication Data

A catalogue record for this book is available from the British Library

ISBN 0-471-95276-1 (cased)

Typeset in 10/12pt Palatino by MHL Typesetting Ltd, Coventry
Printed and bound in Great Britain by Biddles Ltd, Guildford
This book is printed on acid-free paper responsibly manufactured from sustainable forestation,
for which at least two trees are planted for each one used for paper production.

CONTENTS

ABOUT THE EDITORS

David Rose is Professor of Psychology and Head of the Department of Psychology at the University of East London. He has published extensively in the field of neuropsychology, and is a past Secretary of the European Brain and Behaviour Society. He is currently researching in the area of assessment and rehabilitation following brain injury.

David Johnson is Consultant Clinical Psychologist and Head of Neuro-psychology at the Astley Ainslie Hospital in Edinburgh. His particular interest is head injury in children, and in 1988 he founded the Children's Head Injury Trust. He has written extensively in the field of rehabilitation and is soon to publish a book on head injury and litigation.

LIST OF CONTRIBUTORS

DREW ALCOTT   Unsted Park Rehabilitation Centre, Munstead
                       Heath, Godalming, Surrey GU7 1UW

BILL BRAITHWAITE   Exchange Chambers, Pearl Assurance House, Derby
                       Square, Liverpool L2 9XX and 2 Crown Office Row,
                       London

MICHAEL BARNES   Centre for Rehabilitation Engineering Studies,
                       University of Newcastle upon Tyne, Hunters
                       Moor Regional Rehabilitation Centre, Hunters
                       Road, Newcastle upon Tyne NE2 4NR

DAVID JOHNSON   Department of Neuropsychology, Astley Ainslie
                       Hospital, Grange Loan, Edinburgh EH9 2HL

JULIA JOHNSON   Head Injury Rehabilitation Unit, Ticehurst House
                       Hospital, Ticehurst, East Sussex TN5 7HU

WILLIAM W. McKINLAY   Case Management Services Ltd, 17A Main Street,
                       Balerno, Edinburgh EH14 7EQ and Scotcare
                       National Brain Injury Rehabilitation Unit,
                       Edinburgh EH14 7EQ

MICHAEL ODDY   Head Injury Rehabilitation Unit, Ticehurst House
                       Hospital, Ticehurst, East Sussex TN5 7HU

DAVID ROSE   Department of Psychology, University of East
                       London, Romford Road, London E15 4LZ

HELEN SMITH   Head Injury Rehabilitation Unit, Ticehurst House
                       Hospital, Ticehurst, East Sussex TN5 7HU

MARTIN SMITH   Department of Neuroanaesthesia, The National
                       Hospital for Neurology and Neurosurgery, Queen
                       Square, London WC1N 3BG

ANDY TYERMAN   Head Injury Service, Rayners Hedge, Croft Road,
                       Aylesbury, Buckinghamshire HP21 7RD

ANNA J. WATKISS   Case Management Services Ltd, 17A Main Street,
                       Balerno, Edinburgh EH14 7EQ

JUDY YEOMANS   Head Injury Rehabilitation Unit, Ticehurst House
                       Hospital, Ticehurst, East Sussex TN5 7HU

PREFACE

When our proposal for this volume was first being considered by John Wiley & Sons, one reviewer prefaced his/her otherwise favourable comments by exclaiming, 'Oh no — not another book on brain injury!'. We do have some sympathy with this. In the last 15 years there has been a deluge of articles, papers and books on the subject. Ironically it is because there is now so much literature on brain damage that we feel a volume such as this may be of value. Let us explain.

There has always been a need to 'manage' those with head injuries. However, until relatively recently management meant little more than containment of the problem — finding an institutional niche within which those unfortunate enough to sustain disabling brain damage could spend the rest of their days in as much comfort as possible and without undue inconvenience to others. In the last 25 years the situation has changed a great deal (although, in many people's opinion, not sufficiently). Within society generally there has been an increasing acknowledgement of the rights of the disabled. There have been advances in technology, especially computer technology, which have made possible aids for the disabled which allow them to express more fully the capacities they do have. Perhaps most important of all, our view of the brain and its function has changed dramatically.

Traditionally the brain has been viewed as fixed and inflexible with virtually no capacity for repair or to adapt to damage to its own structure. Consequently any functional consequences of brain damage have been regarded as 'incurable'. Research in the last 25 years has shown this to be unduly pessimistic. Damage to the brain is always very serious, of course. However, far from being fixed, unchangable and static, we now know the brain to be a dynamic and interactive organ which is constantly changing in terms of cellular activity, neural circuitry and transmitter chemistry in response to demands placed upon it. As we have gradually come to acknowledge the adaptability and flexibility of the brain, so we have also become more interested in the possibility that the consequences of brain damage are not necessarily incurable — that some degree of recovery of function may be possible after all.

As a consequence of all these developments we have seen the emergence of a much more optimistic approach to the problems caused by head injury. The objectives of care and containment have been extended to embrace rehabilitation and, wherever possible, reintegration into family, social and employment networks. There is now a real commitment to *improving* outcome. Moreover, it is acknowledged that maximising outcome for the head-injured is not within the gift of any one profession. Outcome depends upon the contributions of ambulance personnel, paramedics and staff of accident and emergency departments. Thereafter it depends on neurosurgeons, anaesthetists, neurologists, nurses, physiotherapists, speech therapists, occupational therapists, dieticians, psychologists and psychiatrists. One can identify a further ring of professionals which includes hospital managers, lawyers, teachers and social workers, whose professional expertise can be crucial to the ultimate outcome in any given instance. As many of these groups have developed and expanded their own specialist professional literature relating to the problems of brain injury it has become more and more difficult for the non-expert (most of us, most of the time!) to gain an overview of the whole picture regarding the improvement of outcome. This brings us back to the present volume.

This is not a book for specialists seeking to gain a 'state-of-the-art' assessment of their own area of professional expertise. Rather it is for professionals and their trainees who see the value of keeping up to date with thinking and developments in other professional areas which have an impact on outcome following brain injury. Whilst most of us would applaud the intention to keep abreast of developments beyond our own particular areas, finding the time to do so is a major problem. In providing a collection of short and readable chapters on a variety of different professional areas we hope to facilitate the exchange of information. We have taken as our theme the journey from injury, through acute care, detailed assessment, rehabilitation and long-term management, to final outcome. Along the way we have examined the legal and legislative issues surrounding brain injury.

Inevitably we have failed to cover everything of relevance to improving outcome. There was clearly a case for including chapters devoted to physiotherapy, speech therapy and occupational therapy, for example. That they do not appear here should not be taken to imply that their potential for contributing to outcome is in any way underestimated. It would also have been valuable to hear from the computer scientists and engineers whose work in the area of 'assistive technology' promises to enhance outcome very considerably. It is just a matter of space. Indeed, we believe there is a strong case for an annual publication consisting of short and readable updating reviews of developments in professional areas concerned with outcome within which there would be room for reports from all relevant groups. In the meantime we hope readers will find the following chapters of value.

We should like to thank all our authors for their forbearance whilst we have sought to meet particular criteria regarding coverage, style and readability. We should also like to thank our extremely patient publisher!

David Rose and David Johnson

1

BRAINS, INJURIES AND OUTCOME

DAVID ROSE AND DAVID JOHNSON*

*Department of Psychology, University of East London and *Department of Neuropsychology, Astley Ainslie Hospital, Edinburgh*

INTRODUCTION

The brain, more than any other part of us, defines our individuality. It is the repository of our particular and unique memories, the controller of our defining skills and abilities, the moderator of our characteristic moods and feelings, the facilitator of our interactions with our environment and our communications with our fellow human beings. Consequently, damage to the brain is always serious. All too often it is catastrophic. In total the numbers who sustain damage to the brain from traumatic brain injury, stroke and neurodegenerative diseases are considerable and the costs in economic, social and individual terms are enormous.

In this volume we will confine the discussion to just one of these categories, traumatic brain injury, which is defined as:

> ... an insult to the brain, not of a degenerative on congenital nature, but caused by an external force, that may produce a diminished or altered state of consciousness. (National Head Injury Foundation, 1985)

Frankowski, Annegers & Whitman (1985), in a review of seven major reports on the incidence of traumatic brain injury in the United States, arrived at all average incidence figure of approximately 250 per 100 000 of the population. This figure is in good agreement with statistics from Australasia and the United Kingdom. Males are twice as likely as females to suffer a traumatic brain injury and, since the peak incidence falls in the 15–24 age range, the

Brain Injury and After: Towards Improved Outcome. Edited by F.D. Rose and D.A. Johnson.
© 1996 John Wiley & Sons Ltd.

consequent problems are likely to be very long-term. Road accidents are the biggest single cause, accounting for between a third and a half of all such injuries. Other major causes are assaults and falls.

As medical science becomes more successful in increasing survival rates among those who sustain traumatic brain injury, no doubt aided by the youth and fitness of the sub-group most affected, we must look ever more closely at what lies beyond the immediate medical emergency for these patients. A concept which conveniently encompasses the variety of factors we need to take into account is that of outcome. Outcome refers to:

> ... the cumulative impact of the individual's entire personal history following onset of the condition (Fuhrer, 1987)

In other words, outcome represents the net effect of the brain injury. It refers to the steady state situation which pertains as a result of the interactive effect of a great variety of relevant factors. These include the type, location and severity of the injury, the success of the acute care interventions in the immediate aftermath of the accident and of any subsequent rehabilitation programme, the social support received by the patient from family and friends, the patient's financial state, whether the financial compensation (if any) is suitably structured and covers the costs of necessary care, accommodation and equipment which the patient may need to aid him/her in adjusting to daily life or to resume his/her occupation. However, outcome also depends on factors which are more remote from individual cases, such as the adequacy of legislation concerned with provision for disabled persons, the level of financial support for relevant scientific research, the general level of education of the public and, therefore, people's tolerance of the effects of brain damage.

Within the following pages all of these will be examined. But first we must digress to briefly consider the brain itself.

THE BRAIN

The keen interest in the brain and its workings shown by makers of television documentaries in recent years has been of great benefit to those of us whose teaching duties include the anatomy and physiology of the nervous system. There can be few readers of this volume who, from that source alone, cannot already conjure up in their 'mind's eye' a passable three-dimensional image of the brain. Nevertheless, a brief account here may be of value if only as an aide memoire. Those who wish to examine the structure and function of the brain in more detail will be spoiled for choice of suitable books. England & Wakely (1991) provide a beautifully illustrated account of the anatomy of the brain and both Nathan (1988) and Temple (1993) have written very readable introductory accounts of how function is related to structure. For coverage of structure/function relationships at a more complex level the reader is recommended to look at texts on biological or physiological psychology, for example Kalat (1995) and Pinel (1993).

Figure 1.1 shows a human brain from above, from the side and from below. In colour the brain is greyish-white and has a slightly jelly-like consistency. In a

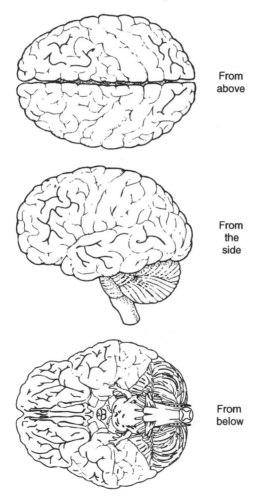

From above

From the side

From below

Figure 1.1: View of the human brain from above, the side and below

young adult male it weighs about 1 400 grams and, reflecting the lower average body weight, 1 280 grams in an equivalently aged female. The brain is protected by the skull, of course, but also by a series of membranes (the meninges) which lie between the outer surface of the brain and the inside of the skull. A third protection for the brain is provided by a fluid, cerebrospinal fluid (CSF). This is found between the middle and inner meningeal coverings (in the subarachnoid space) and also within a complex series of canals and cavities, the ventricular system, found deep within the brain. The presence of CSF both inside and outside the brain means that the whole structure is effectively suspended in fluid and this provides an effective 'cushion' against physical impact.

The brain consists of billions of cells (as well as blood vessels, fluid, etc.). These cells are of numerous different types, the most important of which, from the point of view of overall brain function, are nerve cells or neurons. Nerve cells themselves are of many different types but most have an elongated process (the axon) emanating from the body of the nerve cell and are specialised for the conduction of small electrical signals or nerve impulses which are the units of the code in terms of which the whole nervous system operates. These signals are transmitted between nerve cells by chemical neurotransmitters. Estimates of the number of nerve cells in the brain vary somewhat but 12 billion is a frequently quoted figure. In her recent Royal Institution Children's Lectures (1994), Susan Greenfield sought to emphasise this almost incomprehensible number (and the complexity of the resulting system) by suggesting there are as many nerve cells in the brain as trees in the Amazon rain forest and as many connections between those nerve cells as there are leaves on those trees. It is not clear who did the counting but we are sure you get the general idea!

The brain is made up of two large, more or less symmetrical, cerebral hemispheres mounted on a central core or stalk of tissue which is continuous with the spinal cord. This arrangement can be seen in Figure 1.2 which shows a brain which has been cut vertically from crown to spinal cord (technically a mid-saggital section). Also labelled in the figure are the main structures we would encounter on tracing a pathway from the spinal cord up to the highest parts of the brain.

The spinal cord, at its simplest, can be thought of as the basis of an interconnected horizontal and vertical communication system. Through its ascending and descending nerve pathways, and the 31 pairs of peripheral sensory and motor nerves which connect with it, information can be collected from and instructions relayed to any point within the three dimensional space occupied by the body.

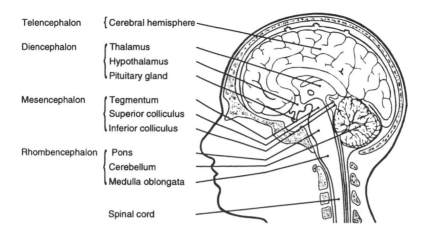

Figure 1.2: Vertical (mid-sagittal) section through the brain showing structures from spinal cord to cerebral cortex

At its upper end the spinal cord gives way to the medulla oblongata, the first part of the hindbrain. Functionally as well as anatomically, the medulla can be seen as an extension of the spinal cord. Vertical communication is via ascending and descending nerve fibre tracts and horizontal communication is via the paired cranial nerves, several of which connect with this part of the brain. However, the medulla is particularly associated with the control of respiration, heart rate and blood pressure and so damage to this part of the brain is frequently fatal.

Above the medulla are the two remaining components of the hindbrain, the pons, which is situated on the ventral aspect of the brain (nearest the front of the head), and the cerebellum, which is situated on the dorsal aspect of the brain (nearest the back of the head). The pons, like the medulla, carries messages from the higher parts of the brain to the spinal cord and vice versa, and also forms the point of connection with several of the cranial nerves. The cerebellum is a highly wrinkled structure associated with sensory motor coordination although its functions extend beyond this to encompass aspects of learning and memory as well.

Although still substantial in cross-sectional area, the midbrain is much smaller than either the hindbrain or the forebrain and can be thought of as a stalk of tissue connecting the two. As we would expect, the midbrain contains nerve pathways linking the spinal cord and hindbrain to the forebrain. These are found on the ventral aspect of the midbrain which is known as the tegmentum. The dorsal aspect of the midbrain is known as the tectum and this contains two pairs of swellings, the inferior and superior colliculi, which form part of the auditory and visual pathways respectively.

The forebrain, the largest and most prominent of the three sections of the brain and which is mounted on this midbrain stalk of tissue, is made up of two main sections, the diencephalon and the telencephalon. The diencephalon, in turn, is made up of two structures, the thalamus and the hypothalamus. The thalamus is the first structure we encounter as we move upwards from the midbrain. It consists of two symmetrical lobes which form a relay station where preliminary analysis is carried out on sensory information travelling from the sense organs to the higher parts of the brain. Additionally it is involved in motor control and in the mediation of a variety of cognitive processes. The hypothalamus is situated on the lower front margin of the thalamus. It is involved in the control of a variety of processes including feeding and drinking, sexual and aggressive behaviour and circadian rhythms. Attached to the base of the hypothalamus is the pituitary gland and through this the hypothalamus has considerable influence on endocrine function generally.

Once we get above the structures of the diencephalon we come to the telencephalon (the 'end brain') which is the part of the brain readily recognisable as the two cerebral hemispheres (Figures 1.1 and 1.2). Although to a large extent mirror images of each other, the hemispheres do differ in anatomical detail and there are certainly important functional differences between them. The most prominent part of the telencephalon is the cerebral cortex, the highly convoluted outer covering of the two hemispheres. However, before discussing this we should note some of the structures which are to be found in the space between the top of the thalamus and the lower margins of the cerebral cortex.

Very apparent from any dissection of this part of the brain would be the profusion of nerve pathways — the 'circuitry' — connecting the cerebral cortex both with underlying (subcortical) structures and with other cortical areas. The major nerve fibre tract connecting the two cerebral hemispheres, the corpus callosum, accounts for much of this. In amongst this tangle of connections we would also find a number of clearly defined neural structures. Broadly these structures form two major systems, the basal ganglia and the limbic system (there are also some diencephalic structures in the latter). The basal ganglia (globus pallidus, caudate nucleus and putamen) are primarily involved in aspects of motor control. The limbic system (hippocampus, septum, mamillary bodies, amygdala and cingulate cortex) is a rather less coherent unit from a functional point of view. Traditionally regarded as involved in emotional/motivational processes, it is clear that some parts of the limbic system have additional functions. For example, for some years the

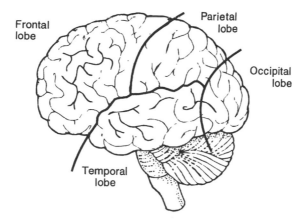

Figure 1.3: Side view of the human brain showing the
four cerebral lobes

hippocampus has been the major focus of attention of scientists investigating the neural basis of memory.

Let us return to the outer covering of the cerebral hemispheres, the cerebral cortex. By virtue of its position this is the part of the brain (especially the frontal and temporal cortex) most likely to be damaged in traumatic brain injury. It is also the area of the brain most closely associated with higher cognitive function. In the human about 80% of the brain consists of cerebral cortex compared with 74% in apes, 68% in monkeys, 50% in prosimians, 43% in carnivores and 30% in rodents. Structurally the cortex is a relatively thin layer of tissue (between 1.5 and 4.0 mm in thickness) made up of columns of nerve cells (most consisting of six cells). Its highly convoluted appearance reflects the quantity of this type of brain tissue. In order to accommodate the required amount of cortex without dramatically increasing the size of the skull the cortical layer has become highly wrinkled and folded into every available space not already occupied by the other telencephalic structures. In total the surface area of the cortex in the human brain is estimated to be approximately 2000 cm^2, not much smaller than a broadsheet newspaper.

In describing the functions of the cerebral cortex it is helpful to divide the surface into four separate areas or lobes which are largely defined by the positions of particular ridges (gyri) and fissures (sulci) in the convoluted cortical surface. The four lobes, frontal, parietal, occipital and temporal are shown in Figure 1.3.

All attempts to summarise the functions of different brain areas necessarily sacrifice detail and subtlety in the interests of producing a manageable overview. Nowhere is this problem more acute than in discussion of the functions of the four lobes of the cerebral cortex. In part this is because of their very considerable complexity but it is also because none of the lobes can be regarded as a functionally coherent entity. Nevertheless we can make some general statements.

Although for many years something of a mystery, the frontal lobes are now known to have a superordinate role in the planning, sequencing and monitoring of a wide variety of behaviours. This aspect of frontal lobe function is well captured in Luria's description of the frontal lobes as the 'executive of the brain' (Luria, 1973). Additionally the frontal lobes contain motor cortex, a vital part of the brain's system for the control of movement, and areas involved in both language and memory. One of the most fascinating aspects of frontal lobe function is its involvement in personality processes. Much of what we know about this derives from the study of patients who underwent the psychosurgical procedure of frontal lobotomy, in which the nerve pathways between the frontal lobes and the underlying thalamus were cut. The procedure was developed as a treatment for a range of psychiatric conditions and has subsequently been much criticised (Valenstein, 1980), partly because of unwanted consequences (side-effects) including apathy, loss of initiative and blunted emotional responses. More recently the role of the frontal lobes in schizophrenia has been the subject of much debate. Frontal lobe function (and dysfunction) is extremely complex (Levin, Eisenberg & Benton, 1991) but since this part of the brain is so frequently damaged in traumatic brain injury it is vital that we increase our understanding of it.

Within the parietal lobes is to be found the primary somatosensory cortex which receives and analyses information from the skin including touch, pressure, heat, cold and some aspects of pain. Damage to this part of the brain can lead not only to impairment of specific aspects of somatosensory processing but also to a fragmented and distorted sense of one's own body and its relationship to the immediate environment — literally to disintegration of one's body image. This can lead to several more specific impairments, of course. However, there is evidence for parietal involvement in many other functions as well, including constructional ability, attention and, again, aspects of language and memory.

The temporal lobes display a similar heterogeneity of function. The auditory cortex is to be found in this part of the brain but some complex visual processing also takes place here and also the integration of visual and auditory systems. Memory is closely associated with the temporal lobes (particularly the transfer of information from short-term to long-term consolidated storage) and, once again, aspects of language processing. Finally, the temporal lobes, like the frontal lobes, appear to be involved in the regulation of personality processes including aspects of sexual and aggressive behaviour.

The cerebral lobes which most closely approach functional coherence are the occipital lobes. This part of the brain receives visual information, already partly analysed by the retina and visual thalamus, and subjects it to even more detailed analysis. This process occurs in stages, the first of which (- primary processing) involves the central area of the occipital lobes, known as area 17. Further analysis (secondary processing) is then carried out by surrounding areas, known as areas 18 and 19. However, there are limits to the functional coherence of even this part of the brain, since it is now known that other areas of the cortex are also involved in visual processing, for example the parietal lobes (in visual object recognition) and the temporal lobes (in tertiary visual processing and in face recognition).

In summary, whilst there is 'division of labour' between the four cerebral lobes they operate in a highly complex, integrated and interactive way in mediating cognitive and behavioural function. This point is of great importance in understanding both the functional consequences of brain damage and recovery of function following brain damage.

BRAIN ORGANISATION AND THE EFFECTS OF BRAIN DAMAGE

Within the brief description of the brain in the preceding section it is clearly implied that sensory, motor and cognitive functions are controlled to a very considerable extent by discrete areas of tissue within the brain. This doctrine of 'localisation of function' (see Finger & Stein, 1982) has been a guiding principle of neuroscience for the last century and a half and has served us well in providing a conceptual framework within which we have accumulated a large body of detailed knowledge about the brain. However, the principle of localisation has not gone unquestioned. Certainly, over the years many scientific and clinical findings have come to light which are difficult to reconcile with the view that psychological and behavioural functions are completely localised within a very specific areas of brain tissue.

For example, there have been many reported instances of brain damage in which several apparently discrete functional areas have been destroyed without the predicted functional losses occurring. A very famous and much quoted example is the case of Phineas Gage, a railway worker in the United States (Harlow, 1848; Bigelow, 1850 — but see Beaumont, 1983, for a more accessible account). In 1848 Phineas Gage had a horrific accident in which an iron bar over an inch in diameter was blown through his head, tracing a trajectory from his lower cheek to his forehead. Following the accident he displayed a marked personality change, becoming wilful, inconsiderate, obstinate and generally intemperate in his manner. However, given the extent of his injury and the number of functional areas which must have been damaged it is not the 'impairment' in Gage's personality but his apparent lack of impairment in terms of any other functions which is remarkable. Reports which appear to be at odds with a strict localisation-of-function view of the brain are to be found in more recent literature also. In the 1980s John Lorber caused quite a stir with his study of adult patients identified by brain scans as having suffered as children from hydrocephalus (a build-up of cerebrospinal fluid in the ventricular system which damages brain tissue by crushing it against the inside of the skull). Within a sample of 253 such subjects he found nine with 'extreme hydrocephalus' (95% of the upper part of the intracranial cavity filled with cerebrospinal fluid). Of these nine, four had an IQ above 100 (i.e. above normal) and two an IQ of 126. One of the latter subjects, described by Lorber as having 'virtually no brain' had gained a first class honours degree in economics, mathematics and computer studies! This study is described by Paterson (1980).

A third finding which appears not to fit with the concept of localisation of function is that of language development in children who have undergone left hemispherectomy. Hemispherectomy is a neurosurgical procedure developed in the 1920s as a radical treatment for malignant gliomas within a cerebral hemisphere and later used in the treatment of intractable epilepsy in children. In this latter context it was found that if the procedure was carried out in young children on the left (which is normally where language is 'localised') language would develop nevertheless (Vargha-Khadem & Polkey, 1992).

There is also experimental evidence which challenges localisation of function. Lashley (1929) published a very famous monograph describing his research on the effects on learning and memory of differing extents of cortical destruction in laboratory rats. On the basis of his results he argued that the cerebral cortex is 'equipotential' with respect to the learning function and the degree of learning impairment which results from damage to the cortex depends not on which part of the cortex is damaged but merely the amount of cortex damaged.

All of these apparently discrepant findings can be challenged, of course. Phineas Gage may well have been shown to be impaired in many respects if subjected to modern methods of neuropsychological investigation, and aspects of John Lorber's work were certainly challenged subsequently (Bower, 1980). In the case of the hemispherectomised children it is now known that language development is not entirely normal and that it anyway occurs at a cost in terms of compromised development of right hemisphere function

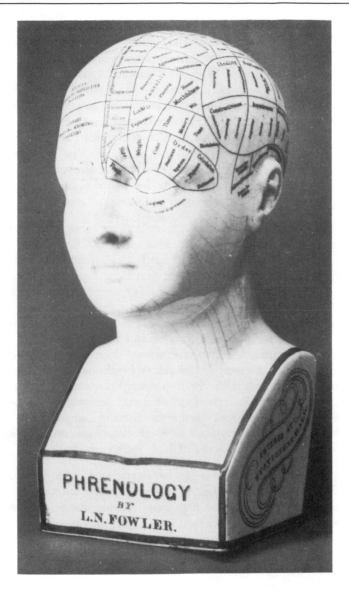

Figure 1.4: The phrenologists' view of localisation of function. Cognitive and behavioural functions were divided into mental 'faculties' which were assigned to very specific regions of the brain. It was further believed that a pronounced faculty in an individual would be detectable because that part of the brain would be enlarged and the overlying area of the skull would protude slightly — hence psychological assessment by 'reading the bumps'. From Clarke & O'Malley (1968), © 1968 The Regents of the University of California, reproduced by permission.

(Vargha-Khadem & Polkey, 1992). Finally, Lashley's interpretation of his findings in terms of mass action and equipotentiality became the subject of one of the most heated debates within the area of brain science in the 1930s and 1940s (see Steele Russell, 1966, for a succinct summary of this debate). However, in the present context it is not important whether these (and many other) discrepant findings have proved to be 'reliable and correct'. Rather their importance lies in the fact that they have caused scientists and clinicians to critically re-examine the strict localisation-of-function view of the brain. Whilst the result of this reappraisal has not been the rejection of the localisation doctrine (quite rightly, since there is incontrovertible evidence of localisation of function in the brain), it has led to the acknowledgement that there are other factors which must also be taken into account.

It is now accepted that the situation is considerably more complex than was at first thought and the concept of localisation of function within the brain must be qualified by other principles of functional organisation. For example, it is now acknowledged that the term 'function' must itself be carefully defined if it is to be used meaningfully in this context. As Luria pointed out many years ago, there is a difference between a specific and discrete function, such as the neural control of particular reflexes, and what he termed a '-functional system' (a complex, multifaceted and variable process in which an invariant objective might be achieved in several different ways — and which might include within it several individual functions) of which learning, memory, language, motivation and emotion might be examples (Luria, 1973). Functions, as opposed to functional systems, may be localised in the sorts of small, well-defined and self-contained areas of tissue familiar to us from the charts of the phrenologists (Figure 1.4) which clearly influenced much of the subsequent more scientific analyses of brain lesion effects.

However, most of what we have so far referred to as psychological and behavioural functions would fit better Luria's definition of functional systems and to the modern brain scientist it is inconceivable that such complex and multifaceted entities could be localised in this strict and specific way. In these cases it is now accepted that localisation is within much more diffuse and multi-structural anatomical systems, perhaps being within a hierarchy or circuit of structures.

This development in our thinking about localisation of function has important implications for our understanding of the consequences of brain damage, of course. Within a strict, phrenology-like, localisation of function, damage to a particular area would be expected to lead to a well-defined and complete functional deficit. In such a system it is difficult to see how sparing of function of the type observed in Phineas Gage and Lorber's patients could occur, still less subsequent recovery of that function. With a more diffuse localisation of function (functional systems subserved by sets of neural structures) our expectations would be different. Because the goal of a functional system can be achieved in more than one way, based upon slightly different neural substrates, both sparing and recovery of function now become realistic possibilities.

Of even greater relevance to our understanding of the consequences of brain damage is a further principle of functional organisation in the brain known as plasticity. This is defined as:

> ... an inferred property of the brain that allows an adaptive change in activity as a result of experience or as a result of damage to one of its parts. (Based on Bullock, Orkand & Grinnell, 1977)

Widespread acknowledgement of this characteristic of brain function is a relatively recent phenomenon. Certainly until the 1960s the brain was generally regarded as a somewhat fixed and inflexible structure which was, to a large extent, 'hard-wired' by birth. Structural damage thereafter was considered to be permanent and any functional loss consequent upon it therefore incurable. As Stein & Glasier (1992) have noted, neurologists and neuropsychologists working in the area of head injury at that time showed little interest in recovery of function, seeing their role largely as one of stabilising the patient and then diagnosing and localising the deficit.

Gradually, however, it became clear that this was an unduly pessimistic view of how the brain functions. The small steady trickle of evidence of brain plasticity, which for many years had been there for those wise enough to appreciate it, now became a torrent which could no longer be ignored. For example, during the 1960s and 1970s studies by Rosenzweig and his colleagues of rats kept in highly interactive enriched environments provided clear evidence that the normal brain, particularly the cerebral cortex, does change very significantly in response to changes in the external environment (Renner & Rosenzweig, 1987). The enriched cerebral cortex was found to be larger, heavier and have a greater surface area than non enriched cortex. Nerve cells within the enriched cortex were bigger, had larger synapses and, generally, had more profuse connections with other nerve cells. At the neurochemical level also, environmental enrichment caused changes which were suggestive of a more efficient and highly developed brain. Plastic changes within both the developing and mature nervous systems and the mechanisms underlying them are now a major focus for research within neuroscience. A good introduction to the topic of plasticity is to be found in the work of Crutcher (1991).

As a consequence of recent work on plasticity, and in response to changing views about localisation of function which we reviewed earlier, we have been forced to modify our view of the brain considerably. Whilst still accepting a degree of localisation of function within the brain, we now know it to be more complex than at first thought. Functions may be specifically localised but functional systems are more widely distributed in terms of their underlying neural substrates. Moreover, this more complex type of localisation can change over time, for example in the course of development but also in response to events occurring within the brain and in the outside environment. In other words, the localisation of function which does exist is subject to a degree of variability and flexibility as a result of the brain's plasticity. In summary, far from being fixed, unchangeable and static, we now know that the brain is a dynamic and interactive organ, constantly changing in terms of cellular activity, neural circuitry and transmitter chemistry in response to demands placed upon it.

Predictably, as we have gradually come to acknowledge the adaptability and flexibility of the brain so we have also become more interested in the possibility that the consequences of brain damage are not necessarily '-incurable' — that recovery of function is possible after all.

Indeed, within the last 10–15 years research on recovery from brain damage has become a major specialist area within neuroscience variously called Restorative Neurology (Stein, 1989) or Neurological Rehabilitation (Wade, 1990). Under these banners we have seen some valuable research carried out, for example in the areas of neural transplantation (Dunnett, 1989; Gray, Sinden & Hodges, 1990), the 'glutamate cascade' which causes so much secondary damage after the primary injury (Zivin & Choi, 1991), other pharmacological treatments for brain damage (Stein, Glasier & Hoffman, 1994), environmental influences on recovery from brain damage (Will, 1981; Rose, 1988; Will & Kelche, 1992) and many others. Elsewhere (Rose & Johnson, 1992) we have noted that:

> Research on recovery is now a multinational, multidisciplinary and multimillion dollar activity, the progress of which can be charted through numerous conferences, in several major books and, more recently, in the emergence of journals devoted to this area ...

We have a great deal of progress still to make, however.

FROM INJURY TO OUTCOME

Traumatic brain injuries can be variously classified as closed (diffuse) or open (penetrating). The former is associated with the rapid deceleration characteristic of car accidents whilst the latter, as the label implies, is the sort of injury associated with gunshot wounds or collisions with sharp objects. Sometimes a third category is distinguished, crushing injuries, in which the head is caught between two surfaces. It is now widely acknowledged that brain injury, whatever the cause, is not an instantaneous process. The damage directly caused by the accident or assault is known as the primary damage. Further damage can then be caused by complications arising from the first insult. For example, if as a result of other injuries the patient's blood pressure falls, this may result in the brain being deprived of oxygen and this may then create further damage to the brain tissue. Similarly if the brain swells or blood clots form within the brain still further tissue damage can result. These types of damage are known as secondary damage. Sometimes it is argued that traumatic brain injury should be seen as involving not two but three separate phases of damage (Gronwall, Wrightson & Waddell, 1990).

Whatever the nature or cause of the damage, changing views of the brain over the last 30 years have provided a clear rationale for attempts to rehabilitate those who have suffered traumatic brain injury. Within neuroscience there is clear evidence that some degree of recovery of function is possible following injury to the brain. However, to the patient and to the patient's family and friends the important measure is outcome and that depends, in part, on factors other than adaptive changes which may be taking place in the brain. In order to maximise outcome we must take account of all the factors involved. A good starting point is to understand the chain of events which links the initial injury and the eventual outcome.

Earlier in this chapter we quoted Fuhrer's definition of outcome. Here we should like to both extend and simplify that definition by suggesting that outcome be regarded as a measure of the extent to which, following traumatic brain injury, a patient is able to resume his/her normal life style. That, in turn, depends upon the pattern of handicaps, disabilities and impairments which result from the brain injury. Each of these terms has a specific definition and from these definitions the chain of connection between initial injury and eventual outcome becomes apparent. An impairment is defined as:

> ... any loss or abnormality of psychological, physiological or anatomical structure or function. (World Health Organisation, 1980, p. 27)

Disability refers to the effect of an impairment upon a person's ability to perform an activity in a normal manner. The definition of this term is:

> ... any restriction or lack (resulting from impairment) of ability to perform an activity in the manner or within the range considered normal for a human being. (World Health Organisation, 1980, p. 29)

The final term, handicap, is defined as:

> ... a disadvantage for a given individual, resulting from an impairment or a disability, that limits or prevents the fulfilment of a role that is normal (- depending on age, sex and social and cultural factors) for the individual. (World Health Organisation, 1980, p. 29)

The terms 'impairment', 'disability' and 'handicap' then define a progression of consequences of traumatic brain injury. The term 'impairment' simply labels the effect of the injury on the brain and its function. The term 'disability' assesses the impairment due to the brain injury in terms of its effects on what would be considered a normal profile of activities for a fit person. Finally, the term 'handicap' places the disability within the personal context of that particular person's previous abilities, expectations and aspirations.

In order to illustrate further the relationship between these terms we can imagine a situation in which a brain injury has caused an impairment (for the sake of argument let us say a reduction in neurotransmitter production in a particular part of the brain) which, because it is not severe, has no immediately discernible effect on the person's behavioural or psychological functions. In this case, then, the impairment causes neither disability nor handicap. Equally one can imagine that the impairment does cause a disability (for the sake of argument a below-normal ability to do mental arithmetic) but that this does not constitute a handicap for that particular person because he/ she never has any need to do mental arithmetic in any case. There is also a third scenario, of course. In this latter example, if the patient happened to be an accountant his/her disability in mental arithmetic would constitute a very real handicap in terms of earning a living. The value of these three terms is that they allow us to examine the consequences of traumatic brain damage, either at the level of biological or psychological mechanisms (impairment), or performance relative to some statistically defined normal population (- disability), or performance relative to the individual's particular personal history and aspirations (handicap). They also define the link between initial injury and eventual outcome.

Impairment, disability and handicap are all potential targets for rehabilitation strategies. Rehabilitation has traditionally been defined in terms of the maximisation of the patient's residual capacities. An example of such a definition is given below:

> ... the restoration of patients to their fullest physical, mental and social capability. (Mair, 1972, p. 5)

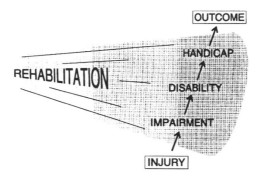

Figure 1.5: The relationship between impairment,
disability and handicap and their positions in the chain
of consequences linking injury and outcome

Today rehabilitation is viewed within a rather broader perspective. Diller (1992) describes the situation in the following way:

> The major innovation in rehabilitation after the Second World War which helps define the modern era is not in its techniques or theories, but in its perspective and aims. The goal of rehabilitation is to assist a person with CNS damage to facilitate recovery and adaptation so that the individual with residual impairments can perform optimally and reduce the burdens on his/her environment. This is usually done by organising a team of specialists to assist the individual to develop skills to overcome the disability imposed by impairments and to organise environmental resources to aid the process. The aims are utterly pragmatic and functional.

This wider perspective clearly means that a great variety of interventions and strategies can be encompassed within the term 'rehabilitation'.

The relationship between injury, impairment, disability, handicap, outcome and rehabilitation is illustrated in Figure 1.5.

TOWARDS IMPROVED OUTCOME — THE AIMS OF THE PRESENT VOLUME

The chain of consequences linking injury and outcome shown in Figure 1.5 also serves to identify a number of points of intervention in attempting to improve outcome following traumatic brain injury. Three of these, impairment, disability and handicap are the traditional focus of rehabilitation strategies. However, there are also approaches to improving outcome which fall outside the usual meaning of rehabilitation. In total the spectrum of potentially useful interventions is very wide and involves many different professional groups. For example in addition to the list of familiar groups such as neurologists, neuropsychologists, neurosurgeons, nurses, physiotherapists, psychiatrists, occupational therapists and speech therapists, the activities of architects, computer scientists, engineers, lawyers, politicians, social workers and teachers can have great relevance to outcome.

It is the diversity of professional expertise and activity having relevance to improving outcome following traumatic brain injury which provides the point of departure for the present volume. It is difficult enough to keep up to date with just one specialist field, let alone several. And yet if we are to maximise our collective impact on outcome it is important that those concerned with traumatic brain injury should be aware of each other's aims and methods. In this book we seek to provide a brief and readable account of current thinking in the main areas of activity relevant to traumatic brain injury. It is not a book for experts who wish to update their knowledge of their own particular area of expertise. Rather, it is intended to help experts in all relevant areas to update their knowledge of recent developments and current practice in areas of expertise other than their own.

We have structured our coverage of the area not according to boundaries between professional groups but in terms of different stages in dealing with traumatic brain injury. Chapter 2 deals with the acute care of patients with head injuries and Chapter 3 with assessment of patients once their condition has stabilised. Chapters 4, 5 and 6 consider rehabilitation, the importance of the social context and long-term management, respectively. Chapters 7 and 8 then examine the importance to outcome of legal, legislative and policy considerations. In our own concluding chapter (Chapter 9) we develop some of the points raised in earlier chapters and present some of our own thoughts on moving towards improved outcome.

REFERENCES

Beaumont, J. G. (1983). *Introduction to Neuropsychology*. Oxford: Blackwell Scientific Publications.

Bigelow, H. J. (1850). Dr Harlow's case of recovery from the passage of an iron bar through the head. *American Journal of the Medical Sciences*, **39**, 13–22.

Bower, A. J. (1980). Is your brain really necessary? A comment. *World Medicine*, **July**, 25–27.

Bullock, T. H., Orkand, R. & Grinnell, A. (1977). *Introduction to Nervous Systems*, San Fransisco: W. H. Freeman and Company.

Clarke, E. & O'Malley, C.D. (1968) Human Brain and Spinal Cord: A Historical Study Illustrated by Writings from Antiquity to the Twentieth Century, Berkeley CA: University of California Press.

Crutcher, K. A. (1991). Anatomical correlates of neuronal plasticity. In *Learning and Memory. A Biological View*, Second Edition (Eds. J. L. Martinez & R. P. Kesner). San Diego: Academic Press, pp. 93–146.

Diller, L. (1992). Neuropsychological Rehabilitation. In *Recovery From Brain Damage. Reflections and Directions* (Eds. F. D. Rose and D. A. Johnson). New York: Plenum Press, pp. 1–22.

Dunnett, S. B. (1989). Neural transplantation: normal brain function and repair after damage. *The Psychologist*, **2**, 4–8.

England, M. A. & Wakely, J. (1991). *A Colour Atlas of the Brain and Spinal Cord*. Aylesbury: Wolfe Publishing.

Finger, S. & Stein, D. G. (1982). *Brain Damage and Recovery. Research and Clinical Perspectives*. London: Academic Press, pp. 1–47.

Frankowski, R. F., Annegers, J. F. & Whitman, S. (1985). Epidemiological and descriptive studies. Part 1: The descriptive epidemiology of head trauma in the United States. In *Central Nervous System Trauma Status Report* (Eds. D. P. Becker and J. T. Povlishock). National Institutes of Health, USA, pp. 33–43.

Fuhrer, M. J. (1987). *Rehabilitation Outcomes: Analysis and Measurement*, Baltimore: Brookes.

Gray, J. A., Sinden, J. D. & Hodges, H. (1990). Cognitive function: neural degeneration and transplantation. *Seminars in the Neurosciences*, **2**, 133–142.

Greenfield, S. (1994). Royal Institution Children's Lectures, London: British Broadcasting Company.

Gronwall, D., Wrightson, P. & Waddell, P. (1990). *Head Injury. The facts*. Oxford: Oxford University Press.

Harlow, J. M. (1848). Passage of an iron bar through the head. *Boston Medical and Surgical Journal*, **39**, 389–393.

Kalat, J. W. (1995). *Biological Psychology*, Fifth Edition. Pacific Grove: Brooks/Cole Publishing Company.

Lashley, K. S. (1929). *Brain Mechanisms and Intelligence*. Chicago: University Press.

Levin, H. S., Eisenberg, H. M. & Benton, A. L. (Eds.) (1991). *Frontal Lobe Function and Dysfunction*. New York: Oxford University Press.

Luria, A. R. (1973). *The Working Brain. An Introduction to Neuropsychology*. Harmondsworth: Penguin.

Mair, A. (1972). *Medical Rehabilitation: The Pattern for the Future*. Report of the sub-committee of the Standing Medical Advisory Committee, Scottish Home and Health Department, HMSO, Edinburgh

Nathan, P. (1988). *The Nervous System*. Oxford: Oxford University Press.

National Head Injury Foundation (1985). *An Educator's Manual: What Educators Need to Know about Students with Traumatic Head Injury*. Framingham, MA: National Head Injury Foundation.

Paterson, D. (1980). Is your brain really necessary? *World Medicine*, **May 3rd**, 21–24.

Pinel, J. P. J. (1993). *Biopsychology*, Second Edition. Boston: Allyn and Bacon.

Renner, M. J. & Rosenzweig, M. R. (1987). *Enriched and Impoverished Environments. Effects on Brain and Behaviour*. New York: Springer-Verlag.

Rose, F. D. (1988). Environmental enrichment and recovery of function following brain damage in the rat. *Medical Science Research*, **16**, 257–263.

Rose, F. D. & Johnson, D. A. (1992). Progress in understanding recovery of function after brain damage: the need for collaboration. *Restorative Neurology and Neuroscience*, **4**, 241–244.

Steele Russell, I. S. (1966). Animal learning and memory. In *Aspects of Learning and Memory*, (Ed. D. Richter). London: Heinemann Medical, pp. 121–171.

Stein, D. G. (1989). Editorial, *Restorative Neurology and Neuroscience,* **1.**

Stein, D. G. & Glasier, M. L. (1992). An overview of developments in research on recovery from brain injury. In *Recovery From Brain Damage. Reflections and Directions* (Eds. F. D. Rose and D. A. Johnson). New York: Plenum Press, pp 1–22.

Stein, D. G., Glasier, M. L. & Hoffman, S. W. (1994). Pharmacological treatments for brain injury and repair: progress and prognosis. In *Brain Injury and Neuropsychological Rehabilitation. International Perspectives* (Eds. A. L. Christensen & B. P. Uzzell). Hillsdale, New Jersey: Lawrence Erlbaum, pp. 17–39.

Temple, C. (1993). *The Brain.* Harmondsworth: Penguin.

Valenstein, E. S. (Ed.) (1980). *The Psychosurgery Debate. Scientific. Legal and Ethical Perspectives.* San Fransisco: W. H. Freeman and Company.

Vargha-Khadem, F. & Polkey, C. E. (1992). A review of cognitive outcome after hemidecortication in humans. In *Recovery From Brain Damage. Reflections and Directions* (Eds. F. D. Rose and D. A. Johnson). New York: Plenum Press, pp. 137–151.

Wade, D. T. (1990). Neurological rehabilitation. In *Recent Advances in Clinical Neurology* (Ed. C. Kennard). Edinburgh: Churchill Livingstone.

Will, B. (1981). The influence of environment on recovery after brain damage in rodents. In *Functional Recovery from Brain Damage* (Eds. M. W. van Hof & G. Mohn). Amsterdam: Elsevier/North Holland, pp. 167–188.

Will, B. & Kelche, C. (1992). Environmental approaches to recovery of function from brain damage: A review of animal studies (1981–1991). In *Recovery from Brain Damage. Reflections and Directions* (Eds. F. D. Rose and D. A. Johnson). New York: Plenum Press, pp. 79–103.

World Health Organisation (1980). *International Classification of Impairments, Disabilities and Handicaps.* Geneva: World Health Organisation.

Zivin, J. A. & Choi, D. W. (1991). Stroke therapy. *Scientific American,* **265,** 56–63.

2

ACUTE CARE

MARTIN SMITH

The National Hospital for Neurology and Neurosurgery, London

INTRODUCTION

This chapter will consider the acute care of patients following head injury. In order to apply rational treatment in the acute phase it is necessary to understand the pathophysiology of brain injury and a brief outline of this will be given. Attention will be focused on therapeutic interventions aimed at the primary cerebral event as well as on the effects of complications affecting other bodily systems. Acute medical treatment will be described and the potential for advances in therapy discussed. Acute care has a major role to play in the neurological outcome of the patient but aspects of longer-term rehabilitation must also be considered in these early stages.

PATHOPHYSIOLOGY OF HEAD INJURY

There are two processes involved in brain damage after head injury — primary and secondary brain injury. Primary injury is the direct result of trauma and occurs immediately. Secondary injury occurs later, results from both intracranial and extracranial complications, and is a significant cause of morbidity and mortality. No intervention can attenuate primary brain injury but secondary injury is preventable in many cases. Subsequent outcome can be improved by prompt and aggressive intervention to prevent or treat the complications which may lead to secondary brain damage.

Brain Injury and After: Towards Improved Outcome. Edited by F.D. Rose and D.A. Johnson.
© 1996 John Wiley & Sons Ltd.

Primary Brain Injury

This results from the mechanical effect of forces applied to the skull and brain at the time of the injury and is manifest within seconds. Primary brain damage may be due to diffuse axonal injury, intracranial blood clot (haematoma) or skull fracture.

Diffuse brain injury occurs because the brain is poorly anchored within the skull and its soft consistency renders it liable to move in response to rapid acceleration or deceleration. Distortion of the brain, caused by internal shearing forces, leads to stretching and tearing of axonal tracts within the white matter (Adams et al., 1977). Such damage is widespread in severe injuries, but mild stretch injury is responsible for the transient disturbances of consciousness known as concussion.

Blood clots may occur within the brain substance itself, between the brain tissue and the meninges (the lining of the brain) or between the meninges and the skull. These are called intracerebral, subdural or extradural haematomas respectively (Bullock & Teasdale, 1990a). Extradural haematomas are usually caused by tearing of the middle menigeal artery (Richards, 1990). Localised lesions may cause lack of oxygen supply to the neurones within that area of the brain and result in neuronal death. The area with limited oxygen supply is called the ischaemic area and becomes surrounded by an area of partial ischaemia known as the ischaemic penumbra. As blood flow becomes reduced there is sequential loss of cellular function (Ishige et al., 1987). First neuronal electrical function ceases, followed by failure of energy-dependent ionic pumps within the cell membrane and finally cessation of all neuronal function. This results in uncontrollable movement of ions (especially potassium) across the cell membrane and cell death. Following an episode of loss of oxygen supply, some brain cells become irreversibly damaged. Those in the ischaemic penumbra, however, may continue to receive enough blood to maintain oxygenation above the level required to maintain ionic pump function but below that required for electrical, and therefore clinical, function. Metabolic failure is likely to occur in the ischaemic penumbra if its precarious oxygen supply is not reversed within 3–4 hours. Ischaemic brain tissue releases biochemical substances which worsen cerebral injury (Aitkenhead, 1986; Desalles et al., 1986). These include excitatory amino acids (e.g. glutamate) and oxygen-free radicals (Faden et al., 1989).

The pathophysiological effects of primary brain injury set up a pattern of compromised oxygen supply to brain cells, cerebral swelling and an increase in intracranial pressure, which may in turn worsen oxygen supply. This vicious cycle is aggravated by a number of factors which lead to secondary brain injury (Gentleman et al., 1993).

Table 2.1:   Intracranial and extracranial complications of head injury

Intracranial
- Changes in cerebral blood flow (areas of high & low flow)
- Reduction in brain oxygen supply
- Swelling of brain substance (cerebral oedema)
- Raised intracranial pressure
- Loss of autoregulation (impaired control of cerebral perfusion)

Extracranial
- Hypoxaemia (low blood oxygen levels)
- Hypercapnoea (high blood carbon dioxide levels)
- Hypotension and hypertension (low & high blood pressure)
- Changes in heart rate (increases & decreases)
- Pulmonary oedema (fluid in air spaces of lungs)

Secondary Brain Injury

Intracranial and extracranial complications of the initial injury may cause secondary brain injury (Mayberg & Lam, 1993) and are shown in Table 2.1. There is no doubt that aggressive treatment in the early stages can influence outcome in those in whom secondary brain injury can be avoided (Murr, Schurer & Baethmann, 1992). Recent attention has focused on so called 'avoidable factors' to highlight the direction in which therapy should be aimed (Jennett & Carlin, 1978; Jeffreys & Jones, 1981; Rose, Valtonen & Jennett, 1977). The most important avoidable factors are lack of oxygen (hypoxia) and low blood pressure (hypotension), expanding intracranial blood clots and raised intracranial pressure (Mendelow et al., 1979; Miller et al., 1978; Price & Murray, 1972). In one study, avoidable factors definitely contributed to death in 30% of cases and possibly contributed in another 24% (Jeffreys & Jones, 1981).

Secondary brain damage is essentially caused by a reduction in the flow of oxygenated blood to the brain (Gisvold & Juul, 1991). It is therefore necessary to gain control of intracranial pressure and to maintain adequate cerebral blood flow to ensure sufficient oxygen supply (Astrup, 1991).

Head injury has many effects on intracranial physiology, discussed in the ensuing sections.

Cerebral blood flow

The cerebral blood flow response to head injury is variable (Astrup, 1991; Facco & Giron, 1993; Mayberg & Lam, 1993). Some areas of the brain develop low blood flow and others an increase in flow. High blood flow may worsen brain swelling and cause further rises in intracranial pressure (Murr, Schurer & Baethmann, 1992).

Under normal circumstances the brain is able to maintain a remarkably constant cerebral blood flow despite wide variations in mean arterial pressure; this is known as cerebral autoregulation (Aitkenhead, 1986). Autoregulation is lost following head injury and the supply of blood to the brain (the cerebral perfusion pressure, CPP) becomes directly related to mean arterial blood pressure (MAP) and intracranial pressure (ICP):

$$CPP = MAP - ICP$$

If intracranial pressure becomes elevated following head injury, it may be necessary to maintain blood pressure at higher than normal levels to ensure adequate cerebral perfusion (Astrup, 1991; Bullock & Teasdale, 1990a). It should be noted that 70% of patients in coma after head injury have significantly raised intracranial pressure (Bullock & Teasdale, 1990a).

Cerebral metabolism

The supply of oxygen is normally closely regulated to fulfil the metabolic demands of the brain. This phenomenon, known as flow-metabolism coupling, may be disrupted after head injury. Cerebral metabolism may be decreased following head injury but cerebral oxygen delivery is usually more severely depressed, and to avoid further ischaemic brain damage it is essential to maintain adequate delivery of oxygen to brain tissue by preservation of cerebral perfusion and maintenance of adequate blood gas tensions (Gentleman et al., 1993). If fits develop, cerebral metabolism is markedly increased and oxygen supply is unlikely to meet demand (Jennett, 1973). Seizures must therefore be treated aggressively.

Raised intracranial pressure

The cranium is a rigid box. In normal individuals, a small increase in the volume of one compartment of intracranial contents is compensated for by a reduction in another, thereby maintaining a constant intracranial pressure. As the brain swells, for example, cerebrospinal fluid (CSF) and blood are driven out of the intracranial cavity. This accounts for the compensation phase of the intracranial compliance curve (A–B in Figure 2.1). As intracranial pressure rises further, a stage of decompensation is reached where small increases in volume cause large increases in pressure (C–D in Figure 2.1). Intracranial compliance falls following head injury and many patients rapidly move to the decompensation phase, when even small further increases in pressure cause shifting of the brain substance. Because the brain is contained within the rigid

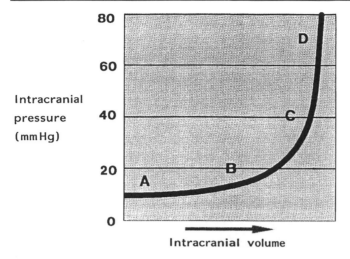

Figure 2.1: Intracranial pressure–volume curve

box of the skull, no expansion outwards is possible. The brain is therefore pushed downwards towards the base of the skull. This may cause severe damage (often permanent) to areas of the brain which are squashed against the opening in the meninges (tentorial hiatus) or the base of the skull (foramen magnum). This process is known as coning and is responsible for the pupillary and other physiological changes seen after severe head injury. Coning adversely affects outcome and is often fatal (Marmarou et al., 1991).

The clinical features of raised intracranial pressure are listed in Table 2.2. Conscious level is the most sensitive indicator but is obviously obscured in a patient already in coma or sedated with drugs. Changes in respiratory pattern are also prevented in patients being artificially ventilated. Blood pressure and heart rate changes occur later and pupillary changes occur when coning is actually taking place. It should be noted that changes in pupil size and reactivity may also occur independently of intracranial pressure as a result of direct trauma to the third cranial nerve which innervates the iris.

It is clear that many of the signs of rising intracranial pressure may be

Table 2.2: Clinical signs of rising intracranial pressure

- Decrease in conscious level
- Fall in respiratory rate or change in respiratory pattern
- Decrease in heart rate
- Rise in blood pressure
- Pupil changes (dilate, become unequal or non-reacting)

Table 2.3: Causes of hypoxaemia after head injury

Neurosurgical
● Abnormal breathing patterns (damage to respiratory centre)
● Apnoea (no respiratory drive)
● Neurologic pulmonary oedema (massive outflow of sympathetic activity affects pulmonary vessels & membranes causing formation of fluid in air spaces of lungs)

Respiratory
● Airway obstruction (facial injuries or patient in coma)
● Aspiration (of gastric contents into lungs in patients in coma)
● Chest wall/lung injuries
● Pneumothorax (rupture of lining of lung leading to collapse of lung)
● Pneumonia

obscured after head injury. Changes which can be observed often occur late when irreversible brain damage has already occurred. Intracranial pressure monitoring may therefore be useful in some patients. A knowledge of intracranial pressure allows treatment to be initiated early in an attempt to prevent coning and trends may be helpful in guiding management (El-Shunnar & Hamlyn, 1993). The response to treatment can also be observed. Additionally, with a knowledge of both intracranial pressure and blood pressure, the cerebral perfusion pressure can be assessed and treatment directed at maintaining this at adequate levels.

Oxygen levels

Hypoxaemia (low oxygen level in the blood) is common following head injury and may be attributable directly to the cerebral lesion or result from pulmonary complications of the injuries (Bullock & Teasdale, 1990a; Gentleman et al., 1993) (Table 2.3). Permanent ischaemic damage occurs if brain tissue is deprived of adequate oxygen levels for more than a few minutes and areas of partial ischaemia may be converted into complete ischaemia. The terminal branches of the cortical vessels have inadequate anastomotic connections and the areas supplied by these vessels (the watershed zones) are the most vulnerable to reductions in cerebral blood flow. This explains why higher cortical functions, such as memory and executive skills, are the most sensitive to hypoxic brain damage.

Carbon dioxide levels

The cerebral blood vessels are responsive to changes in the level of carbon dioxide in the arterial blood (Richards, 1990). High levels of carbon dioxide cause dilation of cerebral vessels which increases cerebral blood volume and hence intracranial pressure. This is deleterious after head injury when brain swelling may be present, and rises in carbon dioxide levels must be prevented by maintenance of adequate ventilation. Conversely, lower than normal carbon dioxide levels cause constriction of cerebral vessels, reduction in cerebral blood flow and a fall in intracranial pressure. This has obvious therapeutic implications, but over-zealous attempts at reduction in carbon dioxide levels may result in excessive falls in cerebral blood flow and worsening of cerebral ischaemia (Obrist et al., 1984). The responsiveness of cerebral vessels to carbon dioxide may be lost following head injury and this can be of prognostic significance. In a recent study, mortality approached 50% and severe disability 36% if carbon dioxide reactivity was lost, whereas its preservation resulted in figures of 19% and 6% respectively (Schalen, Messeter & Nordstrom, 1991).

IMMEDIATE MANAGEMENT OF SEVERE HEAD INJURY

Aggressive treatment of head injury can improve outcome in those in whom secondary brain damage can be avoided. Treatments aimed at the prevention of hypoxia, hypotension and raised intracranial pressure are the most significant (Gisvold & Juul, 1991; Gentleman & Jennett, 1990; Gentleman et al., 1993; Richards, 1990). The goal of initial resuscitation after head injury is to restore blood pressure and blood oxygen and carbon dioxide levels to normal values as rapidly as possible, in order to minimise or prevent secondary brain injury. After effective resuscitation, the aim is to protect the brain by prevention of ischaemia due to intracranial haematomas, rising intracranial pressure or the consequences of brain shift.

Acute management should begin at the site of the accident and be continued during transfer to hospital (Gentleman et al., 1993; Guidelines for initial management after head injury in adults, 1984; Richards, 1990). Competent resuscitation in the field and in the accident department is the single most important aspect of head injury care and, with improvements in the intensive care management of these patients, has lowered mortality from 50% to 35% with similar levels of disability (10–15%) in the survivors (Miller, 1992).

Priorities for immediate management are aimed at minimising the avoidable factors already highlighted (Table 2.4). Airway management, administration of oxygen and treatment of hypotension should commence at the accident site. With the increased provision of paramedics and mobile medical teams in the UK this is now becoming a reality. Definitive management of head injury is usually undertaken in a centre with specialist neurosurgical expertise and this may entail transfer to a district general hospital for initial assessment and

Table 2.4: Priorities for immediate management after head injury

- Evaluation and management of airway
- Administration of oxygen
- Endotracheal intubation and artificial ventilation — if patient in coma
- Cardiovascular resuscitation — with appropriate fluid
- Diagnosis of neurosurgical lesion
- Evaluation and stabilisation of other injuries

stabilisation prior to further transfer to the regional neuroscience centre. This is a critical time (Andrews et al., 1990; Marsh, Maurice-Williams & Hatfield, 1989; Gentleman & Jennett, 1981; Gentleman & Jennett, 1990).

Airway Management

Airway management is crucial in the early stages after head injury as hypoxaemia is so common. Standard care of the unconscious patient includes nursing in the left semi-prone (recovery) position with a clear airway and administration of supplemental oxygen. In patients in coma it is necessary to pass a plastic tube (endotracheal tube) into the trachea (Bullock & Teasdale, 1990a; Gentleman et al., 1993). This allows the lungs to be artificially ventilated and normal arterial oxygen and carbon dioxide levels to be maintained. It also protects the lungs from contamination with stomach contents which may pass into the mouth in unconscious patients. Passage of an endotracheal tube requires the insertion of a special instrument into the mouth (a laryngoscope) which is a stressful procedure and causes a substantial rise in intracranial pressure even in unconscious patients. It is therefore necessary to anaesthetise the patient with a small dose of an intravenous anaesthetic agent to prevent this rise in intracranial pressure. Because there is a risk of an associated injury to the cervical spine in anyone with a head injury, care must be taken during passage of the endotracheal tube to prevent movement of the neck. The head should be stabilised and a cervical collar applied (Gentleman et al., 1993).

Resuscitation

Resuscitation after head injury should be rapid and aggressive (Gentleman et al., 1993; Murr, Schurer & Baethmann, 1992). In adults, closed head injury alone is never the cause of low blood pressure unless there is severe scalp bleeding (Illingworth & Jennet, 1965) and, if there is difficulty in maintaining blood pressure, sites of blood loss from other injuries should be identified

(McLaren, Robertson & Little, 1983). Large bore intravenous cannulae are inserted and blood volume replaced as appropriate (Gentleman et al., 1993). Intravenous solutions such as 0.9% saline require substantial infusion volumes to normalise blood pressure in haemorrhagic shock and blood is the agent of choice. Synthetic solutions, which mimic plasma, are useful substitutes prior to blood being available.

There has been recent interest in the use of so called 'small-volume' resuscitation. This involves the use of a mixture of saline and synthetic 'plasma-like' solutions (dextran) which restore cardiac output and blood pressure more rapidly than other methods. Furthermore, only about 10% of blood loss requires replacement. It also seems likely that such solutions are more effective than conventional methods for normalising cerebral blood flow and oxygen supply and additionally cause a fall in intracranial pressure (Prough et al., 1991; Wisner, Schuster & Quinn, 1990). The use of saline-dextran solutions needs validating in clinical studies.

Assessment

An initial neurological examination is made and a Glasgow coma score (GCS) assigned (Gentleman & Teasdale, 1978; Teasdale & Jennett, 1974). This is a 15-point score based on best eye opening, motor and verbal responses and provides a global assessment of neurological function (Table 2.5). It is easy to perform and remarkably free of inter-operator variation. The initial GCS is important because it allows a baseline against which changes in neurological condition can be monitored and may be useful in predicting outcome. Although the GCS provides a standardised assessment of global neurological function it cannot localise focal lesions. Therefore, pupillary responses and focal neurological deficits should also be clearly documented.

Stabilisation of Other Injuries

About 40% of head-injured patients have associated other injuries (Gentleman, Teasdale & Murray, 1986) which may affect outcome (Bloomfield, 1989; Piek et al., 1992). These should be excluded by clinical examination and appropriate investigation. Injuries of the cervical spine, chest, abdomen and long bones must be considered. Every severely head-injured patient should have radiological examination of the cervical spine as up to 10% may have a concomitant cervical injury (Stullken et al., 1985). The neck should be stabilised in a collar until cervical injury has been excluded. A chest X-ray is also carried out and, if a pneumothorax is present, chest drains inserted prior

Table 2.5: The Glasgow Coma Score

	Score
Best motor response (observed in upper limb)	
Obeys commands	6
Localises to painful stimuli	5
Withdraws from painful stimuli	4
Flexes to painful stimuli	3
Extends to painful stimuli	2
No response	1
Best verbal response	
Orientated	5
Confused speech	4
Inappropriate words	3
Incomprehensible sounds	2
None	1
Best eye-opening response	
Spontaneously	4
To speech	3
To pain	2
None	1

to the initiation of artificial ventilation (Frost, 1977). Pneumothorax is common following trauma yet many patients continue to suffer morbidity, and even death, because of failure to diagnose and treat this complication (Marsh, Maurice-Williams & Hatfield, 1989). Blood should be drawn for routine haematological and biochemical investigations and for blood grouping and cross-matching. Arterial blood gas tensions should also be measured in patients with decreased conscious level or chest injuries.

Extracranial injuries must be dealt with prior to definitive treatment of the head injury (Gentleman, Teasdale & Murray 1986). Active bleeding and pneumothorax should always be treated before transfer to a neurosurgical unit but it is sufficient to stabilise non-life-threatening injuries. The hazards associated with the transfer of multiply injured patients and those in coma can be minimised by adequate resuscitation prior to transfer and appropriate monitoring and management during the journey (Gentleman et al., 1993, Gentleman & Jennett, 1990; Guidelines for initial management of head injury in adults, 1984).

Investigation of Head Injury

Patients with severe head injury require access to cranial CT scanning facilities. In less severe cases, where admission to a district hospital is planned

Table 2.6: Risk of intracranial haematoma — association with skull fracture and conscious level

	No skull fracture	Skull fracture
Fully conscious	1:7 900	1:45
Impaired conscious level	1:180	1:5
Coma	1:27	1:3.5

Data from Teasdale et al. (1990), with permission.

for observation, a skull X-ray may be helpful. The skull X-ray will confirm the presence and site of a fracture and, in association with the neurological condition, may predict whether or not an intracranial haematoma is present (Table 2.6) and therefore whether the patient requires further investigation (Teasdale et al., 1990). Indications for CT scanning and referral to a neurosurgeon have previously been agreed (Guidelines for initial management of head injury in adults, 1984) and are listed in Table 2.7. Patients with a fractured skull in association with neurological symptoms or signs, coma continuing after resuscitation or a deterioration in conscious level require urgent referral. It was suggested in 1989 that every large district general hospital should have CT scanning facilities (Langton Hewer & Wood, 1989) and although the number of scanners has increased since that time some do not operate 'out of hours'. Furthermore, the interpretation of cranial CT may be difficult (Gentleman & Jennett, 1990). Features of raised intracranial pressure can easily be missed by the untrained and it is preferable that CT scanning in head injury be performed under the supervision of a neuro-radiologist or neurosurgeon (Bullock & Teasdale, 1990b). With the advent of digital data transmission via computer links, scans can now be reviewed by appropriate personnel at a distant site, thereby preventing unnecessary patient transfer.

Table 2.7: Indications for neurosurgical consultation and CT scan following initial resuscitation after head injury

Immediate referral
- Patient in coma (GCS < 8)
- Deterioration in conscious level (GCS falls by > 2)
- Focal pupil or limb signs
- Fractured skull with GCS < 15, focal neurological signs or seizures

Urgent referral
- Confusion persisting for > 8 hours
- Depressed or compound skull fracture
- Base of skull fracture
- Signs of rising intracranial pressure (worsening headache or vomiting)

SURGICAL TREATMENT OF HEAD INJURY

Evacuation of a discrete haematoma is the primary goal of surgical treatment after head injury. However, some lesions may be inaccessible to the neurosurgeon or be in such sensitive areas of the brain that the risks of surgery are too great. Alternatively, brain injury may be diffuse and surgical intervention inappropriate.

Surgical evacuation of an expanding extradural haemoatoma should be carried out urgently. An extradural haematoma may not be immediately manifest — 25–30% present as rapid deterioration in neurological status following a lucid interval after the initial injury (Jefferys & Jones, 1981; Jennett & Carlin, 1978). Early surgery can be life-saving and subsequent morbidity and mortality dependent upon early diagnosis and treatment. Delay in surgical treatment was highlighted as a major preventable cause of morbidity as long ago as 1981 (Jeffreys & Jones, 1981). Acute subdural haematomas require urgent evacuation if large and causing significant shift of brain substance. The management of intracerebral haematomas is more controversial. Some neurosurgeons prefer evacuation, whereas others do not operate but apply supportive measures and therapy to control intracranial pressure (Caplan, 1992).

CONTROL OF INTRACRANIAL PRESSURE

The non-surgical principles for the control of raised intracranial pressure (intracranial hypertension) can be related to control of intracranial blood volume, manipulation of metabolic factors and the use of osmotic agents (Cold & Holdgaard, 1992).

Control of Intracranial Blood Volume

Position and venous pressure

A slight head-up tilt (15–30°) with the neck in the neutral position allows maximum venous return from the head and thereby reduces intracranial pressure. However, this position is also accompanied by a decrease in blood pressure which may adversely affect cerebral perfusion pressure.

Hyperventilation

Increase in the amount of ventilation causes a fall in the arterial carbon dioxide level of the blood (hypocapnoea). In patients with raised intracranial pressure, moderate hypocapnoea with arterial carbon dioxide levels of 3.8–4.2 kPa effectively reduces cerebral blood flow and intracranial pressure. The reduction in intracranial pressure occurs secondary to cerebral vaso-constriction and the subsequent fall in cerebral blood volume (Cold & Holdgaard, 1992). Although the decrease in cerebral blood volume is small in comparison with total brain volume, hypocapnoea can be life-saving in patients with an expanding cerebral lesion and hyperventilation is an important tool in the acute management of intracranial hypertension (Bozza, Maspes & Rossanda, 1961). Excessive hyperventilation should, however, be avoided as it causes a dangerous decrease in cerebral blood flow and provokes ischaemia, especially in those areas already compromised (Obrist et al., 1984).

It has previously been suggested that prolonged artificial hyperventilation is an effective tool in the control of intracranial hypertension and may improve neurological outcome following head injury (Gordon, 1979; Rossanda & Selenativ, 1973) but these benefits have not been confirmed in more recent studies (Muizelaar et al., 1993). In any case, adaptation to hyperventilation is complete within 24–30 hours as the pH of the fluid surrounding the brain (the CSF) becomes equilibrated with that in plasma (Christensen, 1974). Its use beyond this time is unhelpful in terms of control of intracranial pressure, but artificial ventilation may be required for longer periods to maintain oxygenation or prevent rises in carbon dioxide levels.

Drug therapy

Indomethacin has been used to control raised intracranial pressure (Cold & Holdgaard, 1992; Jensen et al., 1991). It has an effect on the cerebral circulation similar to that of hyperventilation and reduces body temperature if this is elevated. Dihydroergotamine causes a significant decrease in intracranial pressure because of constriction of capacitance vessels (Cold & Holdgaard, 1992; Grande, 1989). Its effects on intracranial pressure are accompanied by a balanced increase in cerebral blood flow and metabolic rate for oxygen, thereby preventing cerebral ischaemia (Asgeirsson et al., 1991).

Metabolic Control of Intracranial Pressure

The basis for the metabolic control of intracranial pressure is the concept that cerebral blood flow is adjusted to meet the metabolic demands of brain tissue. If the metabolic demand falls so will cerebral blood flow and volume and hence intracranial pressure.

Hypothermia

Moderate hypothermia (30–33 °C) has a protective effect in experimental brain ischaemia. Hypothermia has previously been used in the treatment of severe head injury but in recent years has been abandoned (Cold & Holdgaard, 1992). There has, however, been renewed interest in this technique and recent studies have shown a reduction in intracranial pressure and improvement in outcome in hypothermic patients (Marion et al., 1993; Shiozaki et al., 1993). The National Acute Brain Injury Study: Hypothermia is now under way in the USA.

Hypnotic agents

Barbiturates, which are usually used as intravenous anaesthetic agents, increase cerebrovascular resistance and reduce cerebral blood flow and intracranial pressure secondary to metabolic suppression of oxygen consumption (Aitkenhead, 1986). However, barbiturates may also cause a fall in blood pressure and compromise cerebral perfusion (El-Shunnar & Hamlyn, 1993; Saul & Ducker, 1982; Ward et al., 1985). Chronic administration of barbiturates has been used in the intensive care management of head injuries to prevent or attenuate intracranial hypertension. In several uncontrolled studies, barbiturates have been demonstrated to improve outcome (Eisenberg et al., 1988; Rockoff, Marshall & Shapiro, 1979; Saul & Ducker, 1982) but in controlled studies these findings are not supported (Ward et al., 1985).

Propofol, a new intravenous anaesthetic agent, is gaining support for the sedation and control of intracranial hypertension after head injury (Smith, 1994). Because of its rapid metabolism and ideal pharmacological profile it is associated with good control of sedation levels as well as rapid wake-up when the drug is stopped. It causes a dose-dependent fall in intracranial pressure (Herregods et al., 1988) and cerebral perfusion pressure is maintained at modest doses (Artru, Shapira & Bowdle, 1992). There is an associated fall in cerebral metabolic rate for oxygen, and unlike with barbiturates, the responsiveness of cerebral vessels to carbon dioxide is maintained (Craen et al., 1992). This has obvious implications for the concurrent use of hyperventilation. Disadvantages of propofol include a fall in blood pressure (Farling, Johnston & Coppel, 1989). There has also been some concern about a link between propofol and seizures (Hodkinson, Frith & Mee, 1987), but at normal clinical doses this drug is an anti-convulsant and has been successfully used in the treatment of status epilepticus resistant to other therapies (Mackenzie, Kapadia & Grant, 1990; McBurney, Teiken & Moon, 1994).

Osmotic agents

Mannitol, an osmotic diuretic, is widely used to control intracranial pressure. When given as a single dose on demand it lowers intracranial pressure, whereas cerebral blood flow may increase (Astrup, 1991). The effect of mannitol on outcome has yet to be documented and chronic mannitol therapy has never been shown to be useful (Smith et al., 1986). Mannitol, in common with other osmotic diuretics, relies on the presence of an intact blood–brain barrier across which to exert its osmotic effect. Following disruption of the blood–brain barrier, mannitol may actually worsen brain swelling but this is likely to occur in focal areas where neuronal death has already occurred. Mannitol also lowers blood viscosity and improves blood flow in the cerebral microcirculation (Burke et al., 1981) It is also an oxygen free radical scavenger.

More recently, saline-dextran solutions have been used to control intracranial hypertension (Prough et al., 1991; Worthley, Cooper & Jones, 1988) as described above.

OTHER NON-SURGICAL MANAGEMENT OF HEAD INJURY

Non-surgical treatments may be required following surgery or in those in whom surgical intervention is impossible or inappropriate.

Blood Pressure

As the brain requires continuous perfusion with well oxygenated blood, permanent ischaemic damage occurs if this is reduced below a critical threshold for more than a few minutes. Autoregulation may be lost following head injury and hypotension must be avoided to ensure maintenance of an adequate cerebral perfusion pressure (Bouma et al., 1992). What the level of CPP should be after head injury is a matter of debate, but most clinicians aim for levels between 60 and 80 mmHg (Astrup, 1991). Cardiac output and blood pressure must be optimised by appropriate administration of intravenous fluids. In the presence of a raised intracranial pressure it may be necessary to increase blood pressure with drugs which improve the function of the heart, to maintain cerebral perfusion (Bouma et al., 1992; Richards, 1990). It has been shown that a systolic blood pressure of < 60 mmHg in head-injured patients in coma is rarely associated with survival (Miller et al., 1978). Excessive rises in blood pressure should also be avoided, as these may worsen brain swelling. Invasive monitoring of the cardiovascular system is essential if cardiovascular support is required (Smith, 1994). This entails placement of arterial and central venous cannulae to measure blood pressure and central venous pressure continuously. Occasionally a sophisticated cannula which measures the pressures in the heart and lungs (a pulmonary artery catheter) is required and this is usually passed via a large vein in the neck.

Ventilation

Respiratory abnormalities are common following head injury and hypoxaemia and elevation of the carbon dioxide level in the blood (hypercapnia) are bad for the injured brain. Artificial ventilation is essential if blood gas tensions are abnormal. Because such abnormalities are so common after severe head injury, it is the view of some that all patients in whom conscious level is impaired should be electively ventilated (Miller, 1977). Endotracheal intubation also protects the airway and allows easy clearance of chest secretions by the physiotherapist.

Fluid Balance

Previously it was common practice to restrict fluids after head injury in order to minimise brain swelling or cerebral oedema (Pfenninger & Himmelseher, 1991). This view has recently been questioned. Severe fluid restriction is rarely indicated as it leads to a reduced circulating blood volume, low blood pressure and a rise in the viscosity of the blood. These may all prevent adequate blood flow to 'at risk' areas of the brain (Smith, 1994).

To maintain adequate cerebral flow, circulating blood volume should be normalised as described above. Flow through the cerebral microcirculation is improved if blood viscosity is reduced and a haematocrit (a measure of the ratio of red blood cells to plasma) of 30–35% is optimal — blood flow is maximised whilst oxygen-carrying capacity by the red blood cells is maintained (Smith, 1994). Fluid replacement therapy is best carried out with 0.9% saline.

The use of glucose-containing solutions should generally be avoided (Mayberg & Lam, 1993; Smith, 1994). A high level of glucose in the blood (hyperglycaemia) augments ischaemic neuronal damage by an increase in the formation of lactic acid by the neurones. This accumulates locally and leads to deregulation of ionic membrane pumps and the formation of other biochemical substances responsible for further neuronal injury. On the other hand, adequate supplies of glucose are essential for undamaged areas of brain. Glucose levels are therefore routinely monitored after head injury and maintained between 4 and 8 mmol/l. There is now evidence to suggest that blood glucose levels may be of prognostic significance after head injury (Lam et al., 1991).

Control of Plasma Electrolytes

The hypothalamus synthesises antidiuretic hormone (ADH), also known as vasopressin, which acts on the kidney to control loss of water and sodium (Seckl & Lightman, 1989). Disturbances of electrolytes are common following head injury (Piek et al., 1992; Stullken et al., 1985). Disorders of sodium control are of particular importance because high and low sodium levels cause a decrease in conscious level and coma (Smith, 1994). Low sodium levels may additionally be a cause of seizures after head injury.

The neurones in the hypothalamus responsible for the synthesis of ADH may become non-functional after head injury, leading to a failure of water retention by the kidney. This causes a condition known as diabetes insipidus (DI) which is characterised by a high urine output with severe water loss and a secondary rise in blood sodium levels (Seckl & Lightman, 1989). This may worsen the damage to injured brain tissue. DI is readily treated with a synthetic preparation of ADH called desmopressin acetate (DDAVP). DI usually resolves spontaneously but may persist in a minority of patients. Chronic therapy with DDAVP in the form of a nasal spray provides convenient and efficient control in such patients.

Under other circumstances, there is an abnormal and persistent release of ADH resulting in water retention and an associated loss of sodium in the urine. This is called the syndrome of inappropriate antidiuretic hormone secretion (SIADH) and is characterised by a low blood sodium level. Fluid restriction results in a slow return of sodium levels to normal and is often the only treatment required (Arieff, 1993; Smith, 1994).

Hyponatraemia after head injury may be associated not only with a loss of sodium in the urine but also of water. This leads to a significant reduction in circulating volume and is known as the cerebral salt-wasting syndrome (CSW). It may be difficult to differentiate CSW from SIADH but this is essential as the treatment regimens are diametrically opposed (Lolin & Jackowski, 1992). Fluid restriction in CSW will worsen the already reduced circulating volume. The sodium deficit in CSW should be corrected by slow infusion of solutions containing high concentrations of sodium.

Nutrition

The importance of maintaining an adequate calorific intake after head injury is now without dispute (Clifton et al., 1984). There is evidence that the outcome after head injury can be improved by early feeding so long as the blood glucose level is not allowed to rise too high.

Gastro-intestinal tract function remains intact in most patients after head injury and a naso-gastric tube should be passed to allow administration of drugs and commercial liquid feeds which are high in calories (Mendelow, 1990). Skull fractures affecting the skull base may penetrate to the nasal bones and a naso-gastric tube should not be inserted in such patients because of the risk of infection or of the tube passing into brain substance. In such patients the oro-gastric route or percutaneous gastrostomy should be chosen. A gastric tube also allows decompression of the stomach — acute dilatation of the stomach is common in unconscious patients.

Control of Seizures

The continuous neuronal firing which occurs during seizure activity causes a massive increase in the brain's requirement for oxygen. As these demands can rarely be met by a corresponding increase in the supply of oxygen, further ischaemia and neuronal death may occur. Seizures must therefore be rapidly terminated with the usual pharmacological agents such as barbiturates and benzodiazepines (Jewkes, 1987; Smith, 1994). Following a seizure, the patient must be started on a long-acting anticonvulsant such as phenytoin, in a dose sufficient to produce an immediate pharmacological effect. The use of prophylactic anticonvulsants remains a matter of much debate, although certain patient groups are particularly at risk of developing seizures and many recommend prophylaxis in such patients. This includes those with a depressed skull fracture, haematomas in epileptogenic areas (parietal and temporal lobes) or in those having suffered a high-velocity penetrating injury such as a gunshot.

Coagulopathies

Ischaemic brain tissue releases substances which prevent normal clotting of the blood (coagulopathy) and the risk of spontaneous haemorrhage is increased. The incidence of coagulopathies after head injury has been reported to be between 19 and 24% (Piek et al., 1992) and patients with abnormal clotting are more likely to develop delayed brain injury (Stein et al., 1992). It is therefore recommended that coagulation studies be performed in all severely brain injured patients and aggressive replacement of clotting factors is advised in the face of abnormalities.

Other Therapies

Steroids

Although steroids are useful in the treatment of brain oedema associated with intracerebral tumours, they are not helpful following head injury (Dearden et al., 1986).

Brain Protection

Excitatory amino acids, such as glutamate, act as transmitters in the central nervous system but are released in excess after ischaemic injury and cause neuronal death. Animal experiments have shown that during incomplete ischaemia, antagonists of the N-methyl-D-aspartate (NMDA) glutamate receptor can lessen the damage and improve subsequent neurological function (Faden et al., 1989). The results of human studies are awaited. Oxygen free radicals are also generated in excess in ischaemic brain and contribute significantly to further neuronal damage and death. Many compounds are of interest as being potentially protective against ischaemic damage caused by these highly toxic molecules. Free radical scavengers, such as superoxide dismutase, have been investigated in animal models of ischaemia and preliminary data in man show a decrease in mortality but no improvement in outcome (Muizelaar et al., 1993).

The cerebro-specific calcium channel blocker nimodipine is commonly used for the reversal of vasospasm following subarachnoid haemorrhage and may also have a cytoprotective effect via interaction with the cell membrane calcium cascade. A recent multi-centre trial, however, has failed to show improvement in outcome when nimodipine is given after head injury (European Study Group, 1994).

A novel group of compounds have been designed which are potent inhibitors of oxygen free radical induced lipid peroxidation. One such drug, tirilazid, has shown some protective benefit in animal experiments of cerebral ischaemia (Hall et al., 1992) and clinical trials are awaited with interest.

Gastrointestinal tract protection

Treatment to prevent stress induced gastrointestinal bleeding is often necessary after head injury. Ranitidine, an H_2 antagonist, has been widely used, although this drug reduces gastric acid secretion and predisposes to pulmonary infection with upper gastrointestinal tract bacteria. Acid in the stomach is essential to prevent bacteria from passing from the gastrointestinal tract into the mouth and then into the lungs, thereby causing pneumonia. Sucralfate provides an alternative method without affecting gastric acid but reduces the absorption of many drugs including anticonvulsants. The increased use of early feeding via gastric tubes is also useful in decreasing the incidence of upper gastrointestinal tract erosions and ulceration.

Anti-embolic prophylaxis

Neurosurgical patients fall into a high risk group for the development of deep vein thrombosis (blood clots in the calf veins) and pulmonary embolus (blood clot in the lungs), and prophylaxis against thromboembolism must be undertaken (Smith, 1994). Many neurosurgeons are unhappy to use small doses of heparin, a drug which reduces the clotting of the blood, because of the risk of catastrophic haemorrhage, but it has rececntly been shown to be safe when started on the first post-operative day (Frim et al., 1992). The combined use of anti-embolic stockings and intermittent calf compression is equally effective and entirely without risk. They should be started as soon as is practical and continued throughout the period during which the patient is bed-bound.

Physiotherapy

The physiotherapist plays a key role in the management of patients after head injury (Richards, 1990). In the acute phase, the physiotherapist will be active in the prevention or treatment of chest infection. Early physiotherapy to the limbs and trunk prevents later development of contractures and patients should be sat and stood as soon as their general condition allows. This may even be possible when patients are still being artificially ventilated. Such manoeuvres ensure maintenance of good autonomic control of blood pressure and heart rate reflexes and maintain body and limb alignment. Early input from a skilled neurophysiotherapist is essential for the long-term rehabilitation of the patient.

MONITORING OF THE HEAD INJURED PATIENT

Monitoring of head-injured patients should include continuous electrocardiogram, oxygen saturation, direct arterial blood pressure and end tidal carbon dioxide (for ventilated patients) on the Intensive Care Unit (Richards, 1990; Smith, 1994). In patients with multiple trauma or cardiovascular instability, central venous pressure monitoring is mandatory and, in some, pulmonary artery catheterisation may be required.

Intracranial pressure monitoring is now easily carried out with miniature fibreoptic sensors which can be inserted on the ICU (El-Shunnar & Hamlyn, 1993; Ostrup et al., 1987).

Cerebral metabolic parameters can be monitored in a variety of ways. The placement of a catheter in the jugular bulb (which contains venous blood draining from the cerebral hemisphere on the same side) allows simultaneous measurement of arterial and jugular bulb oxygen saturation and enables the arteriovenous oxygen content difference to be calculated (Dearden, 1991). More recently, small fibreoptic catheters have been used to continuously measure cerebral oxygen saturation, which is a sensitive indicator of cerebral hypoxia (Berridge, 1993). Blood samples can also be aspirated for measurement of cerebral lactate levels, which are used as a marker of poor oxygen supply to metabolising brain tissue.

Continuous non-invasive monitoring of the linear velocity of blood through the middle cerebral artery using transcranial doppler may be used as an indirect assessment of cerebral blood flow after brain injury (Bishop et al., 1986; Martin & Naylor, 1994). Near infra-red spectroscopy (NIRS) is a relatively new technique for the non-invasive measurement of cerebral oxygenation and perfusion. This technique uses transmission spectroscopy of light in the near infra-red range of the spectrum which is able to penetrate human tissue. Although the technique is in the early stages of evaluation it is likely that it will provide a continuous, bedside and non-invasive monitor of cerebral haemodynamics and oxygenation (McCormick et al., 1991).

If the patient is at risk of developing seizures, continuous monitoring of brain electrical activity should be carried out. The usual technique of monitoring brain electrical function is to record the electroencephalogram (EEG). This is a time-consuming process which generates large amounts of paper record which is difficult to interpret by the untrained. New methods allow computerised processing of the large amounts of data generated by the EEG and present it in a user-friendly display. Such processed techniques must always be supplemented at intervals by formal 16-lead EEG recordings.

Despite advances in monitoring techniques for head-injured patients the most important aspect is the reliance on skilled observation carried out by a trained neurological nurse (Smith, 1994).

OUTCOME AFTER HEAD INJURY

It should now be clear that outcome after head injury can be improved by appropriate therapy in the acute phase. No intervention can attenuate the primary brain injury but recovery and survival can be jeopardised by complications of this primary insult. Such complications arise from the cerebral insult itself or from the effect of this or associated injuries on other bodily systems.

The mortality after severe head injury is about 35% (Miller, 1992). This includes those with primary injuries severe enough to cause instant death and those in whom early resuscitation has not been adequate. If the patient survives the initial injury, prompt medical attention at the accident site and then in hospital may prevent secondary brain injury and may reduce subsequent neurological impairment and prevent death (Miller et al., 1992). Early resuscitation is crucial in this respect and reduces subsequent mortality. Of the patients who reach hospital in coma, 50% will make a good recovery whereas 50% will either die or remain severely disabled (Richards, 1990). It is not possible in the early stages after injury to predict those in whom a full functional recovery is possible, but prevention of avoidable factors of secondary brain injury is of crucial importance. In one study, outcome was poor for 76% of patients with hypoxia and hypotension but for only 44% of those without these features (Gentleman & Jennett, 1990).

The major predictors of outcome after head injury are the initial Glasgow coma score, pupillary size and reaction and age (Bullock & Teasdale, 1990b). Age is by far the most important factor, with young adults having the best chance of a good outcome. The elderly have a decreased cerebral reserve and are less able to withstand even minor injury (Galbraith, 1987) as are the very young who have immature brains. GCS below 8 after initial resuscitation is associated with a worse prognosis than higher scores and about 40% of patients in coma after 6 hours will die (Bullock & Teasdale, 1990b). Prognosis should not be estimated too soon because early resuscitation and stabilisation can dramatically improve conscious level and outcome prospects. Outcome will also be improved if mediators of secondary injury, such as raised intracranial pressure, hypoxia and hypotension, have been avoided. A recent study showed that an ICP > 20 mmHg and a mean arterial pressure < 90 mmHg were both independently predictive of a poor outcome (Piek et al., 1992).

Outcome after head injury can be quantified using the Glasgow outcome score (Jennett & Bond, 1975). A moderate or good outcome is generally accepted to be one which allows the patient to return to independent living. It should be noted that this includes those with residual cognitive impairment who do not retain many of the executive skills they previously possessed. Some patients do of course return to an essentially normal life.

Mental disabilities are far more important to patients and their families than physical impairment. Personality changes, poor memory and concentration, lack of motivation and poor control of emotions are frequently seen after head injury. Minor deficiencies may be detected by psychometric testing even in those who have apparently returned to their premorbid state. Residual physical impairments after head injury may include hemiparesis, ataxia, speech difficulties and isolated cranial nerve problems such as loss of smell, double vision, deafness and tinnitus. Seizures remain a problem in some patients (Bullock & Teasdale, 1990b).

Recovery from brain injury has three main components — physical, mental and social. Most physical recovery takes place within the first 6 months but improvements in mental state and social adaptation may be slower. In general terms, however, about 80% of recovery is achieved within the first 6 months (Bullock & Teasdale, 1990b). Rehabilitation must be considered in the early stages. It is all too easy to forget long-term outcome during the high technology phase of acute medical care, but input from a multi-disciplinary team, including physiotherapists, psychologists, dieticians, occupational therapists and rehabilitation specialists, as well as members of the acute medical team, is essential. It allows seamless transition from the acute environment into the longer-term rehabilitation process.

SUMMARY

Despite the considerable progress in resuscitation and intensive care of patients with severe head injury during the last decade, the resulting morbidity and mortality remains high. Up to 40% of patients with severe brain injury will die and many of the survivors are left with permanent brain damage (Working Party Report of the Medical Disability Society, 1988). Their average age is 30 years and many will never work again.

Improvement in pre-hospital emergency care, the rapid diagnosis of intracranial lesions and the initiation of early treatment in the accident department has contributed significantly to improvement in outcome by minimising secondary brain damage. It is now clear that secondary insults to the brain from ischaemia or hypoxia are best avoided or attenuated by efficient primary care, including aggressive fluid resuscitation and airway management. Progress is being made in the monitoring of intracranial hypertension and non-invasive methods of measuring cerebral blood flow and metabolism. New and more efficient therapeutic modalities are also likely to be introduced.

Outcome has been improved during the last decade by minimising secondary brain damage with efficient primary care and early resuscitation. It is likely that the next decade will see the introduction of specific treatments for secondary brain damage with drugs which antagonise the mediators of ischaemic cerebral injury.

REFERENCES

Adams, J. H., Mitchell, D. E., Graham, D. I. & Doyle, D. (1977). Diffuse brain damage of intermediate impact type. *Brain*, **100**, 489–502.

Aitkenhead, A. (1986). Cerebral protection. *Brit. J. Hosp. Med.*, 1986, **35**, 290–298.

Andrews, P. J. D., Piper, I. R., Dearden, N. M. & Miller, J.D. (1990). Secondary insults during intrahospital transfer of head injured patients. *Lancet*, **335**, 327–330.

Arieff, A. I. (1993). Management of hyponatraemia. *Brit. Med. J.*, **307**, 305–308.

Artru, A. A., Shapira, Y. & Bowdle, T. A. (1992). Electroencephalogram, cerebral metabolic and vascular responses to propofol anaesthesia in dogs. *Journal of Neurosurgical Anesthesiology*, **2**, 99–109.

Asgeirsson, B., Bertman, L., Grande, P. O., et al. (1991). Role of dihydroergotamine in the treatment of raised intracranial pressure after severe head injury. *8th International Symposium on Intracranial Pressure*, Amsterdam, The Netherlands, June.

Astrup, J. (1991). Drug treatment in head injury. *Current Opinion in Anesthesiology*, **4**, 653–656.

Berridge, J. C. (1993). Jugular bulb venous oxygen saturation monitoring in head injury. *Care of the Critically Ill*, **9**, 159–161.

Bishop, C. C. R., Powell. S., Rutt, D. & Browse, N. L. (1986). Transcranial doppler measurements of middle cerebral artery flow velocity: a validation study. *Stroke*, **17**, 913–915.

Bloomfield, E. L. (1989). Extracerebral complications of head injury. *Crit. Care Clin.*, **5**, 881–892.

Bouma, G. J., Muizelaar, J. P., Bandoh, K. & Marmarou, A. (1992). Blood pressure and intracranial pressure–volume dynamics in severe head injury: relationship with cerebral blood flow. *J. Neurosurg.*, **77**, 15–19.

Bozza, M. M., Maspes, P. E. & Rossanda, M. (1961). The control of brain volume and tension during intracranial operations. *Br. J. Anaesth.*, **33**, 132–147.

Bullock, R. & Teasdale, G. (1990a). Head injuries — I. *Brit. Med. J.*, **300**, 1515–1518.

Bullock, R. & Teasdale, G. (1990b). Head injuries — II. *Brit. Med. J.*, **300**, 1576–1579.

Burke, A. M., Quest D. O., Chien, S. & Cerri, C. (1981). The effects of mannitol on blood viscocity. *J. Neurosurg.*, **55**, 550–553.

Caplan, L. R. (1992). Intracerebral haemorrhage. *Lancet*, **339**, 656–658.

Christensen, M. S. (1974). Acid–base changes in cerebrospinal fluid and blood, and blood volume changes during prolonged hyperventilation in man. *Br. J. Anaesth.*, **46**, 348–357.

Clifton, G. L., Robertson, C. S., Grossmand, R. G., Hodge, S., Foltz, R. & Garaza, G. (1984). The metabolic response to severe head injury. *J. Neurosurg.*, **60**, 687–696.

Cold, G. E. & Holdgaard, H. O. (1992). Treatment of intracranial-hypertension in acute head injury with special reference to the role of hyperventilation and sedation with barbiturates; a review. *Intensive Care World*, **9**, 172–178.

Craen, R. A., Gelb, A. W., Murkin, J. M. & Chong, K. Y. (1992). CO_2 responsiveness of cerebral blood flow is maintained during propofol anaesthesia. *Canadian Journal of Anaesthesia*, **39**, A7.

Dearden, N. M., Gibson, J. S., McDowall, D. G., Gibson, R. M. & Cameron, M. M. (1986). Effect of high-dose dexamethasone on outcome from severe head injury. *J. Neurosurg.*, **64**, 81–88.

Dearden, N. M. (1991). Jugular bulb venous oxygen saturation in the management of severe head injury. *Current Opinion in Anaesthesiology*, **4**, 279–286.

Desalles, A. A. F., Kontos, H. A., Becker, D. P. et al. (1986). Prognostic significance of ventricular CSF lactic acidosis in severe head injury. *J. Neurosurg.*, **65**, 615–624.

Eisenberg, H. M., Frankowski, R. F., Contant, C. F., Marshall, L. F. & Walker, M. D. (1988). High-dose barbiturate control of elevated intracranial pressure in patients with severe head injury. *J. Neurosurg.*, **69**, 15–23.

El-Shunnar, K. S. & Hamlyn, P. J. (1993). Intensive management and monitoring techniques in severe brain injury. *Care of the Critically Ill*, **9**, 146–149.

European Study Group on Nimodipine in Severe Head Injury (1994). A multicenter trial of the efficacy of nimodipine on outcome after severe head injury. *J. Neurosurg.*, **80**, 797–804.

Facco, E. & Giron, G. P. (1993). Cerebral blood flow monitoring in head trauma. *Care of the Critically Ill*, **9**, 144–145.

Faden, A. I., Demediuk, P., Panter, S. S. & Vink, R. (1989). The role of excitatory amino acids and NMDA receptors in traumatic brain injury. *Science*, **244**, 798–800.

Farling, P. A., Johnston, J. R. & Coppel, D. L. (1989). Propofol infusion for sedation of patients with head injury. *Anaesthesia*, **44**, 222–226.

Frim, D. M., Barker, F. G., Poletti, C. E. & Hamilton, A. J. (1992). Postoperative low-dose heparin decreases thromboembolic complications in neurosurgical patients. *Neurosurgery*, **30**, 830–832.

Frost, E. A. M. (1977). Respiratory problems associated with head trauma. *Neurosurgery*, **1**, 300–305.

Galbraith, S. (1987). Head injuries in the elderly. *Brit. Med. J.*, **294**, 325.

Gentleman, D. & Jennett, B. (1981). Hazards of inter-hospital transfer of comatose head-injured patients. *Lancet*, **2**, 853–855.

Gentleman, D. & Jennett, B. (1990). Audit of transfer of unconscious head-injured patients to a neurosurgical unit. *Lancet*, **1**, 330–333.

Gentleman, D. & Teasdale, G. (1978). Adoption of the Glasgow coma score in the British Isles. *Brit. Med. J.*, **283**, 408.

Gentleman, D., Dearden, M., Midgley, S. & Maclean, D. (1993). Guidelines for resuscitation and transfer of patients with serious head injury. *Brit. Med. J.*, **307**, 547–552.

Gentleman, D., Teasdale, G. & Murray, L. (1986). Cause of severe head injury and risk of complications. *Brit. Med. J.*, **292**, 449.

Gisvold, S. E. & Juul, R. (1991). Acute management of head injuries: cerebral protection. *Current Opinion in Anaesthesiology*, **4**, 229–234.

Gordon, E. (1979). Non-operative treatment of acute head injuries: the Karolinska experience. *Int. Anaesthesiol. Clin.*, **17**, 181–189.

Grande, P. O. (1989). The effects of dihydroergotamine in patients with head injury and raised intracranial pressure. *Intensive Care Med.*, **15**, 523–527.

Guidelines for initial management after head injury in adults (1984). Suggestions from a group of neurosurgeons. *Brit. Med. J.*, **288**, 983–985.

Hall, E. D., Yonkers, P. A., Andrus, P. K., Cox, J. W. & Anderson, D. K. (1992). Biochemistry and pharmacology of lipid antioxidants in acute brain and spinal cord injury. *J. Neurotrauma*, **9** (suppl 2), 425–442.

Herregods, L., Verbeke, J., Rolly, G. & Colardyn, F. (1988). Effects of propofol on elevated intracranial pressure. Preliminary results. *Anaesthesia*, **44**, 107–109.

Hodkinson, B. P., Frith, R. W. & Mee, E. W. (1987). Propofol and the electroencephalogram. *Lancet*, **2**, 1518.

Illingworth, G. & Jennett, B. (1965) The shocked head injury. *Lancet*, **2**, 511–514.

Ishige, N., Pitts, L. H., Hashimoto, T., Nishimura, M. C. & Bartowski, H. N. (1987). Effect of hypoxia on traumatic brain injury in rats. *Neurosurgery*, **20**, 848–858.

Jeffreys, R. V. & Jones, J. J, (1981). Avoidable factors contributing to the death of head injury patients in general hospitals in Mersey region. *Lancet*, **2**, 459–461.

Jennett, B. (1973). Epilepsy after non-missile head injuries. *Scot. Med.*, **18**, 8–13.

Jennett, B. & Bond, M. (1975). Assessment of outcome after severe brain damage. A practical scale. *Lancet*, **1**, 1031–1034.

Jennett, B, & Carlin, J. (1978). Preventable mortality and morbidity after head injury. *Injury*, **10**, 31–39.

Jensen, K., Ohrstrom, J., Cold, G. E. & Astrup, J. (1991). The effects of indomethacin on intracranial pressure, cerebral blood flow and cerebral metabolism in patients with severe head injury and intracranial hypertension. *Acta Neurochir. (Wien)*, **108**, 116–121.

Jewkes, D. A. (1987). The postoperative period — some important complications. *Clinical Anaesthesiology*, **1**, 517–531.

Lam, A. M., Winn, H. R., Cullen, B. F, & Sundling, N. (1991). Hyperglycaemia and neurological outcome in patients with head injury. *J. Neurosurg.*, **75**, 545–551.

Langton Hewer, R. & Wood, V. A. (1989). Availability of computed tomography of the brain in the United Kingdom. *Brit. Med. J.*, **298**, 1219–1220.

Lolin, Y. & Jackowski, A. (1992). Hyponatraemia in neurosurgical patients: diagnosis using derived parameters of sodium and water homeostasis. *Brit. J. Neurosurg.*, **6**, 457–466.

Mackenzie, S. J., Kapadia, F. & Grant, I. S. (1990). Propofol infusion for control of status epileticus. *Anaesthesia*, **45**, 1043–1045.

Marion, D. W., Obrist, W. D., Carlier, P. M. et al. (1993). The use of moderate therapeutic hypothermia for patients with severe head injuries: a preliminary report. *J. Neurosurg.*, **79**, 354–362.

Marmarou, A., Anderson, R. L., Wood, J. D., Choi, S. C. & Young, H. F. (1991). Impact of ICP instability and hypotension on outcome in patients with severe head trauma. *J. Neurosurg.*, **75**, 59–66.

Martin, P. J. & Naylor, A. R. (1994). Transcranial sonography and its clinical applications. *Hospital Update*, **20**, 479–486.

Marsh, H., Maurice-Williams, R. S. & Hatfield, R. (1989). Closed head injuries: where does delay occur in the process of transfer to neurosurgical care? *Brit. J. Neurosurg.*, **3**, 13–20.

Mayberg, T. S. & Lam, A. M. (1993). Management of central nervous system trauma. *Current Opinion in Anaesthesiology*, **6**, 764–771.

McBurney, J. W., Teiken, P. J, & Moon, M. R. (1994). Propofol for treating status epilepticus. *Journal of Epilepsy*, **7**, 21–22.

McCormick, P. W., Stewart, M., Goetting, M. G., Dujouny, M., Lewis, G. & Ausma, J. I. (1991). Non-invasive cerebral optical spectroscopy for monitoring cerebral oxygen delivery and haemodynamics. *Crit Care Med.*, **19**, 89–97.

McLaren, C. A. N., Robertson, C. & Little, K. (1983). Missed orthopaedic injuries in the resuscitation room. *J. R. Coll. Surg. Edinb.*, **28**, 399–401.

Mendelow, A. D., Karoni, M. Z., Paul, K. S., Fuller, G. A. G. & Gillingham, F. J. (1979). Extradural haematoma: effect of delayed treatment. *Brit. Med. J.*, **1**, 1240–1242.

Mendelow, A. D. (1990). Management of head injury. *Hospital Update*, **16**, 195–206.

Miller, J. D. (1977). The search for the optimal management of head injury. *Med Coll. Virginia Q.*, **13**, 97–106.

Miller, J. D., Sweet, R. C., Narayan, R. & Becker, D. P. (1978). Early insults to the injured brain. *JAMA*, **240**, 439–442.

Miller, J. D. (1992). Evaluation and treatment of head injury in adults. *Neurosurgery Quarterly*, **2**, 28–43.

Miller, J. D., Jones, P. A., Dearden, N. M. & Tocher, J. L. (1992). Progress in the management of head injury. *Brit. J. Surg.*, **79**, 60–64.

Muizelaar, J. P., Marmarou, A. & Ward, J. D. (1991). Adverse effects of prolonged hyperventilation in patients with severe head injury: a randomized clinical trial. *J. Neurosurg.*, **75**, 731–739.

Muizelaar, J.P., Marmarou, A., Young, H. F. et al. (1993). Improving outcome of severe head injury with oxygen radical scavenger, polyethylene glycol-conjugated superoxide dismutase: a phase II trial. *J. Neurosurg.*, **78**, 375–382.

Murr, R., Schurer, L. & Baethmann, A. (1992). Acute management of severe head injury. *Current Opinion in Anaesthesiology*, **5**, 284–291.

Obrist, W. D., Langfitt, T. W., Jaggi, J. L., Cruz, J. & Gennarelli, T. A. (1984). Cerebral blood flow and metabolism in comatose patients with acute head injury: relationship to intracranial hypertension. *J. Neurosurg.*, **61**, 241–253.

Ostrup, R. C., Luerssen, T. C., Marshall, L. F. & Zornow, M. H. (1987). Continuous monitoring of intracranial pressure with a miniaturised fibreoptic device. *J. Neurosurg.*, **67**, 206–209.

Pfenninger, E. & Himmelseher, S. (1991). Perioperative fluid management in neurosurgical anaesthesia. *Current Opinion in Anaesthesiology*, **4**, 649–652.

Piek, J., Randall, M., Chesnut, R. M., et al. (1992). Extracranial complications of severe head injury. *J. Neurosurg.*, **77**, 901–907.

Price, D. J. E. & Murray, A. (1972). The influence of hypoxia and hypotension on recovery from head injury. *Injury*, **3**, 218–223.

Prough, D. S., Whitley, J. M., Taylor, C. I., Deal, D. D. & Dewitt, D. S. (1991). Regional cerebral blood flow following resuscitation from hemorrhagic shock with hypertonic saline — influence of a subdural mass. *Anesthesiology*, **75**, 319–327.

Richards, P. (1990). Management of head injury. *Current Anaesthesia and Critical Care*, **1**, 99–104.

Rockoff, M. A., Marshall, L. F. & Shapiro, H. M. (1979). High-dose barbiturate therapy in humans: a clinical review of 60 patients. *Ann. Neurol.*, **6**, 194–199.

Rose, J., Valtonen, S. & Jennett, B. (1977). Avoidable factors contributing to death after head injury. *Brit. Med. J.*, **2**, 615–618.

Rossanda, M., Selenativ, A., Villa, C. & Beduschi, A. (1973). Role of automatic ventilation in treatment of severe head injuries. *J. Neurosurg. Sci.*, **17**, 265–270.

Saul, T. G. & Ducker, T. B. (1982). Effect of intracranial pressure monitoring and aggressive treatment on mortality in severe head injury. *J. Neurosurg.*, **56**, 498–503.

Seckl, J. & Lightman, S. (1989). Neuroendocrinology of posterior pituitary function. *Hospital Update*, **9**, 103–114.

Schalen, W., Messeter, K. & Nordstrom, C. H. (1991). Cerebral vasoreactivity and the prediction of outcome in severe traumatic brain lesions. *Acta Anaesthesiol. Scand.*, **35**, 148–152.

Shiozaki, T., Sugimotot, H., Taneda, M. et al. (1993). Effect of mild hypothermia on uncontrollable intracranial hypertension after severe head injury. *J. Neurosurg.*, **79**, 363–368.

Smith, H. P., Kelly, D. L., McWhorter, J. M. et al. (1986). Comparison of mannitol regimens in patients with severe head injury undergoing intracranial monitoring. *J. Neurosurg.*, **65**, 820–824.

Smith, M. (1994). Postoperative neurosurgical care. *Current Anaesthesia and Critical Care*, **5**, 29–35.

Stein, S. C., Young, G. S., Talucci, R. C., Greenbaum, B. H. & Ross, S. E. (1992). Delayed brain injury after head trauma: significance of coagulopathy. *Neurosurgery*, **30**, 160–165.

Stullken, E. H., Balestrieri, F. J., McWhorter, J. M. & Prough, D. S. (1985). Anesthetic management of intracranial trauma. *Seminars in Anesthesia*, **4**, 154–161.

Teasdale, G. & Jennett, B. (1974). Assessment of coma and impaired consciousness. *Lancet*, **2**, 81–84.

Teasdale, G. M., Murray, G., Anderson, E. et al. (1990). Risks of acute traumatic intracranial haematoma in children and adults: implications for managing head injuries. *Brit. Med. J.*, **300**, 363–367.

Ward, J. D., Becker, D. P., Miller, J. D. et al. (1985). Failure of prophylactic barbiturate coma in the treatment of severe head injury. *J. Neurosurg.*, **62**, 383–388.

Wisner, D. H., Schuster, L. & Quinn, C. (1990). Hypertonic saline resuscitation of head injury; effects on cerebral water content. *J. Trauma*, **30**, 75–78.

Working Party Report of the Medical Disabilty Society. (1988). The management of traumatic brain injury, London: The Medical Disability Society, pp. 1–29.

Worthley, L. I. G., Cooper, D. J. & Jones, N. (1988). Treatment of resistant intracranial hypertension with hypertonic saline. Report of two cases. *J. Neurosurg.*, **68**, 478–481.

SUGGESTED OTHER READING

Baethmann, A. (1989). Secondary brain damage from severe head injury and cerebral ischaemia — the role of glutamate. *Current Opinion in Anaesthesiology*, **2**, 567–571.

Deshpande, J. K. (1993). Cerebral ischaemia and neuronal protection. *Current Opinion in Anaesthesiology*, **6**, 772–778.

Ingram, G. S. (1994). Neurophysiology. In *Anaesthesia and Intensive Care for the Neurosurgical Patient* (Eds F. J. M. Walters, G. S. Ingram and J. L. Jenkinson). London: Blackwell Scientific Publications, pp. 25–45.

Jennett, B. & Teasdale, G. (1981). *Management of Head Injuries.* Contemporary Neurology Series No. 20. F. A. Davis Co., Philadelphia, PA.

Kreimeier, U., Frey, L. & Messmer, K. (1993). Small-volume resuscitation. *Current Opinion in Anaesthesiology*, **6**, 400–408.

McCormick, P. W. (1991). Monitoring cerebral oxygen delivery and hemodymamics. *Current Opinion in Anaesthesiology*, **4**, 657–661.

Midgley, S. & Dearden, N. M. (1994). Head injuries. In *Anaesthesia and Intensive Care for the Neurosurgical Patient* (Eds F. J. M. Walters, G. S. Ingram & J. L. Jenkinson). London: Blackwell Scientific Publications, pp. 373–403.

Nevin, M. (1994). Cerebral metabolism. In *Anaesthesia and Intensive Care for the Neurosurgical Patient* (Eds F. J. M. Walters, G. S. Ingram & J. L. Jenkinson). London: Blackwell Scientific Publications, pp. 46–69.

North, B. & Reilly, P. (1990). *Raised Intracranial Pressure — A Clinical Guide.* Oxford: Heinemann Medical Books.

Vandesteene, A. & de Rood, M. (1989). Brain monitoring. *Current Opinion in Anaesthesiology*, **2**, 537–543.

3

ASSESSMENT

MICHAEL ODDY AND DREW ALCOTT*

*Head Injury Rehabilitation Unit, Ticehurst House Hospital, Ticehurst, and *Unsted Park Rehabilitation Centre, Godalming*

INTRODUCTION

Assessment following brain injury is a wide-ranging and complex topic. Assessment may be carried out for many different purposes and at many different stages. The consequences of brain injury vary widely in terms of nature and degree. There is, therefore, an almost insatiable need for appropriate measures. Ideally, there is a need for assessment procedures to have demonstrated properties of reliability, validity and sensitivity and in many cases to be standardised on appropriate samples. These requirements are rarely met and attempts to develop appropriate measures continue.

In an attempt to impose some order on a somewhat chaotic field, this chapter will be divided according to the International Classification of Illness, Disease and Health (ICIDH); impairment, disability and handicap. The allocation of assessment procedures to these headings is somewhat arbitrary, partly because many measures have been developed without reference to this classification and partly because different theoretical standpoints would place measures under different categories. However, this classification is in increasing use and does provide a framework for thinking about different levels of analysis.

In this chapter, we will consider measurement of motor function, sensory function, cognition, mood and behaviour under the heading of 'impairment'. Under the heading of 'disability', we will consider so-called 'functional scales', such as scales of activities of daily living and those global outcome scales which concentrate upon disability rather than handicap. Under the heading 'handicap', we will consider those procedures which attempt to measure the

Brain Injury and After: Towards Improved Outcome. Edited by F.D. Rose and D.A. Johnson.
© 1996 John Wiley & Sons Ltd.

quality of an individual's life. This will include social adjustment measures and measures of psychological well-being. There are certain other measures, such as measures of motivation or personality considered relevant to progress in rehabilitation, which do not fall easily under any of these headings.

The choice of an appropriate measure clearly depends on the stage of recovery. In the acute stage of recovery from brain injury measures of impairment tend to predominate whereas in later stages measures of disability and handicap come to the fore.

THE NEED FOR ASSESSMENT

There are a number of quite distinct reasons for conducting a formal assessment and these place different requirements on the measurement instrument.

Diagnosis/Formulation

Assessment may be carried out in order to arrive at a formulation which attempts to explain the patient's complaints or observations of the patient's state or behaviour. This may be in terms of aetiology or in terms of a theoretical model of malfunction, not necessarily linked to a specific cause. Normally, such a formulation would have implications for both treatment and prognosis. For example, a measure of depth of early coma may be used as a criterion for determining whether the patient should be transferred to a neurosurgical centre. It is also an indicator of the severity of the injury and hence has (broad-band) implications for the long-term recovery of the patient.

Monitoring

Measures are also required which allow progress to be monitored. In the early stages of recovery (at least the first 2 years) such progress is always likely to reflect an element of natural recovery, but may also reflect treatment effects. Such monitoring is invariably carried out in order to indicate whether the current management strategies are having the desired effect or whether a different or additional intervention is required.

In some cases, the measures being used for monitoring are broad and reflect the overall state of the patient. In other cases, they are narrow and reflect a particular aspect of the presentation which is seen as an important target for modification. For example, a patient who is sexually molesting female staff and visitors may have the frequency of this behaviour recorded in order to ensure that treatment programmes intended to reduce this behaviour are being effective.

Prediction and Planning

This aim often overlaps with other aims. However, many assessment procedures represent ways of predicting from behaviour in a time-limited, structured environment to behaviour in wider, natural settings. For example, neuropsychological assessments of memory would have the aim, amongst others, of predicting the person's ability to function in a wide range of situations — at home, in the community and at work. Such information can assist in making appropriate plans for a return home or a return to work, ensuring that the need for support, assistance or supervision are correctly pitched. The dramatic changes often resulting from a brain injury mean that careful planning for the future is a crucial element of brain injury rehabilitation.

Formal measures have a less than perfect correlation with ability in real life situations. Attempts have been made to improve the predictive power by designing tests with greater 'ecological validity'. This is normally achieved by designing tasks which more directly reflect everyday situations rather than deriving from theoretical models of impairment. Hence these procedures tend to cross the boundary between measurement of impairment and of disability.

Programme or Service Evaluation

With the introduction of competition between providers of health and social services in the UK, the requirement to measure service performance routinely is increasing. The choice of measures will depend on the nature of the service and the stage in the recovery process at which it is delivered. However, the emphasis tends to be upon measures of disability or handicap as these represent 'outcome' rather than process.

Epidemiology

Present changes in health and social services in the UK have led to an increased requirement for epidemiological information, by both providers and purchasers of services. Essentially this is a need for information about the incidence and prevalence of impairment, disability and handicap rather than information allowing evaluation of services as described in the previous section. There has been a tendency in the past for epidemiological studies to focus on measures of impairment or disability, but the increased involvement of social services as purchasers and providers of community/long-term care appears likely to shift the emphasis towards disability and handicap.

ISSUES IN MEASUREMENT

There are a number of problems associated with the design of measures which tend to recur across the spectrum of assessment methods. Any measurement instrument needs to possess certain properties.

Reliability

The instrument should give the same result when it is repeated under conditions in which the underlying variable is not expected to have changed. For example, it should produce stable findings after a short interval (test–retest reliability) or when applied by two different people (inter-rater reliability). Another way in which the reliability of an instrument is gauged is by dividing the test in half and correlating the two resultant scores (split-half reliability).

Validity

This is usually defined as the ability of the instrument to measure what it is supposed to measure. An assessment of a test's validity is normally made by correlating the test results with some external criterion. This may be another test designed to measure the same characteristic or it may be some other criterion. Validity may further be assessed by looking at the instrument's ability to distinguish between two groups considered or known to differ on the relevant characteristic.

Norms

For many instruments interpretation of the results may only make sense when compared to some reference group. Normally this would be the healthy population matched for variables such as age and sex. The performance of a representative sample from the normal population is tested and a scoring system is devised for the test based on the mean and standard deviation obtained from this normative sample.

Sensitivity

Obviously a measure needs to be sensitive enough to measure the phenomenon under investigation. In some circumstances measures need to be sensitive to changes over a period of time (for example in rehabilitation). In other cases, the crucial form of sensitivity is the ability to discriminate between a 'normal' result (one that may be obtained by a member of the healthy population) and an abnormal result (i.e. indicative of brain dysfunction).

Increasing sensitivity to change can result in lower reliability, hence measures which are appropriate for one purpose may not be ideal for another. This is basically the problem of Type 1 (false positive) and Type 2 (false negative) errors. In some circumstances it may be important to avoid false positive errors (e.g. when hazardous, uncomfortable or expensive treatment would be indicated) and in others to avoid false negatives (e.g. when dangers to the patient could arise from not identifying an impairment).

All measures will have a limited range over which they are sensitive and there will be 'floor' and 'ceiling' effects at the bottom and top of the range.

Range of Measurement

Measurement instruments may be wide and inclusive or they may be narrow and specific. The latter normally produce more accurate results. However, most instruments have a range within which they are sensitive and are less so beyond this range. For example, a coma scale may be sensitive to changes when the patient is in the very early stages of recovery but less so as the patient is emerging from coma. Some instruments may have floor or ceiling effects which represent absolute limits to their ability to discriminate.

Measurement instruments may attempt to assess a single dimension or to provide a composite measure of a number of dimensions. Multidimensional measures have to contend with the weightings which should be accorded to the different dimensions providing the composite measure. Selection of the number of items is in itself a form of weighting.

Ease of administration

In practice what makes a good measure depends a great deal on the time the instrument takes to administer. If the instrument is to provide a useful basis for intervention or planning it must be easy to apply. If it is not, it is unlikely to be applied consistently and its value will be lost.

The administration of measures almost always requires training; it is vital that the requisite training is clearly stated and only those with this training should administer the measure. In some cases the requirement for training may be met by the administrator's basic professional training. In other cases there may be a need for specific training in the use of a particular instrument. There have been recent attempts to devise measures that can be administered by those with a range of professional backgrounds.

MEASURES OF IMPAIRMENT

The selection of a measure of impairment depends not only upon the stage of recovery but also on the type and severity of impairment from which the patient is suffering. Following traumatic brain injury the first measure normally applied is a scale indicating depth of coma.

The most widely used scale is the Glasgow Coma Scale (Teasdale & Jennett, 1974). This rates the patient's responsiveness in terms of eye opening, motor responses and verbal responsiveness. It has a maximum score of 15 and is used to monitor the depth of coma and to plot deterioration and recovery. It also has some utility as a predictive measure in that indices, such as the lowest Glasgow Coma Scale (GCS) score or GCS score on admission may be used to indicate the severity of the initial injury.

Once a patient is conscious, but still confused, he/she would normally score 14 out of the 15 points. At this stage, measures of orientation and amnesia may be used.

Although the GCS remains by far the most commonly used, a number of other scales have been developed to assess the patient and monitor progress during coma and in the early stages of recovery. The Ranchos Los Amigos Levels of Cognitive Function Scale (Malkmus, 1980) requires ratings to be made placing the patient's behaviour in one of eight categories.

1. Completely unresponsive
2. Inconsistent and non-purposeful responses only
3. Engages in purposeful behaviour and/or follows simple commands inconsistently
4. Confused/agitated
5. Confused/inappropriate
6. Confused/appropriate
7. Automatic/appropriate
8. Purposeful/appropriate

As can be seen from these levels, the Ranchos Scales cover both coma and the period of confusion and disorientation which follows. This scale has been criticised on the grounds that the categories are broad and, hence, insensitive to subtle changes in level of functioning. There is also some overlap between the different levels on the scale and Horn et al. (1993) have pointed out that environmental stimuli alone may determine which point on the scale the patient demonstrates. For example, in Level 4, the patient must be rated as 'confused, agitated'. Clearly, the extent of agitation may be determined by the nature of the environment in which the patient is recovering.

An excellent review of eight other measures of recovery in and after coma is provided by Horn et al. (1993). The authors conclude that the GCS remains the best method of monitoring the level of response in the early stages of coma after severe head injury. However, they question the validity of using the summated score of the three sub-scales, rather than each sub-scale separately. They also point to difficulties with this scale when there are complicating factors, such as motor or speech deficits or amongst patients who remain minimally responsive for days or longer. In order to address these problems, the authors are in the process of developing a Visual Awareness Scale (Horn et al., 1992, 1993). This is based upon very careful observation of the patient during coma and after. A series of items based on these observations is being developed, placed in the order of a normal recovery sequence. For example, the first two suggested items are:

1. Eyes opened briefly (spontaneous eye opening lasting only a few seconds)
2. Eyes opened for an extended period (more than 30 seconds)

Items at the other end of the scale concern attention and appear harder to rate reliably, for example, 'Is able to ignore distraction'. As stated above, this scale is not yet fully developed, but promises to be a useful addition to the rating of coma, particularly during the indeterminate phase when the patient is emerging from coma.

Post-traumatic Amnesia

As the patient emerges from coma there is a phase of confusion, disorientation and often agitation. When the patient emerges from this phase he/she is normally unable to recall any events during it. It has therefore traditionally been referred to as 'the period of post-traumatic amnesia' (Russell & Smith, 1961). Several attempts have been made to devise measures to assess and monitor recovery during this phase. By far the most commonly used scale is the Galveston Orientation and Amnesia Test (GOAT) (Levin et al., 1979). As the name implies, this procedure tends to measure two distinct aspects of awareness and cognition. One is the extent to which the patient is orientated in person, place and time. The other is the extent to which they are amnesic for recent events. The reason for this is that traditionally patients have been seen as emerging from unconsciousness into a further, but higher, state of altered awareness, commonly known as the phase of post-traumatic amnesia. The term post-traumatic amnesia (PTA) is used because the termination of this phase is marked by a return of day-to-day memory. However, recent studies (e.g. Corrigan et al., 1992) suggest there are at least three distinct features of this early stage of recovery which can be measured separately and which imperfectly correlate with each other. These are orientation, amnesia and agitation. The Westmead PTA Scale (Shores et al., 1986) attempts to measure only the amnesia. Corrigan (1989) has devised a scale for assessing agitation during this phase. Orientation can be measured by the simple clinical procedure of asking the person's name, some simple details about where the patient is and the nature of the place and details of the day of the week, day of the month, month and the year. The Westmead Scale omits some of the questions concerning orientation, included in the GOAT. It also omits questions concerning the patient's last memory prior to the accident and first memory subsequent to it. However, the Westmead includes a recognition component which is used if the patient is unable to give answers by recalling information, and it includes a learning component, whereby patients are tested on whether they remember pictures of common objects from one session to another.

The measurement of cognitive impairment and confusion at this early stage in recovery is a developing field and new methods are currently under development.

Motor and Sensory Impairment

This area has been expertly reviewed by Wade (1992, 1993). It is an area in which traditionally clinical judgement rather than formal measurement devices has been applied. However, in rehabilitation there is a clear need for measurements to be taken at different times, often months apart and frequently carried out by different clinicians. To meet this need, a number of formal assessment procedures have been devised recently. For example, dynamometers have been employed to measure muscle power (e.g. Sunderland et al., 1989, Andres et al., 1986). Measures of mobility have been developed. The Rivermead Mobility Index covers activities such as walking or going upstairs, as well as various aspects of balance and of transferring. Once again, this index cannot be considered to be a pure measure of impairment since it includes functional activities (disability), such as getting in and out of the bath or shower. This highlights the difficulty of defining the exact point where impairment ends and disability begins.

Standard measures of walking speed have been developed. These may be over short distances, such as the time to walk 10 metres or over a set timespan, where the emphasis is upon endurance and cardio-respiratory fitness. Such measures have been criticised on the grounds that speed is less important than the quality of the gait. However, Wade & Langton Hewer (1987) have argued that good gait is associated with faster speed. Some normative data is available concerning walking speed in the general population (Cunningham et al., 1982; Wade & Langton Hewer, 1987). Attempts have been made to develop measures of the quality of gait, but these tend to be highly complex and time-consuming and no method is available for general clinical use.

Bond (1976) published a brief neurophysical scale for use with head-injured patients. This provides a quick method of obtaining a composite score based on motor and sensory impairment. However, it also includes some high level functions, such as dysphasia. Whilst it is attractive as a brief and simple way to describe the neurophysical recovery of patients, there have been no reliability data published on this instrument.

A standardised measure of the tactile kinaesthetic sensory system has been developed by Lincoln et al., (1991). However, the authors obtained very poor inter-rater reliability on this scale and suggest that poor reliability may well be a problem on the more usual clinical assessments carried out. The authors are revising their scale in the light of these findings in an attempt to develop a more reliable instrument.

Cognition

This is a large and complex area and there are a growing number of texts dealing with it (e.g. Lezak, 1995; Spreen & Strauss, 1991; Crawford, Parker & McKinlay, 1992). Once the patient has recovered from the early stage of confusion and disorientation, a full cognitive assessment will include consideration of memory and learning, attention, verbal abilities, perceptual abilities, reasoning and the elusive executive or organisational abilities. Many of the most commonly used tests were not devised as measures of brain injury, but as general measures of intellectual function. Most prominent amongst these are the Wechsler Adult Intelligence Scales. The extensive standardisation and normative data available for this test, together with its familiarity amongst clinical psychologists, has ensured its longevity. The last 10 years has seen the development of a number of specialised tests of cognition with good reliability, validity and normative data available. However, many of the tests used by clinical neuropsychologists in the assessment of brain-injured patients have been designed in the course of experimental investigations, and normative data are often limited. The Wechsler Adult Intelligence Scales-Revised (WAIS-R) contain a number of sub-tests, few of which correspond to specific cognitive functions as currently conceptualised. A development of this scale designed specifically for neuropsychological patients is due to be published shortly (Psychological Corporation).

Recent developments in cognitive neuropsychology have led to an increased fractionation of cognitive processes. These developments have also led to new assessment techniques. An earlier emphasis upon the use of neuropsychological tests to identify the location of lesions in the brain has been replaced, since the advent of more effective imaging techniques during the last 20 years, by an emphasis upon the identification of the precise nature of the cognitive deficits in relation to current theories of brain–behaviour relationships. Clearly, such tests play a major role in specifying the exact nature of underlying impairment in patients suffering a brain injury. The utility of such tests in predicting the ability to perform in real life situations has been enhanced recently by the development of 'ecologically valid' tests of cognition, such as the Rivermead Behavioural Memory Test (Wilson et al., 1985) and the Test of Everyday Attention (Robertson et al., 1994). These tests are standardised procedures carried out in formal settings, but include items which simulate real-life circumstances rather than testing abstract abilities. For example, rather than learning a list of words, the patient is required to learn the name of a person in a photograph.

Mood

There are very few tests of mood designed specifically for the brain-injured population. Many of the tests used with other populations, such as the General Health Questionnaire (GHQ; Goldberg & Hillier, 1979) or the Beck Scales (Beck, 1961) can be used with brain injured patients. However, scales such as the Wimbledon Self-report Scale (Coughlan & Storey, 1988) and the Hospital Anxiety and Depression Scales (Zigmond & Snaith, 1983) have been designed to exclude items which may have different interpretations in a neurological population. For example, items referring to dizziness or fatigue have been omitted from these scales. Such tests are clearly to be preferred but if general mood scales are used, care must be taken to ensure that items are not checked other than for reasons of mood disturbance.

Kinsella et al. (1988) investigated the use of the GHQ, the Leeds Scale of Depression and Anxiety and Visual Analogue Scales of Depression and Anxiety. They concluded that head-injured patients were able reliably to complete the self-report scales of mood disturbance. When compared with 'close-other ratings' there were moderately high correlations on both the GHQ and the Leeds Scale. Correlations on the Visual Analogue Scales were low. Test–retest scores for the head-injured patients on all three measures were high, particularly on the Leeds Scales. Other authors (e.g. McKinlay &

Brooks, 1984) have expressed reservations about self-rating instruments, because of the problem of lack of awareness which is greater amongst the more severely injured.

Behaviour

This is a most important area, but there are few formal measures. It is in this area that the problem of lack of awareness of impairment (at least in the more severely brain injured) is most acute (McGlynn & Schacter, 1987; Prigatano & Altman, 1990; Klonoff et al., 1989; Crosson et al., 1989; Lam et al., 1988). Hence many measures rely on ratings by staff or relatives.

The Neurobehavioral Rating Scale (Levin et al., 1987) is a scale for use by professional staff to rate various aspects of the behaviour of brain-injured individuals, based on observation in a rehabilitation setting. As such it is slanted towards those behaviours characteristic of the more severely damaged.

Other methods rely on relatives' ratings. The Katz Adjustment Scales, originally designed for those with psychotic illnesses, have been used with the brain-injured (Oddy, Humphrey & Uttley, 1978; Prigatano, 1984). Jackson et al. (1991) carried out a factor analysis on a sample of brain-injured individuals.

Kinsella et al. (1991) devised a scale specifically for parents to rate the behavioural characteristics of their brain-injured sons and daughters. This measures two main factors, loss of emotional control and loss of motivation. Whilst these factors emerged from a principal components analysis, it is interesting that the results closely match suggested classifications for behavioural impairment following brain injury (Eames, 1989).

The above measures make use of ratings by staff or relatives. Self-report measures have been used despite the difficulties in the interpretation of results due to brain-injured patients' lack of awareness of their behavioural problems. The Minnesota Multiphasic Personality Inventory has been used by a number of authors. This is a very lengthy procedure which has not been standardised on a brain injury sample and therefore its usefulness is limited to those with more moderate or milder brain injuries. Many studies have used simple checklists, with reliability or validity data rarely reported. Tyerman & Humphrey (1984) used a Semantic Differential with a head-injured sample and this method has the potential for development.

A number of authors have reported on the use of Symptom Checklists (e.g. Oddy et al., 1978; Van Zomeren & Berg, 1985; Brooks & McKinlay, 1983). These typically include items of a neurophysical, cognitive and emotional nature as well as those concerned with behaviour and personality change. Gouvier et al. (1988) have investigated the psychometric properties of these instruments.

Most of the above instruments have been designed for use with the moderately or severely brain-injured. Gouvier et al. (1992) have devised a scale for the measurement of the somewhat controversial post-concussional syndrome. This includes subjective symptoms of a sensory, motor, cognitive and behavioural kind.

MEASURES OF DISABILITY

The assessment of disability is particularly important because it is commonly considered to be the main focus of rehabilitation. Although rehabilitation aims to minimise handicap (i.e. maximise fulfilment of social roles), it normally achieves this by reducing disability (Wade, 1992).

Disability measures are of little use during the early phase following a head injury when pathology and impairment are more relevant. It is in later phases when disability measures become useful. They may be used for any of the purposes mentioned earlier, however, some are designed for a single primary purpose. The Office of Population Censuses and Surveys (OPCS) disability scales for example are designed for epidemiological use.

Commonly Used Disability Measures

As there is a wide range of disability measures it is not possible to review them all here (see Wade, 1992; Hall, 1992). Some of the commonly used measures will be described as well as more recent measures which may become more widely used.

Barthel Index

The Barthel Index was first introduced in the mid-1960s (Mahoney & Barthel, 1965) and is now said to be one of the most commonly used activities of daily living (ADL) measures in Britain (Wade, 1993). It was intended particularly for patients with impaired use of their limbs (e.g. hemiparesis). It covers 10 basic aspects of daily function (e.g. toilet use, feeding, mobility and dressing) which were selected because of their importance for social independence. Each of the items is a rating scale (ranging from 2 to 4 points) indicating dependence or independence, and in some cases an intermediate level (e.g. 'needs help').

The reliability and validity of the Barthel Index is acceptable (Hall, 1992; Wade, 1993), although Dewing (1992) has commented on some weaknesses in the results of reliability studies.

The sensitivity of the Barthel Index is poorer in cases of milder impairment as it has a relatively low 'ceiling' (e.g. Wade et al., 1983). A maximum score indicates functional independence but not necessarily normality (Wade & Langton Hewer, 1987). It also lacks sufficient sensitivity to be a useful measure of progress in rehabilitation. This particularly concerns head injury, as the Barthel Index focuses on a few activities of daily living but does not provide an adequate measure of cognitive problems for head-injured patients.

The particular strength of the Barthel Index is the simplicity of its design. It is easy and quick to learn and use. It provides a broad picture of an individual's level of independence which is very useful in deciding one of the most common clinical questions (i.e. 'do they require nursing care?'). There are other possible uses of the Barthel Index including prediction of outcome. There are indications that a formula using the Barthel results may be useful in predicting eventual outcome (Wade & Langton Hewer, 1987; Wade et al., 1983). This has limitations, such as the fact that the maximum reliability of prediction is not a great deal higher than 50% (e.g. 63%) as well as the fact that prediction is considerably less reliable in cases of milder disability. A modified version for use as a postal questionnaire (Gompertz, Pound & Ebrahim, 1994) also allows the Barthel Index to be used for epidemiological research.

Disability Rating Scale

The Disability Rating Scale (DRS) was developed by Rappaport and colleagues (1982) for use with severe head trauma patients. It was intended to improve upon other existing measures (e.g. the Glasgow Outcome Scale).

The DRS consists of 8 items divided into 4 categories. The first category relates to arousability, awareness and responsivity and incorporates a modified version of the Glasgow Coma Scale (GCS). The second category concerns cognitive ability for self-care activities (feeding, toileting and grooming). The third category (dependence on others) assesses severity in terms of physical dependence. The fourth category (psychosocial adaptability) measures ability to carry out domestic, academic or employment responsibilities. It was designed for ease of use and sensitivity, since it was intended for use in monitoring rehabilitation progress across the range from coma to return to the community.

There is evidence that the metric characteristics of the DRS are good (Hall et al., 1993). Both reliability and validity are acceptable. Although it is more sensitive than the Glasgow Outcome Scale it is less sensitive in cases of mild

disability than other, more detailed measures (e.g. the Functional Independence Measure; FIM). Its sensitivity is better in the lower part of the range
(i.e. more severe disability).

One strength of the DRS is its potential for use across a wide range of
disability. Its brevity also makes it easy to use. It has been advocated as a
suitable measure for monitoring progress during the acute phase (Hall et al.,
1993).

Functional Independence Measure

The Functional Independence Measure (FIM) was developed in the USA in a
multi-centre project (Forer, 1992). It is now being used in other countries
including the UK (DiTunno, 1992), where it is becoming increasingly
common.

The FIM was designed as a measure of disability and rehabilitation outcome.
Its 18 scales are intended to represent relevant disabilities commonly
addressed in rehabilitation. The measure is sub-divided into motor (n = 13)
and cognitive (n = 5) scales. Each scale is a 7-point rating scale extending
from total dependence to complete independence. Its purposes include the
evaluation of rehabilitation progress and measurement of the level of
disability. It is intended to provide an indication of the level of care needed to
enable the person to fulfil basic daily activities effectively. It can also be used
for follow-up review (e.g. by telephone interview).

Functional Assessment Measure

The Functional Assessment Measure (FAM) was developed as an extension of
the FIM to improve its usefulness with brain-injured patients. It is not a
separate measure as it includes the FIM scales. It particularly enhances the
FIM by including cognitive and psychosocial factors (e.g. reading, emotional
status, employability) (Hall, 1992, 1993).

The FAM's metric characteristics have yet to be demonstrated. There is
evidence supporting its validity, but reliability was poor (Hall et al., 1993).
Those who have used the FAM have reported some difficulty in clinical
usage, especially with scales of a more abstract quality (Hall et al., 1993). This
experience has been reported by users in Britain (Pentland & McPherson,
1994; Turner-Stokes, 1995, personal communication); however, difficulties
were not restricted to FAM scales (e.g. emotional disturbance; adjustment to
limitations) but also included some FIM scales (e.g. expression; problem-
solving). As it is still a research protocol it is not surprising that further
research will be needed to address its reliability, sensitivity and clinical utility.

Assessment of Motor and Process Skills

The Assessment of Motor and Process Skills (AMPS) is designed for the use of occupational therapists as a clinical tool for the analysis of the causes of functional disabilities (Fisher, 1993). Although it provides some indication of the degree of disability, its intended primary use is to guide rehabilitation intervention (i.e. formulation and treatment design). A total of 35 skills are identified, 15 of which are motor (e.g. lifts, endures, calibrates) and the remainder are 'processes' (e.g. searches/locates, chooses, heeds). An instrumental activity of daily living (IADL) is chosen which is likely to be relevant and acceptable to the patient (to maximise motivation). Any of a wide variety of IADLs (e.g. bathing, toileting, polishing shoes or making a sandwich) might be selected. Following observation of the person's performance, each of the 35 skill competencies are rated on a 4-point scale (competent — questionable — ineffective — defective). In theory this allows the therapist to use any of a variety of activities as the source of observations for identifying the impairments which are causing disability.

Although the AMPS model is appealing as a method of assessing functional ability it is not as well suited as other tools mentioned here for measuring disability more generally. It also has the drawback of using terms which do not easily fit with existing models of cognitive functions (e.g. needs and benefits).

The OPCS Disability Scales

The Office of Population Censuses and Surveys (OPCS) Scales were designed for use as an epidemiological tool for surveying the prevalence of disability in the general population (Martin, Meltzer & Elliot, 1988). The OPCS has 12 disability scales which were selected from a longer initial list. Severity of disability can be measured in order to study the degree of needs within the community.

It is suited to the categorisation of individual cases but it lacks sensitivity for other purposes, such as measuring change during rehabilitation. Because it aims to measure the overall severity of disability, various areas have been combined (e.g. walking plus steps and stairs) or excluded (e.g. anxiety and depression). Other scales such as the FIM have a greater number of separate scales which increases their potential sensitivity for measuring progress in rehabilitation.

Because items on the scales have been given weightings to reflect the degree of impact upon daily living, the scales can be to some extent treated as interval scales (see below). This allows comparisons between different types of disabilities.

General Issues About Disabilities Measures

There are several general issues which should be considered when using disability measures. Some dangers to avoid in the interpretation of results have been summarised by Wade (1993). Disability measures do not necessarily indicate what impairments underlie dependency. They are unlikely to be sensitive enough to measure detailed changes in specific abilities. Although they help to indicate broad goals they do not indicate a specific treatment approach for achieving the goals.

Almost all measures of disability are ordinal scales. Although the difference between two points on the scale represents improvement or deterioration, it does not indicate the size of this difference. In some cases the increment between points may be small, while in others it may be relatively large. It would, for example, be inappropriate to conclude that a change from 2 to 4 on one scale represented a greater degree of improvement than a change from 2 to 3 on another scale.

There have been efforts to convert some measures into interval scales. In the case of the OPCS scales, for example, an attempt was made to specify the 'weightings' of different items. Even this must be interpreted with caution as the weightings were derived from judgements of perceived impact on independence. Studies of the impact of disability on care-givers not only reveal counterintuitive weightings (e.g. repetitive questioning is experienced as worse than incontinence), but also considerable variation between individuals in their weighting of the burden of different disabilities (e.g. Sanford, 1975).

Statistical methods have also been used in an attempt to convert an ordinal into an interval scale. This would help to overcome the weakness of ordinal scales, which indicate the relative order of items without indicating the size of the distance between items in a scale, as does an interval scale. Rasch scaling techniques have been applied to the AMPS (Fisher, 1993) and the FIM (Heinemann et al., 1993). The validity of this approach hinges on the assumption that there is a single underlying dimension (e.g. disability or activities of daily living). The assumption that activities of daily living do represent a unidimensional phenomenon (Wade & Langton Hewer, 1987; Wade, 1993) is questionable.

Another related issue is the clarity with which disabilities can be distinguished from other phenomena, such as handicaps or impairments. It is accepted that it is not always possible to make clear distinctions (Wade, 1993). This probably contributes to the fact that not all measures focus solely on disability. The Disability Rating Scale (DRS) is an example of a scale which mixes impairment and disability. There is also an overlap in measures of deficient memory which may be viewed as an impairment (see above) or a disability (e.g. the FIM).

MEASURES OF HANDICAP: QUALITY OF LIFE AND SOCIAL ADJUSTMENT

The ICIDH concept of handicap is a disadvantage resulting from impairment or disability that limits or prevents the fulfilment of a role that is normal, depending on age, sex, social and cultural factors for that individual. Some authors consider ADL scales to reflect handicap (see Collin, 1993; Wade, 1993). In this chapter we have considered these measures to reflect disability and will consider measures of 'social adjustment' and quality of life as reflecting handicap.

Weissman (1975) defines social adjustment 'as commonly accepted roles which the individual performs in his/her social environment', a definition which is very close to the 'disadvantage' as defined in the ICIDH system. Such roles are seen as a function of age and, at least in Western society, an adult will function in several roles, for example occupational, marital (as spouse and parent), within an extended family (parents, siblings and close relatives) and in the community.

Social adjustment scales typically assess the degree and quality of the individual's participation in work, social, leisure, marital, wider family and economic activities. Many of these instruments have been devised for use in the psychiatric field. However, since they do not address symptomatology directly but assess the person's performance of generally accepted social roles, they can be validly applied to any group. Oddy, Humphrey & Uttley (1978) successfully used an adaptation of the Social Adjustment Scale (Paykel et al., 1971) in a study of quality of life following head injury. More recent studies (e.g. Marsh, Knight & Godfrey, 1990) have used a self-report version developed from this scale, the Social Adjustment Scale Self-report (Weissman & Bothwell, 1976).

There is some overlap between social adjustment and quality of life measures. For example, the social role approach is implicit in the personal needs approach to measuring quality of life. This approach also includes reference to the physical and financial aspects of the person's circumstances and his/her degree of choice. For example, whether the person has an adequate diet and an appropriate degree of choice of good quality food is considered. For those requiring on-going care the quality of this care is an important aspect of quality of life (Gibbs & Bradshaw, 1990).

'Quality of life' has been assessed in a variety of ways. Some measures cut across different ICIDH categories. For example, Klonoff, Costa & Snow (1986) used a variety of tests to measure quality of life. One of these was the Sickness Impact Profile (Bergner et al., 1976), which measures health-related dysfunction in 12 categories of activity; ambulation, mobility, body control and movement, social interaction, communication, alertness behaviour, emotional behaviour, sleep and rest, eating, home management, recreation and pastimes, and work. Smith (1992) has reviewed the usefulness of this measure in brain injury. Many studies in areas other than brain injury have included symptoms such as pain or fatigue in quality of life measures.

Klonoff et al. (1986) used the Minnesota Multiphasic Personality Inventory (MMPI) as a measure of quality of life. This is basically a measure of psychiatric symptomatology or, at best, a measure of personality and emotional functioning. Measures of affective state are frequently used as indicators of quality of life (McSweeny, Grant & Heaton, 1982).

There are a number of measures which address one aspect of quality of life or social adjustment alone. For example, Kinsella et al. (1989) used the Interview Schedule for Social Interactions (Henderson, Byrne & Duncan-Jones, 1981) with a brain-injured population. This interview assesses the perceived availability and perceived adequacy of close interpersonal relationships and of more superficial relationships involved in social integration. Other studies have used measures of social support (Leach et al., 1994) or measures of family functioning (Kreutzer et al., 1994; Florian, Katz & Lahav, 1989.

Other simple informal measures often used to indicate degree of handicap or quality of life include categorisation of the type of employment to which the person has been able to return (same or superior to premorbid status; normal employment, but down-graded from previous level; part-time employment; sheltered employment; etc). The type of accommodation the person is living in may also be used as a measure (e.g. living independently; living with support of relatives; living with support of professional carers; living in residential care; living in nursing home; etc).

Measurement of the quality of life is perhaps the most difficult area of all. There are wide cultural and individual variations in aspirations, values and expectations which make the task of finding a universally applicable measure impossible. It is interesting that there has been very little attempt to develop adequate measures of this kind in the field of brain injury. This is in marked contrast to the number of studies addressing quality of life in AIDS, cardiovascular or cancer research. This is presumably because these are life-threatening conditions whereas brain injury has little effect on life expectancy. Treatment regimes for the former may prolong life but not necessarily improve the quality of that life. It can be argued, however, that there is an even stronger reason for closely investigating the quality of life where life expectancy is normal. Whether to treat may not be at issue, but the search for methods of improving the quality of that life surely is.

Within a given culture there is some agreement on basic underlying factors which constitute a minimal quality of life. More work is needed to identify and devise adequate measurement techniques.

Much of the above discussion has implied an objective concept of quality of life but it can be argued that the concept is inherently subjective. One study which looked at quality of life in aphasic patients (Lomas et al., 1987) found that the patients themselves were able to generate more specific and concrete items for a quality of life measure than clinicians. Furthermore, the clinicians' values were not fully representative of the patients'. Subjective quality of life has been suggested to be a characteristic more stable than mood but less enduring than personality (McCauley & Bremer, 1991). Whilst such scales have been developed, Gill & Feinstein (1994) have suggested that a simple visual analogue rating asking the person to rate 'How happy are you with life?' may be the best way of tapping subjective quality of life.

CONCLUSIONS

In this chapter we have set ourselves the ambitious target of a tour through the range of formal assessment procedures used in brain injury. We have not limited ourselves to a particular area of interest (e.g. cognitive function, coma state, activities of daily living) or to a particular stage of recovery. There is a vast and increasing number of assessments, hence only a few have been selected to try to illustrate what is available. We have not attempted a critical or exhaustive review of these measures. There are many instruments we have not mentioned, in some cases because they do not fit into the classificatory system we have adopted. One procedure which should be mentioned here is the European Chart for Evaluation of Patients with Traumatic Brain Injury (Truelle et al., 1994). This is an ambitious multi-national attempt to provide guidelines for a 'minimum assessment of head injured people'. The first section is concerned with the collation of initial information and the second deals with impairment, disability and handicap. Some existing measures have been incorporated in the Chart (e.g. Glasgow Coma Scale), but since it attempts to encompass the whole gamut of brain injury assessment it is necessarily cursory in its handling of certain areas. Data on reliability and validity are already available, but the Chart is the subject of further development and certainly it is proposed that this is widely adopted throughout Europe and ideally in other continents.

Ideally, most assessment measures should be based on theory and be adequately standardised. It is often the case, however, that adequately standardised measures are not related to current theory and that theoretically based measures are really experimental procedures which lack standardisation. At best, there should be means and standard deviations derived from normal controls and from a brain-injured group. The Wechsler Intelligence Scales are examples of well-standardised assessment tools, but where there is little relationship to current neuropsychological theory. Test development is costly and time-consuming, but there is a need for standardised tests which are based on current theory of function and dysfunction.

Arguably, the most important development which could occur in brain injury assessment is the development of an adequate measure of disability. The recognition of the importance of disability is reflected in the development of such 'ecologically valid tests' as the Rivermead Behavioural Memory Test (RBMT). Tests such as the RBMT bridge a gap between impairment and disability. They also recognise the importance of standardisation. In many cases, however, there is a need for further research to broaden the normative database.

There is a need for further development of the underlying conceptual model upon which the WHO/ICIDH model is based. The present model developed from work in the field of physical disability.

Applying this to the cognitive realm (e.g. the FAM) has proved to be problematic and points to the need for a more sophisticated conceptual base. For example, there is an assumption that physical dependence is a greater disability than the dependence on another for initiating and prompting behaviour. In terms of degree of handicap, this is almost certainly not the case. There is a much more direct and constant relationship between physical impairment and disability than there is for cognitive and behavioural impairment. Naturally, test design must begin from an assumption about what constitutes different degrees of dependency in activities of daily living. The problem of how to include disabilities which result from cognitive and behavioural impairment has not really been solved. Further conceptual and research work is required. However, further research is needed to test and/or demonstrate the validity of these assumptions.

There is a need for the development of a taxonomy of the activities of daily living which underlie the concept of disability. At present there is no more than a list which could be extended indefinitely. It is important to continue progressing towards a clearer framework of the variety of activities of daily living and how these may best be structured to understand relationships between the various activities.

There is a similar need for theoretical and empirical links to be established between assessment outcomes in the realms of impairment, disability and handicap. There will never be total predictability from one realm to another and if there were, there would be no need for separate measures. However, a better understanding of the nature of the relationships between the different domains needs to be established in order to develop the validity and usefulness of assessment tools.

REFERENCES

Andres, P. L., Hedlund, W., Finison, L., Conlon, T., Felmus, M., & Munsat, T. L. (1986). Quantitative motor assessment in amyotrophic lateral sclerosis. *Neurology*, **36**, 937–941.

Beck A. (1961). Measurement of depression. *Archives of General Psychiatry*, **4**, 561–571.

Bergner, M. (1976). The sickness impact profile: conceptual formulation and methodology for the development of a health status measure. *International Journal of Health Services*, **6**, 393–415.

Bond, M. R. (1976). Assessment of the psychosocial outcome of severe head injury. *Acta Neurochirurgica*, **34**, 57–70.

Brooks, D. N. & McKinley, W. W. (1983). Personality and behavioural change after severe blunt head injury — a relative's view. *Journal of Neurology, Neurosurgery and Psychiatry*, **46**, 336–344.

Collin, C. (1993). Measurement of disability and handicap. In *Neurological Rehabilitation* (Eds P. B. R. Greenwood, T. M. McMillan & C. D. Ward) New York: Churchill Livingstone, pp. 137–145.

Corrigan, J. D. (1989). Development of a scale for the assessment of agitation following traumatic brain injury. *Journal of Clinical and Experimental Neuropsychology*, **11**, 261–277.

Corrigan, J. D., Mysiw, W. J., Gribble, M. W. & Chocks, S. K. L. (1992). Agitation, cognition and attention during post-traumatic amnesia. *Brain Injury*, **6**(2), 155–160.

Coughlan, A. K. & Storey, P. (1988). The Wimbledon Self-report Scale: emotional and mood appraisal. *Clinical Rehabilitation*, **2**, 207–213.

Crosson, B., Barco, P. P., Velozo, C. A., Bolesta, M. M., Cooper, P. V. Werts, D. & Brobeck, T. C. (1989). Awareness and compensation in postacute head injury rehabilitation. *Journal of Head Trauma Rehabilitation*, **4**(3), 46–54.

Cunningham, D. A., Rechnitzer, P. A., Pearce, M. E. & Donner, A. P. (1982). Determinants of self-selected walking pace across ages 19 to 66. *Journal of Gerontology*, **37**, 560–564.

Dewing, J. (1992). A critique of the Barthel Index. *British Journal of Nursing*, **1**(7), 325–329.

DiTunno, J. F. (1992). Functional assessment measures in CNS trauma. *Journal of Neurotrauma*, **9**(1), 301–305.

Eames, P. (1980). Head injury. In *Rehabilitation of the Physically Disabled Adult* (Eds C. J. G. & M. A. Chamberlain). London, Croom Helm, pp. 399–425.

Fisher, A. G. (1993). The assessment of IADL motor skills: an application of many-faceted Rasch analysis. *American Journal of Occupational Therapy*, **47**(4), 319–29.

Florian, V., Katz, S., & Lahav, V. (1989). Impact of traumatic brain damage on family dynamics and functioning: a review. *Brain Injury*, **3**(3), 219–233.

Forer, S. F. (1992). How to make program evaluation work for you: utilization for program service management. *Neurological Rehabilitation*, **2**, 52–71.

Gibbs, I. & Bradshaw, J. (1990). Quality of life and changes in private old people's homes in Great Britain. *Social Indicators Research*, **23**(3), 269–282.

Gill, T. & Feinstein, A. (1994). A critical appraisal of the quality of Quality-of-Life measures. *Journal of the American Medical Association*, **272**, 619–626.

Goldberg D. P. & Hillier, V. F. (1979). A scaled version of the General Health Questionnaire. *Psychological Medicine*, **9**, 139–145.

Gompertz, P., Pound, P. & Ebrahim, S. (1994). A postal version of the Barthel Index. *Clinical Rehabilitation*, **8**, 233–239.

Gouvier, W. D., Uddo-Crane, M. & Brown, L. M. (1988). Base rates of post-concussional symptoms. *Archives of Clinical Neuropsychology*, **3**, 273–278.

Hall, K. M. (1992). Overview of functional assessment scales of brain injury. *Neurological Rehabilitation*, **2**, 98–113.

Hall, K. M., Hamilton, B. B., Gordon, W. A. & Zasler, N. D. (1993). Characteristics and comparisons of functional assessment indices: Disability Rating Scale, Functional Independence Measure, and Functional Assessment Measure. *Journal of Head Trauma Rehabilitation*, **8**(2), 60–74.

Heinemann, A. W., Linacre, J. M., Wright, B. D., Hamilton, B. B. & Granger, C. (1993). Relationships between impairment and physical disability as measured by the Functional Independence Measure. *Archives of Physical Medicine and Rehabilitation*, **74**, 566–573.

Henderson, S., Byrne, D. G. & Duncan-Jones, P. (1981). *Neurosis and the Social Environment*. Sydney: Academic Press.

Horn, S., Shiel, A., McLellan, L., Campbell, M., Watson, M. & Wilson, B. (1993). Assessment scales for monitoring recovery in and after coma with pilot data on a new scale of visual awareness. *Neuropsychological Rehabilitation*, **3**(2), 121–138.

Horn, S., Watson, M., Wilson, B. A. & McLellan, D. L. (1992). The development of new techniques in the assessment and monitoring of recovery from severe head injury: a preliminary report and case history. *Brain Injury*, **6**(4), 321–325.

Jackson, H. F., Hopewell, C. A., Glass, C. A., Warburg, R., Dewey, M. & Ghadiali, E. (1992). The Katz Adjustment Scale: modification for use with victims of traumatic brain and spinal injury. *Brain Injury*, **6**(2), 109–127.

Kinsella, G., Moran, C., Ford, B. & Ponsford, J. (1988). Emotional disorder and its assessment within the severe head injured population. *Psychological Medicine*, **18**, 57–63.

Kinsella, G., Packer, S. & Olver, J. (1991). Maternal reporting of behaviour following very severe blunt head injury. *Journal of Neurology, Neurosurgery, and Psychiatry*, **54**, 422–426.

Klonoff, P. S., Costa, L. D. & Snow, W. G. (1986). Predictors and indicators of quality of life in patients with closed-head injury. *Journal of Clinical and Experimental Neuropsychology*, **8**(5), 469–485.

Klonoff, P. S., O'Brien, K. P., Prigatano, G. P., Chiapello, D. A. & Cunningham, M. (1989). Cognitive retraining after traumatic brain injury and its role in facilitating awareness. *Journal of Head Trauma Rehabilitation*, **4**(3), 37–45.

Kreutzer, J. S., Gervasio, A. H. & Camplair, P. S. (1994). Patient correlates of caregiver's distress and family functioning after traumatic brain injury. *Brain Injury*, **8**(3), 211–230.

Lam, C. S., McMahon, B. T., Priddy, D. A. & Gehred-Schultz, A. (1988). Deficit awareness and treatment performance among traumatic head injury adults. *Brain Injury*, **2**(3), 235–242.

Leach, L. R., Frank, R. G., Bouman, D. E. & Farmer, J. (1994). Family functioning, social support and depression after traumatic brain injury. *Brain Injury*, **8**(7), 599–606.

Levin, H. S., High, W. M., Goethe, K. E., Sisson, R. A., Overall, J. E., Rhoades, H. M., Eisenberg, H. M., Kalisky, Z. & Gary, H. E. (1987). The neurobehavioural rating scale: assessment of the behavioural sequelae of head injury by the clinician. *Journal of Neurology, Neurosurgery, and Psychiatry*, **50**, 183–193.

Levin, H. S., O'Donnell, V. M. & Grossman, R. G. (1979). The Galveston Orientation and Amnesia Test. *The Journal of Nervous and Mental Disease*, **167**(11), 675–684.

Lezak, M. D. (1995). *Neuropsychological Assessment*, Third Edition. New York: Oxford University Press.

Lincoln, N. B., Crowe, J. L., Waters, G. R. et al., (1991). The unreliability of sensory assessments. *Clinical Rehabilitation*, **5**, 273–282.

Lomas, J., Pickard, L. & Mohide, A. (1987). Patient versus clinician item generation for quality-of-life measures: the case of language-disabled adults. *Medical Care*, **25**(8), 764–769.

Mahoney, F. I. & Barthel, D. W. (1965). Functional evaluation: the Barthel Index. *Maryland State Medical Journal*, February, 61–65.

Malkmus, D. (1980) Cognitive assessment and goal setting. In *Rehabilitation of the Head-injured Adult: Comprehensive Management*. Professional staff association of Rancho Los Amigos Hospital Inc.

Marsh, N. V., Knight, R. G. & Godfrey, H. P. D. (1990). Long-term psychosocial adjustment following very severe closed head injury. *Neuropsychology*, **4**, 13–27.

Martin, J., Meltzer, H. & Elliot, D. (1988). *The Prevalence of Disability Among Adults*. London: Office of Population Censuses and Surveys: HMSO.

McCauley, C. & Bremer, B. A. (1991). Subjective quality-of-life measures for evaluating medical intervention. *Evaluation and the Health Projections*, **14**(4), 371–387.

McGlynn, S. M. & Schacter, D. L. (1987). Unawareness of Deficits in Neuropsychological Syndromes. *Journal of Clinical and Experimental Neuropsychology*, **11**, 143–205.

McKinlay, W. W. & Brooks, D. N. (1984). Methodological problems in assessing psychosocial recovery following severe head injury. *Journal of Clinical Neuropsychology*, **6**(1), 87–89.

McSweeney, A. J., Grant, I. & Heaton, R. K. (1982). Life quality of patients with chronic obstructive pulmonary disease. *Archives of Internal Medicine*, **142**, 473–478.

Oddy, M., Humphrey, M. & Uttley, D. (1978). Subjective impairment and social recovery after closed head injury. *Journal of Neurology, Neurosurgery and Psychiatry*, **41**(7), 611–616.

Paykel, E. S., Weissman, M., Prusoff, B. A. & Tonks, C. M. (1971). Dimensions of social adjustment in depressed women. *Journal of Nervous and Mental Disease*, **152**(3), 158–172.

Pentland, B. & McPherson, K. (1994). An attempt to measure the effectiveness of early brain injury rehabilitation. *Health Bulletin*, **52**, 438–445.

Prigatano, G. (1984). Neuropsychological rehabilitation after closed head injury in young adults. *Journal of Neurology, Neurosurgery and Psychiatry*, **47**, 505–513.

Prigatano, G. P. & Altman, I. M. (1990). Impaired awareness of behavioral limitations after traumatic brain injury. *Arch. Phys. Med. Rehabil.*, **71**(December), 1058–1064.

Rappaport, M., Hall, K. M. & Hopkins, K. (1982). Disability rating scale for severe head trauma: coma to community. *Archives of Physical Medicine and Rehabilitation*, **63**, 118–23.

Robertson, I. A., Ward, T., Ridgeway, V. and Nimmo-Smith, I. (1994). *The Test of Everyday Attention*. Bury St Edmunds: Thames Valley Publishing Co.

Russell, W. R. & Smith, A. (1961). Post-traumatic amnesia in closed head injury. *Archives of Neuroloqy*, **5**, 16–29.

Sanford, J. (1975). Tolerance of debility in elderly dependents by supporters at home: its significance for hospital practice. *British Medical Journal*, **3**, 471–473.

Shores, E. A., Marosszeky, J. E., Sandanam, J. & Batchelor, J. (1986). Preliminary validation of a clinical scale for measuring the duration of post-traumatic amnesia. *The Medical Journal of Australia*, **144**(May 26), 569–573.

Smith, H. (1992). Head injury follow-up: is the Sickness Impact Profile a useful clinical tool? *Clinical Rehabilitation*, **6**(1), 31–40.

Spreen, O. & Strauss, E. (1991). *A Compendium of Neuropsychologial Tests*. New York: Oxford University Press.

Sunderland, A., Tinson, D., Bradley, L. & Langton Hewer, R. (1989). Arm function after stroke: an evaluation of grip strength as a measure of recovery and a prognosic indicator. *Journal of Neurology, Neurosurgery and Psychiatry*, **52**, 1267–1272.

Teasdale, G. & Jennett, B. (1974). Assessment of coma and impaired consciousness: a practical scale. *The Lancet*, **2**, 81–84.

Turner-Stokes, L. (1995). Results of a survey of users of the Functional Assessment Measure in the UK (personal communication).

Truelle, J.-L., Brooks, D. N., Potagas, C. & Joseph, P.-A. (1994). A European chart for evaluation of patients with traumatic brain injury. In A.-L. Christensen & B. P. Uzzell (Eds.), *Neuropsychological Rehabilitation: international perspectives*. Hillsdale, New Jersey: Lawrence Erlbaum Associates.

Tyerman, A. & Humphrey, M. (1984). Changes in self-concept following severe head injury. *Int. J. Rehab. Research*, **7**(1), 11–23.

Van Zomeren, A. H. & van den Burg, W. (1985). Residual complaints of patients two years after severe head injury. *Journal of Neurology, Neurosurgery and Psychiatry*, **48**, 21–28.

Wade, D. (1992). *Measurement in Neurological Rehabilitation*. Oxford: Oxford University Press.

Wade, D. (1993). Assessment of motor function: impairment and disability. In *Neurological Rehabilitation* (Eds M. P. B. R. Greenwood, T. M. McMillan and C. D. Ward). New York: Churchill Livingstone, pp. 147–160.

Wade, D. & Langton Hewer, R. (1987). Functional abilities after a stroke: measurement, natural history and prognosis. *Journal of Neurology, Neurosurgery and Psychiatry*, **50**, 171–182.

Wade, D., Skilbeck, C. E. & Langton Hewer, R. (1983). Predicting Barthel ADL scores at six months after an acute stroke. *Archives of Physical Medicine and Rehabilitation*, **64**, 24–28.

Weissman, M. M. (1975). The assessment of social adjustment. *Archives of General Psychiatry*, **32**(March), 357–365.

Wilson, B. Cockburn, J. & Baddeley, A. (1985). *The Rivermead Behavioural Memory Test*. Reading: Thames Valley Publishing C.

Zigmond, A. S. & Snaith, R. P. (1983). The Hospital Anxiety and Depression Scale. *Acta Psychiatrica Scandinavica*, **67**, 361–370.

4

REHABILITATION

MICHAEL ODDY, JUDY YEOMANS, HELEN SMITH AND JULIA JOHNSON

Head Injury Rehabilitation Unit, Ticehurst House Hospital, Ticehurst

INTRODUCTION

There have been considerable changes in brain injury rehabilitation over the last 25 years, in terms of both the volume of activity in the field and the approaches to rehabilitation employed. There has been increasing recognition of the need for rehabilitation for those suffering brain injury, and the preponderance of closed head injury in the younger population has meant that more vigorous and intensive methods have been advocated. There has been an increased emphasis upon specialised services for brain-injured patients and more widespread attempts to deal with cognitive and emotional as well as physical aspects of impairment.

One major way in which approaches to rehabilitation of brain-injured people have changed in recent years can be illustrated with reference to the World Health Organisation International Classification of Impairments, Disabilities and Handicaps (World Health Organisation, 1980). The aim of rehabilitation can be seen as the reduction of the effects of disease or injury on daily life (Ward & McIntosh, 1993). This goal can potentially be achieved by reducing pathology/impairment, disability or handicap. Until recently attempts at formal rehabilitation tended to be directed at the alleviation of impairment. An emphasis at this level usually assumes a biological model of the rehabilitation process. Such models emphasise rehabilitation as early as possible after injury. The first aim is the prevention of secondary effects of the original injury (see Chapter 2). This includes surgical or pharmacological methods of preventing oedema, ensuring adequate oxygenation, etc. However, the prevention of contractures, pressure sores and behaviour problems can also be seen in this light.

Brain Injury and After: Towards Improved Outcome. Edited by F.D. Rose and D.A. Johnson.
© 1996 John Wiley & Sons Ltd.

The second aim is based on the possibility that the injury produces a temporary inhibition of function, the removal of which can he assisted by treatment. The task here is to identify medical treatments, therapeutic activities or environments which release this inhibition.

The advantage of an approach based on the reduction of pathology or impairment is that any gains are likely to have widespread implications for disability and handicap. Beyond the acute stage, rightly or wrongly, there has been a trend away from approaches at this level towards those aimed at reducing disability (or increasing function) and handicaps (Mills, Nesbeda & Katz, 1992; Vogenthaler et al., 1989). An educational approach is inherent in this form of rehabilitation. Interventions can he placed along a spectrum, from those emphasising relearning of previously held skills to those emphasising adjustment, both of goals and the means by which these may be achieved. Such an approach normally begins only when (a) the patient is medically stable and (b) he/she has regained full consciousness. This approach has developed because of the problems which are frequently encountered in achieving generalisation of learning from artificial rehabilitation settings to real life circumstances. A 'functional approach' is directed at teaching practical skills such as shopping or use of public transport, usually in real rather than simulated situations. The advantage is that no generalisation from abstract task to practical application is required since the latter is addressed from the start. The disadvantage is that the skill is narrow in scope and hence the potential widespread benefits of, for example, 'memory retraining' are sacrificed. The evidence for the superior efficacy of functional approaches (Mills, Nesbeda & Katz, 1992; Voganthaler et al., 1989) is persuasive and suggests that this should be the preferred approach at this stage in the development of brain injury rehabilitation methods.

AIMS OF REHABILITATION

Rehabilitation can be seen as an attempt to achieve the following:

1. To provide medical, social and environmental conditions which maximise natural recovery
2. To provide conditions which prevent changes antagonistic to recovery
3. To provide appropriate stimulation for the processes of recovery
4. To assist the individual and the family to adjust emotionally to their change in circumstances
5. To teach compensatory strategies and techniques
6. To provide an environment in which the person can be as independent as possible

At present there is little research to guide the design of rehabilitation programmes to provide those social and environmental conditions which maximise natural recovery. The family's involvement is normally seen as being important in reassuring the patient and improving his/her motivation. There are however, many untested assumptions. The family may have a detrimental as well as a beneficial effect on recovery if they themselves are having difficulty coping. If a patient is in a diminished state of consciousness the presence of the family may be irrelevant to the patient's recovery at that stage, although it may be helpful for the family's well-being.

The amount of stimulation and the 'normality' of the environment may be significant. An acute hospital ward is an unfamiliar environment for most people and may provide confusing rather than helpful stimulation. The needs of other patients and for the normal running of the ward may mean that patients have to be managed in a restrictive way, unhelpful to their recovery. Such needs may lead to problematic behaviour being inadvertently reinforced. For example, patients may receive little attention until they attempt to leave the ward. At this point several staff may rush towards them and engage them in solicitous conversation to coax them back to their bed.

At later stages in the recovery process, the absence of rehabilitation may allow the development of problems, particularly of a behavioural or emotional nature. For mild or moderate head injury, Wrightson (1989) and McMillan & Glucksman (1987) found that a brief period of rehabilitation involving mental exercises and explanation prevented the development of longer-term problems.

What constitutes appropriate stimulation at each stage in recovery is equally unclear at present. The not unreasonable assumption that patients should be exposed to tasks which are mildly or moderately challenging but not beyond their current capability is normally followed, but perhaps in a less formal fashion than is desirable. Attempts to reduce the duration of coma by focusing on basic stimulation of all sensory modalities have been evaluated, with mixed results (Wood et al., 1992; Wilson & McMillan, 1993).

The emotional impact following any form of disability cannot be neglected. After brain injury it poses even greater problems because the person frequently has a reduced capacity to make adjustments. Consequences of brain injury, such as concrete thinking, poor memory and an inability to profit from experience, mean that the victim is often unaware of the extent of the changes he/she has suffered and is baffled when it becomes evident that others see him/her differently. Clearly a satisfactory emotional adjustment to disability must be founded on a reasonably clear understanding of the nature of impairment. In brain injury rehabilitation direct approaches are required to tackle the lack of awareness of deficit (Klonoff et al., 1989; Crosson et al., 1989; Lam et al., 1988; Prigatano & Altman, 1990) and to deal with other motivational and cognitive deficits.

Such an awareness is also an important prerequisite for teaching compensatory strategies and techniques. Wilson (1992) has found that strategies for poor memory taught during formal rehabilitation were not being used when patients were followed up several years later. However the patients had devised other strategies of their own. This may be because at the time their awareness of their deficits and the relevance of the strategies was limited. It may also be another reason for the greater success of functionally-based rehabilitation, as the relevance of the tasks taught may be more readily grasped.

Rehabilitation embraces not only a focus on the individual but also on his/her environment. The concept of an adaptive or a prosthetic environment takes many forms depending upon the particular impairments and disabilities the individual suffers. For those with physical disabilities a prosthetic environment would consist of specially designed physical features. For those with cognitive or behavioural impairment a prosthetic environment might include interpersonal features or devices such as tape recorders, alarms, timers, etc. (Hart & Jacobs, 1993). It will also include an appropriate degree of care or supervision, adequate access to leisure and social activity and work or work substitute.

DOES REHABILITATION WORK?

Given the diversity of rehabilitation as described above and the complexity of the process involved as Ward & McIntosh (1993) have observed, '... there is often little more sense in the question "does rehabilitation work" than in the question "does medical treatment work"?' On the other hand, in order to justify services financially and to improve services over time, this question cannot be ignored. It is clear that the ideal of a double-blind, randomised, controlled, prospective study of efficacy cannot be applied in this area. Therapists cannot be blind to the treatment they are giving nor patients unaware of its nature. In theory, it is possible to allocate patients randomly to treatment and control conditions but in practice this has rarely been achieved (Brooks, 1991; Robertson, 1994).

In broad terms two approaches have been pursued. One is to treat a rehabilitation service as an entity and to gauge the extent to which it can produce beneficial results in broad terms, such as reduction in dependence or return to home or work. The other approach is to formulate very specific goals, devise techniques to address these and measure the extent to which the goals are achieved. In both cases clearly some control or comparison group is needed, even if in many cases this may be no more than a stable baseline. Over the last two decades there have been many studies of this second kind, with varying degrees of scientific acceptability. The former approach has been utilised less and requires a larger-scale study, but several examples of this approach have been published recently (Cope et al., 1991a, 1991b; Johnston & Lewis, 1991; Johnston, 1991).

GENERAL STUDIES OF OUTCOME

Prigatano et al. (1984, 1986) compared outcome following 'holistic' brain injury rehabilitation with that in matched controls who underwent traditional, physically orientated rehabilitation only. They found little effect on cognition *per se* but did find the experimental group were significantly less emotionally distressed. Aronow (1987) compared severe traumatic brain injury patients who were given specialised in-patient brain injury rehabilitation with another group who had suffered severe traumatic brain injury but did not receive rehabilitation. There was no significant difference in outcome between the two groups as measured by variables such as vocational status, living arrangements, hours of daytime care required and independence in mobility, despite the fact that the non-rehabilitation group was more independent in self-care and had fewer memory problems. The author therefore concludes that rehabilitation was effective in bringing the outcome for the rehabilitation group closer to that of the non-rehabilitation controls.

Eames & Wood (1985) described a token economy-based programme of rehabilitation for patients with very severe behaviour disturbances. The results suggested that improvement in behaviour could he achieved and that patients became more independent in terms of the extent of care or supervision they required.

A number of studies have suggested that an approach based upon training patients directly in real-life activities yields more positive results than attempting to address the underlying impairment (Fryer & Haffey, 1987; Mills et al., 1992). Intensity of rehabilitation (defined as high levels of treatment delivered in a relatively short time) has been found to be associated with a better outcome (Blackerby, 1990; Spivack, Spettell & Ellis, 1992). Longer stay in a rehabilitation programme was found to improve outcome by Spivack, Spettell & Ellis (1992) and Tuel et al. (1992), but not by Johnston (1991).

Two recent larger-scale studies have investigated rehabilitation outcome across a number of centres. Cope et al. (1991a) attempted to assess the impact of several post-acute rehabilitation programmes, including both day and residential facilities. Improvement was obtained on all three measures (residential status, the extent to which subjects were engaged in productive activity and the number of hours of attendant care needed on admission) and there was no evidence of deterioration over time following discharge. In a sub-group who commenced their rehabilitation more than a year post-injury, a reduced number were living at home at follow-up, but an increased proportion were engaged in productive activity (Cope et al., 1991b). The former finding is likely to be due to the fact that if those living at home were considered to require rehabilitation, this was clearly an unstable situation.

Johnston & Lewis (1991) conducted a similar study in which telephone follow-up was conducted a year after discharge from nine 'transitional living', 'education' and 'employment' rehabilitation programmes in the USA. Once again, outcome measures were the extent to which subjects were engaged in productive activity and a rating of the extent of supervision and care needed. A significant decrease in the extent of supervision required at follow-up was found. A similar but smaller effect for productive activity was obtained.

Both Cope et al. (1991a, b) and Johnston (1991) consider the costs of rehabilitation. Johnston found that the average cost was $106 000 for an average length of stay of 267 days. Cope et al. estimated the average annual savings on reduced care per person. These were greatest for those with severe disability ($41 288) and least for those with mild disability ($2 696). They suggest that the costs of rehabilitation can be recouped within 3 years. Teasdale, Christensen & Pinner (1993) have reported savings following rehabilitation which can be recouped within 5 years. These were broken down into savings in health and social care. Spending on educational services increased slightly as more patients were able to take advantage of such opportunities.

SPECIFIC STUDIES OF OUTCOME

As there have been a great many studies in this area, an attempt will not be made to provide a comprehensive review, but rather to illustrate the sort of studies which have been conducted. In general, experimental single case designs have been used in which the patient is used as his/her own control. Such studies enable the evaluation of treatment programmes tailored to the needs of the individual, require limited resources and are a more practical proposition in the clinical setting. Their main limitations are the fact that spontaneous recovery may be a confounding variable and that the effects of treatment may be expected to take effect during and *after* the treatment has been administered. In rehabilitation this is a particular difficulty as treatments are often intended to teach strategies and approaches which continue to be implemented. Reversal designs (where a change or withdrawal of treatment is expected to produce a return to baseline levels) is rarely either ethical or possible.

Maximising a Cognitive Ability in Order to Enhance Function Across a Range of Tasks

Gray, Robertson & Pentland (1992) conducted a large-scale study of the effectiveness of attentional retraining. Thirty-one patients were allocated randomly to the treatment and control groups. Studies of this scale are difficult to carry out with the brain-injured population, therefore this study makes an important contribution to a field dominated by single-case designs. Measures included common standardised neuropsychological tests. Little difference between groups was shown immediately after the training, but there were differences at a 6-month follow-up. This study highlights the difficulty in quantifying a process such as 'attention'. The precise relationship between available tests and the pure 'attention function' is far from clear. The tests which showed improvement were complex tasks tapping a number of cognitive functions. Large-scale studies employing both laboratory measures and real-life performance would he helpful.

An earlier study by Ponsford & Kinsella (1988) used a multiple baseline design to evaluate a computer-based attention training programme. This approach was not found to produce any improvement, but the study did suggest that the addition of feedback and social reinforcement led to a significant improvement in attention.

Ruff et al. (1994) reviewed 11 studies of attention training of which 8 found this to be effective. One of their main criticisms of this type of study was that there was a frequent failure to explore generalisation of effects to tasks in day-to-day living.

Maximising Function in Real Life Tasks

The majority of published studies have looked at ways to help individuals function better at specific tasks or categories of tasks. Zencius et al., (1991) gave four patients with memory deficits memory notebooks and trained them to use them. The pre- and post-training methods and the training itself all involved simple familiar activities (housework assignments and keeping appointments). Significant improvements were demonstrated within days.

This study demonstrates that external aids can be highly effective, but it also points to the need to give such aids in the context of training which acknowledges the neuropsychological basis of the functional impairment.

Daniel, Bolter & Long (1992) reported an intervention to help an individual to read again, which consisted of a combination of behavioural and cognitive strategies. Improvement was marked, but the reason for improvement is difficult to pinpoint because of the contribution of spontaneous recovery and an improvement in mood, as well as the components of the intervention. This is a common problem for this kind of study. The most effective intervention for an individual may be a multi-factorial one, but it is then difficult to identify the most salient elements of treatment. Multiple-baseline designs can be of assistance here. In such studies a number of measures are taken over a period of time and interventions are introduced at different stages, each targeted at one of the measures. An example of this approach is a home-based intervention for reading difficulty based on an attention deficit by Wilson & Robertson (1992). Through the use of careful measurement and two different interventions, the authors were able to disentangle the different contributions of the components of the intervention. Whilst one intervention led to targeted improvement without generalisation, the second led to targeted improvement and generalisation. Pre- and post-treatment change on neuropsychological tests was not addressed in this study.

Some promising results have come from what is known as the 'vanishing cues' technique. This was devised by Glisky, Schacter & Tulving (1986) and based on the finding that patients with amnesic syndromes had relatively preserved implicit memory. Patients have been taught to use computers and success has been achieved in commercial work settings (Glisky & Schacter, 1989).

The use of computer-provided cues as prompts for the patient to perform a functional task is another promising development which could reduce the need for supervision and guidance in patients with problems of memory, attention, initiation and time-monitoring. Kirsh et al. (1992) described the use of an interactive cueing system mounted on a cleaner's trolley. This presented prompts, one at a time, with an auditory time cue. Improvement was achieved in two of the four subjects although, even in these cases, performance was too slow for competitive employment. Motivation and level of awareness of deficits were cited as prime factors influencing the success of this programme.

Pharmacological Intervention

Medication is commonly used for post-traumatic epilepsy, the reduction of muscle tone, to address complications of multiple injuries and to address behavioural problems. However, the complexity of the effects of medication on a damaged nervous system, in particular frequent adverse effects on cognitive function, has led to cautious use in this population. However, Zasler (1992) points to accumulating evidence for the effectiveness of pharmacological intervention following brain injury, for disorders such as ataxia, dysphasia and sexual dysfunction.

Maximising Emotional Adjustment

Rehabilitation staff are frequently frustrated by the client's refusal to accept an aid or strategy of proven effectiveness. Skilled counselling or psychotherapy, holistic care and time may be crucial in bringing the individual to the point of setting aside past abilities and becoming curious about new activities. If an approach is perceived as unattractive or out of keeping with his/her self-image and goals, it will be rejected. Given the concrete thinking and impaired learning capabilities of many patients, timing the introduction of an intervention and maintaining the patient's interest are extremely delicate. Studies of successful approaches to these problems have been few and far between. Conventional psychotherapy with appropriate modifications may be appropriate or may need to be replaced by approaches which are more firmly based in the neuropsychological status of the individual (Prigatano & Klonoff, 1988). Some simple practical techniques are being reported which are more acceptable to the client than psychotherapy or repetitive training. In a review of computer-assisted rehabilitation Gianutsos (1992) pointed out that whatever the cognitive outcome, patients involved in computer-aided intervention are likely to develop greater awareness of their problems, which will subsequently help them to accept that the same technology can be used in a compensatory manner. Computers are able to provide non-judgmental, positive feedback, allowing patients to work at their own pace. This may play an increasingly important part in helping patients to increase their awareness of their deficits and their emotional adjustment.

Klonoff et al. (1989) described the use of a variety of activities which appear to be aimed at strengthening cognitive functions, but whose real value lies in their potential for increasing awareness. Out-patients in a rehabilitation programme may deny certain cognitive deficits until they have explored these along with their strengths in a group setting and on a daily basis. This may be perceived as less threatening than simply being given information concerning their poor performance on neuropsychological tests. The approach of these authors is essentially educational, treating their clients as respected adults and allowing them to discover their needs alongside peers with similar difficulties. Such an approach can have considerable impact on the rehabilitation process if, for example, acknowledgement of a memory deficit means that the person accepts the need to use memory aids or undergo repetitive training. Fluharty & Priddy (1993) made the simple, but important, point that memory aids which look normal or attractive to the client will be more likely to be used consistently (for example a filofax rather than an institutional A4 diary).

Integration of the Above Approaches

There is a need for the skilful combination of the approaches outlined above, if brain-injured individuals are to derive maximum benefit. Intervention requires a basic understanding of neurological and neuropsychological deficit coupled with a commitment to client-centred interventions with high face validity. Reducing emotional disturbance and increasing awareness of deficits are important prerequisites of much rehabilitation. Drug therapy, in combination with psychological or educational approaches may be considerably more effective than either alone. Attempts to find methods of improving underlying cognitive abilities should not be abandoned in favour of functional retraining alone because the currently available methods appear to be less successful. If methods for retraining basic abilities can be developed there is a great deal to be gained through their potential for widespread effects on practical performance.

Some explicit attempts to combine approaches have been reported. McDonald (1992) reviewing assessment and rehabilitation for communication disorders, advocated a 'cognitive–pragmatic approach'. She suggests that examining the impact of cognitive deficits on communication skills in natural environments may lead to more successful rehabilitative attempts. This approach focuses on the patient's strengths and weaknesses across various social situations in order to identify specific targets for remediation. In this study, McDonald only described tasks designed to focus on the impact of frontal lobe deficits. Lawson & Rice (1989) devised 'executive strategy training' which was also designed to compensate for the problems caused by injury to the frontal lobes. The patients were trained to identify a problem, initiate a search strategy for dealing with it, and select, initiate and monitor an appropriate strategy. Sohlberg, Mateer & Stuss (1993), reviewing studies of frontal lobe dysfunction, proposed a model to bring together these complex functions into a hierarchy which clinicians can use to select and direct intervention. The important point here is that whilst an understanding of this complex field is far from complete, working from a model or framework will assist us in applying existing techniques systematically and evaluating them more accurately. The model may need major revision, but its value lies in bringing order and direction to an otherwise bewildering field.

RETURN TO WORK

Whereas for the very severely injured the goal of rehabilitation is to reduce the amount of personal care required, for the majority the prime objective is a successful return to work. In the absence of rehabilitation there have been consistent findings of a low rate of return. The rate of return varies between studies, primarily as a function of severity of the injuries sustained by the sample (Humphrey & Oddy, 1980). The length of time post-injury when the follow-up is conducted is also important, although there is evidence that few return to work without the benefit of intensive rehabilitation more than 2 years after injury (Oddy et al., 1985).

Rates of 30% or less have been found in some samples (Jacobs, 1989; Brooks et al., 1987). Even where patients have received rehabilitation, if this has been too short (Johnston, 1989) or focused primarily on physical impairment (Oddy, et al., 1985) rates of return to work have been low.

In the last 10 years a number of attempts have been made to design rehabilitation specifically intended to improve vocational approaches based on day patient programmes of cognitive retraining, psychotherapy groups and occupational trials (Prigatano, 1984; Ben Yishay, Silver & Piatesky, 1987). This, described as the 'milieu' approach, has been reported by Prigatano et al. (1984) with indications of positive results. More recently Prigatano et al. (1994) have evaluated a work re-entry programme using this approach. Patients undergoing a programme aimed at returning them to work (or education) were compared with patients followed up at the same hospital, prior to the development of this rehabilitation programme.

Approximately 50% of 'graduates' of the programme were working full-time at follow-up, but when part-time and volunteer work was considered as productive work, the figure rose to 77%. The corresponding control group level of productivity was only 47%. The quality of the therapeutic alliance between patient and therapist in working towards specific goals was found to relate to the level of productivity achieved by the patient. The working alliance between the patient's families and the therapeutic team was also found to be significantly related to outcome.

Although not a randomised control study, this comparison between one form of rehabilitation and what might be described as normal clinical care is an ethically appropriate one, although the results can only be suggestive of efficacy of one rehabilitation programme over another.

Others have used a 'supportive employment model' (Wehman et al., 1988, 1989a, 1990). This approach involves the use of a job coach who focuses exclusively on one client. The emphasis is upon helping the client at the workplace. There is a careful process of matching the client to the job and identifying potential areas of difficulty. Training may be provided prior to going to the actual workplace. The job coach or employment specialist provides training and counselling at the workplace as well as liaison with the employers over a number of weeks or months, and then gradually reduces the amount of involvement as the client settles.

Once again there are no randomised controlled studies of this approach, but initial results where individuals with poor records of post-injury employment receive such rehabilitation suggest that success rates may be significantly increased. Wehman et al. (1989b) cited successful placement rates of 77% and Haffey & Abrams (1991) of 68%.

It is often not the work itself which prevents brain-injured people from making a successful return but associated problems, such as failing to get to work on time and inappropriate verbal or sexual behaviour in the workplace (Wehman et al., 1989a; Haffey & Abrams, 1991; Sale et al., 1991). The aspirations of brain-injured people can also present a formidable barrier in that they may be too high or too prone to change (Oddy, 1993).

REHABILITATION SERVICES

At present there is no consistent view on how rehabilitation services should be delivered. Services differ in terms of whom they seek to serve, where the service is provided, how it is provided, by whom it is provided and when it is provided.

The Client Group

There has been a trend for rehabilitation centres to become more specialised in recent years. Traditionally, many rehabilitation centres have catered for orthopaedic patients as well as neurological patients. Rehabilitation following brain injury differs from orthopaedic or other neurological rehabilitation in a number of respects. The nature of the impairment is different, the most common and difficult problems being cognitive and behavioural rather than physical. Such deficits require a very different approach in a very different environment. Problems of lack of awareness of deficit and motivation need to be tackled. Behaviour problems are common and on a continuum of severity. Even dedicated brain injury services vary in the severity of behaviour problems they can accept.

There has been a debate as to whether rehabilitation should occur early after injury to optimise effectiveness. Cope & Hall (1982) found that patients who entered a rehabilitation programme less than 35 days after injury required less than half the amount of rehabilitation required by a group who entered the programme more than 35 days after injury. The long-term outcome was similar for both groups, although there was a trend for the early rehabilitation group to do better. The need for early rehabilitation is a frequently stated maxim and is a reasonable prediction if rehabilitation is seen as influencing brain pathology directly. However, there is little empirical evidence to support the superiority of early versus later rehabilitation. Indeed, this was a retrospective study and although no clear difference in severity of initial injury in the two groups was evident, there may well have been selective factors at work. A study by Tuel et al. (1992) demonstrated that amongst a group of patients readmitted for rehabilitation, time since injury was not related to rehabilitation success. In general the type of rehabilitation indicated is different in the early stages before the patient becomes medically stable, and comparing early and later rehabilitation may be comparing two rather different endeavours.

A recent study has identified several factors which suggest that older people (50 +) sustaining head injuries may require different hospital procedures and management techniques to those applied to younger adults. The recovery patterns may well be different and necessitate, for instance, closer monitoring of moderately injured older patients, whom Goldstein et al. (1994) found to be at greater risk of delayed neurosurgical complications. The development of post-traumatic dementia has been associated with head injury in older adults (Heyman et al., 1984) .

The timing and nature of rehabilitation for victims of head injury at different ages clearly warrants further research.

The Rehabilitation Setting

The wider environment in which rehabilitation is provided varies considerably and often greatly influences the nature of the rehabilitation within the centre. Some programmes are based within an acute hospital. Whilst this is desirable during the early stages of rehabilitation because of the need for medical or surgical support, at a later stage the need is to create a participative, educational environment. This may be difficult in a setting in which people tend to slip into the passive role of recipient of treatment.

The size of rehabilitation centres varies widely. A unit may consist of no more than a dozen places on a specific, homogeneous programme or it may be a large centre with as many as 500 beds providing rehabilitation for many diagnostic groups. For the brain-injured, where confusion, disorientation and ability to process information present problems, a smaller, more home-like environment is much to be preferred, particularly for those who remain in a disorientated state for weeks or months.

As indicated above, some aspects of rehabilitation need to be conducted in the target environment such as the workplace or the home.

The tradition of residential rehabilitation centres is gradually being replaced or at least complemented by services run as day centres or provided within the client's own community by community rehabilitation teams. A number of programmes in Europe and in the USA have started to run as training courses (Christensen et al., 1988; Ben Yishay & Lakin, 1989). Participants enrol as a group at the beginning of a course which typically lasts 4 or 5 months. No new participants are admitted once the course has commenced. A repeat cycle may be indicated for those who do not achieve their goals after one cycle (Ben Yishay, Silver & Piatesky, 1987).

The involvement of the family in rehabilitation is a crucial ingredient which is becoming common practice and is clearly more readily achieved where services are provided on a local basis. Access to community resources is important in the planning of any service, especially in the light of the current need for an emphasis on retraining in real rather than simulated situations.

This diversification of the means by which services are delivered is to be welcomed and may lead to the emergence of innovative and cost-effective programmes.

Who Delivers the Service?

There are major differences in the constitution of the rehabilitation team from centre to centre, in terms of both patient:staff ratios and the skill mix. This reflects the differing philosophies and foci of centres. There is, however, considerable if not universal agreement that a team approach is vital in rehabilitation (Ragnarsson, Thomas & Zasler, 1993; Eames, 1989; Frey, 1992). A team may be defined as a group of professionals working in a coordinated fashion towards shared goals. Wood (1993) has enumerated the benefits of a team approach as follows:

1. Improved communication between the individuals involved in treatment
2. Shared knowledge between individuals of different disciplines allowing more efficient treatment of the individual patient
3. A more consistent goal-oriented approach and better continuity of care for the patient as a whole
4. Promotion of a broader perspective for health care provision
5. Provision of a stimulating environment, enhancing the contribution of team members, improving motivation and increasing individual effectiveness
6. Creation of an esprit de corps which leads to a mutually supporting atmosphere

What is less certain is how a team should organise itself, and a number of models have been suggested. Melvin (1980) describes a *multidisciplinary* team as one in which members exchange information but work separately, despite being located on the same premises. Such a team results in the '. . . sum of each discipline providing its own unique activity'. An *interdisciplinary* team is defined as one which works towards common goals with joint responsibility for achieving an outcome which is greater than if each discipline functioned separately. In trying to achieve the status of an interdisciplinary team, the problem of blurring of role boundaries arises. Most management texts are agreed that team members need to have a clear understanding of the scope and limits of their role. It is illogical to argue that a team needs to be made up of different disciplines if roles are totally blurred and the special expertise of individual team members is lost or reduced to the lowest common denominator. Hence joint responsibility for shared goals cannot mean a loss of professional identity. The issue of role ambiguity and differentiation must be explicitly and frequently addressed. Team-building exercises such as journal clubs, in-service training and team meetings can promote the cohesion of the team.

A question which receives frequent comment is that of leadership. This can be divided into clinical and managerial or administrative leadership. Good management skills are transferable and as long as the individual's managerial style fits the particular context this role can be fulfilled by someone without a clinical background. Clinical leadership is more contentious. In most countries there is a strong tradition of medical leadership which is often generalised to the rehabilitation setting. However, much brain injury rehabilitation is educational rather than medical and indeed, in the case of vocational rehabilitation, may have little medical connection at all. The doctor's role is frequently advisory, rather than central to the work of the rehabilitation team.

The practice has grown, therefore, of appointing clinical leaders from the therapy or psychology professions rather than from medicine. This is not to ignore the vital contribution of various medical specialists to the rehabilitation process. However, as Ward & McIntosh (1993) have pointed out, '... there is no reason why a (neurologist) should not make an effective clinical contribution in a non-leading role'.

Duration of Rehabilitation

There is great variation in the length of time for which it is considered rehabilitation should last. In practice, this boils down to a consideration of the optimal time over which in-patient or day-patient rehabilitation should take place. The slogan 'brain injury is for ever' is a truism suggesting that the process of rehabilitation never ends. However, intensive or comprehensive rehabilitation is an expensive process which can only be justified in financial terms for a limited period. There is conflicting evidence as to whether increasing the duration of rehabilitation improves outcome. Spivack, Spettell & Ellis (1992) suggest it does, whilst Johnston (1991) found no such association. No studies have varied duration of rehabilitation in a prospective way and therefore it is impossible to distinguish cause from effect. An ideal rule of thumb would suggest that rehabilitation continue until a plateau had been reached. However, financial constraints rarely allow this luxury and hence the hunt for brief but effective intervention strategies continues with some urgency.

There is a grey area in which intensive rehabilitation tapers into long-term disability management by way of what is often referred to as slow-stream rehabilitation. Different services focus on different parts of the rehabilitation spectrum from acute medical care to vocational rehabilitation and residential care.

A Model Service

A number of suggestions have been made in recent years for the optimal rehabilitation service for those suffering a brain injury (British Psychological Society, 1989; Medical Disabilities Society, 1988; Oddy et al., 1989; Greenwood & McMillan, 1993; McMillan & Greenwood, 1993). McMillan & Greenwood (1993) have recently highlighted the main elements such a service would need to include:

1. *Acute rehabilitation*   Patients in the United Kingdom are initially admitted

to a neurosurgical centre or to a District General Hospital. In addition to medical and surgical care, it is important that coordinated multi-disciplinary rehabilitation should begin during this phase.

2. *Brain injury rehabilitation units*   McMillan & Greenwood suggest that a small but clinically significant group of patients with persisting deficits require several months of in-patient rehabilitation. The authors envisage that at this stage physical therapy and the rehabilitation of daily living skills will be the main focus, but the assessment and management of cognitive deficits and behaviour disorders may also be necessary.

3. *Non-residential rehabilitation centres*   For most brain-injured individuals there are clinical as well as financial advantages to their rehabilitation being conducted on a day-patient basis. For these patients the primary and most disabling problems will be cognitive and personality changes. Such centres would focus on psychosocial aspects of rehabilitation. Patients would progress to these either from the acute hospital stage or via a residential rehabilitation unit. A small number of patients require admission to a specialist unit where active attempts are made to return the individual to the community.

4. *Supported living*   Residential facilities which provide appropriate support (supervision rather than care), are necessary for those who are unable or do not wish to live with their families.

5. *Work centres/daytime activity*   Day centres and sheltered work are important for those who will never be able to return to open employment. Such centres should aim to provide stimulating, enjoyable and satisfying activities for these clients. This is not easily achieved, but it is possible and voluntary organisations such as Headway have been very successful in this respect.

6. *Respite care*   Finally, but in many cases most important of all, respite care should be available in a variety of forms. It is to relatives that the stressful responsibility of care ultimately falls, and any service to make this task a little easier is clearly money well spent.

This model stresses 'centres' where rehabilitation is carried out. The discussion above suggests that rehabilitation services may increasingly be carried out in the community with professionals working directly with employees, families and members of the general public to bring about a return to the most normal and satisfactory life possible.

THE FAMILY

From the moment of injury the family cannot be ignored. The family must be considered both for its own needs and for its role in the rehabilitation process.

These two perspectives are not incompatible, since the family in many cases plays the largest part in the care and rehabilitation of the patient. If the family's own needs are not met its capacity to play this role effectively will be reduced.

It is easy for rehabilitation professionals to come into conflict with the family. Their aims may be different; there may be inadvertent competition between professional and the family. The family is under tremendous pressure and going through a protracted process of adaptation to change and loss. Relatives may feel they need to fight to protect the interests of the patient who is rendered unable to protect him/herself. Such conflict must be avoided. Professionals have a responsibility to understand the family's frustration and distress, find ways to reduce this and harness the family's potential for enhancing the recovery of the brain-injured person.

The engagement of the family in the rehabilitation process varies according to practical constraints, such as their other commitments and the distance they live from the centre. Some centres insist upon a considerable level of involvement as a condition of treatment. Families must be helped with the pain of emotional adjustment to their new circumstances and involved in the planning and decision-making process.

THE FUTURE OF BRAIN INJURY REHABILITATION

It is unlikely there will ever be studies which provide unambiguous evidence for the efficacy of all facets of brain injury rehabilitation. At present it can be concluded that, whilst all studies fall short of true scientific designs, there is accumulating evidence that brain injury rehabilitation can be effective. Despite the best attempts at prevention, brain injuries will continue to occur and to represent a tragedy for the victims and their families. Attempts to alleviate this can be supported on both financial and humanitarian grounds. There are strong grounds for continuing to pursue both general studies of rehabilitation programmes and studies of specific techniques.

The field of brain injury rehabilitation is immensely challenging. It involves the potential to influence outcomes at a number of levels. There remains the possibility, although as yet unproven, that the recovery of the biological function of the brain after injury can be influenced by environmental means. Pharmacological intervention may allow the brain to function more effectively after injury. Theories of cognitive function may allow a technology to develop which enables different cognitive processes or external strategies to improve the person's ability to function. There is also a developing field addressing the person's adjustment to disability.

These fields are not mutually exclusive. Nor are developments in one likely to lead to a reduction in the importance of others. Opportunities need to be available for research in all these areas. For some the pay-off is likely to be more immediate but in others the longer-term results may be more dramatic. There has certainly been an increase in clinical work in specialised brain injury rehabilitation. This needs to be accompanied by a corresponding increase in research activity. The current commercial emphasis on demonstrating favourable outcome for service purchasers does not encourage the dispassionate approach to clinical research which is required. None of us has the answers at present and there needs to be continuing opportunity for experiment and objective evaluation. Such evaluation cannot be achieved where there is a danger that lack of positive outcome may result not in a change of approach, but in the service or centre being disbanded.

At present, the extent to which underlying brain function can be remediated is limited. The greatest contribution that can be made to the well-being of the patient and the family is in helping them adjust emotionally and practically to the changes which severe brain injury inevitably leads. This aspect of rehabilitation tends to be undervalued. It does not have the clinical prestige of attempts to influence brain function. It does not meet the wishes of the patient, the family or indeed health purchasers for 'cure'. Nevertheless, such attempts to help the person forge a different but satisfactory life should be afforded greater importance both clinically and for research.

REFERENCES

Aronow, H. U. (19X7). Rehabilitation effectiveness with severe brain injury: translating research into policy. *Journal of Head Trauma Rehabilitation*, 2(3), 24–36.

Ben-Yishay, Y. & Lakin, P. (1989). Structured group treatment for brain injury survivors. In *Neuropsychological Treatment After Brain Injury* (Eds D. W. Ellis & A.-L. Christensen). Boston: Kluwer Academic Publishing Company, pp. 211–295.

Ben-Yishay, Y., Silver, S. M., & Piatesky, E. (1987). Relationship between employability and vocational outcome after intensive holistic cognitive rehabilitation. *Journal of Head Trauma Rehabilitation*, 2, 35–48.

Blackerby, W. F. (1990). Intensity of rehabilitation and length of stay. *Brain Injury* 4(2), 167–173.

British Psychological Society (1989). *Services for Young Adult Patients with Acquired Brain Damage*. Leicester: British Psychological Society.

Brooks, N. (1991). The effectiveness of post-acute rehabilitation. *Brain Injury*, 5(2), 1–7.

Brooks, N., McKinley, W., Symington, C., Beattie, A. & Campsey, L. (1987). Return to work within the first 7 years of severe head injury. *Brain Injury*, 1, 5–19.

Christensen, A.-L., Pinner, E. M., & Pedersen, P. M. (1988). Program for rehabilitation for brain damage in Denmark. In *Neuropsychological Rehabilitation. Current knowledge and future directions* (Eds. A.-L. Christensen & B. P. Uzell). Boston:

Kluwer, pp. 115–124.

Cope, D. N., Cole, J. R., Hall, K. M. & Barkan, H. (1991a). Brain injury: analysis of outcome in a post-acute rehabilitation system. Part 2. General analysis. *Brain Injury*, **5**, 111–126.

Cope, D. N., Cole, J. R., Hall, K. M. & Barkan, H. (1991b). Brain injury: analysis of outcome in post-acute rehabilitation system. Part 1. *Brain Injury*, **5**, 127-140.

Cope, D. N. & Hall, K. (1982). Head injury rehabilitation: benefit of early intervention. *Arch. Phys. Med. Rehabil.*, **63**(Sept.), 433–437.

Crosson, B., Barco, P. P., Velozo, C. A., Bolesta, M. M., Cooper, P. V., Werts, D. & Brobeck, T. C. (1989). Awareness and compensation in postacute head injury rehabilitation. *Journal of Head Trauma Rehabilitation*, **4**(3), 46–54.

Daniel, M. S., Bolter, J. F. & Long, C. J. (1992). Remediation of alexia without agraphia: a case study. *Journal of Head Trauma Rehabilitation*, **6**(6), 529–542.

Eames, P. (1989). Head injury rehabilitation: Towards a model service. In *Models of Brain Injury Rehabilitation* (Eds. R. L. Wood & P. Eames). London: Chapman and Hall.

Eames, P. & Wood, R. (1985). Rehabilitation after severe brain injury: a follow-up study of a behaviour modification approach. *Journal of Neurology, Neurosurgery and Psychiatry*, **48**, 613–619.

Fluharty, G. & Priddy, D. (1993). Metllods of increasing client acceptance of a memory book. *Brain Injury*, **7**(1), 85–88.

Frey, W. R. (1992). Quality management: protecting and enhancing quality in brain injury rehabilitation. *Brain Injury*, **7**(4), 1–10.

Fryer, J. & Haffey, W. (1987). Cognitive rehabilitation and community readaption: outcome from two program models. *Journal of Head Trauma Rehabilitation*, **2**, 51–63.

Gianutsos, R. (1992). The computer in cognitive rehabilitation: it's not just a tool anymore. *Journal of Head Trauma Rehabilitation*, **7**(3), 26–35.

Glisky, E. L. & Schacter, D. L. (1989). Extending the limits of complex learning in organic amnesia: computer training in a vocational domain. *Neuropsychologia*, **27**(1), 107–120.

Glisky, E. L., Schacter, D. L. & Tulving, E. (1986). Computer learning by memory-impaired patients: acquisition and retention of complex knowledge. *Neuropsychologia*, **24**(3), 313–328.

Goldstein, F. C., Levin, H. S., Presley, R. M., Searcy, J., Golohan, A. R. T., Eisenberg, H. M., Jann, B. & Bertolino-Kusnerik, L. (1994). Neurobehavioral consequences of closed head injury in older adults. *Journal of Neurology, Neurosurgery and Psychiatry*, **57**, 961–966.

Gray, J., Robertson, I. & Pentland, B. (1992). Microcomputer-based attentional retraining after brain damage: a randomised control group design. *Neuropsychological Rehabilitation*, **2**, 97–115.

Greenwood, R. J. & McMillan, T. M. (1993). Models of rehabilitation programmes for the brain-injured adult. 1: Current provision, efficacy and good practice. *Clinical Rehabilitation*, **7**, 248–255.

Haffey, W. J. & Abrams, D. L. (1991). Employment outcomes for participants in a brain injury work reentry program: preliminary findings. *Journal of Head Trauma Rehabilitation*, **6**(3), 24–34.

Hart, T. & Jacobs, H. E. (1993). Rehabilitation and management of behavioral disturbances following frontal lobe injury. *Journal of Head Trauma Rehabilitation*, **8**(1), 1–12.

Heyman, A., Wilkinson, W. E., Stafford, J. A., Helms, M. J., Sigmon, A. H. &

Weinberg, T. (1984). Alzheimer's disease: a study of epidemiological aspects. *Annals of Neurology*, **15**, 335–341.

Humphrey, M. & Oddy, M. (1980). Return to work after head injury: a review of post-war studies. *Injury*, **12**, 107–114.

Jacobs, H. E. (1989). Adult community integration. In *Traumatic Brain Injury* (Ed. P. Bach-y-Rita). New York: Demos.

Johnson, R. (1989). Employment after severe head injury: do the manpower services commission schemes help? *Injury: the British Journal of Accident Surgery*, **20**(1), 5–9.

Johnston, M. V. (1991) Analysis of outcome in a post-acute rehabilitation system II: Subanalyses. *Brain Injury*, **5**, 155–168.

Johnston, M. V. & Lewis, F. D. (1991). Outcomes of community re-entry programmes for brain injury survivors. Part 1: Independent living and productive activities. *Brain Injury*, **5**(2), 141–154.

Kirsch, N. L., Levine, S. P., Lajiness-O'Neill, R. & Schnyder, M. (1992). Computer assisted interactive task guidance: facilitating the performance of a simulated vocational task. *Journal of Head Trauma Rehabilitation*, **7**(3), 13–25.

Klonoff, P. S., O'Brien, K. P., Prigatano, G. P., Chiapello, D. A. & Cunningham, M. (1989) Cognitive retraining after traumatic brain injury and its role in facilitating awareness. *Journal of Head Trauma Rehabilitation*, **4**(3), 37–45.

Lam, C. S., McMahony, B.T., Priddy, D. A. & Gehred-Schultze, A. (1988). Deficit awareness and treatment performance among traumatic head injury adults. *Brain Injury*, **2**(3), 235–242.

Lawson, M. J. & Rice, D. N. (1989). Effects of training in use of executive strategies on a verbal memory problem resulting from closed head injury. *Journal of Head Trauma Rehabilitation*, **2**, 842–854.

McDonald, S. (1992). Communication disorders following head injury: new approaches to assessment and rehabilitation. *Brain Injury*, **6**(3), 283–292.

McMillan, T. & Greenwood, R. (1993). Models of rehabilitation programmes for the brain injured adult: II: Model services and suggestions for change in the U.K. *Clinical Rehabilitation*, **7**(4), 256–263.

McMillan, T. M. & Glucksman, E. E. (1987). The neuropsychology of moderate head injury. *Journal of Neurology, Neurosurgery and Psychiatry*, **50**, 393–397.

Medical Disabilities Society (1988). *The Management of Traumatic Brain Injury*. A report of a working party. London: Development Trust for the Young Disabled.

Melvin, J. L. (1980). Interdisciplinary and multidisciplinary activities and the ACRM. *Archives of Physical Medicine and Rehabilitation*, **61**, 379–380.

Mills, V. M., Nesbeda, T. & Katz, D. (1992). Outcomes for traumatically brain-injured patients following post-acute rehabilitation programmes. *Brain Injury*, **6**, 219–228.

Oddy, M. (1993). Psychosocial consequences of brain injury. In *Neurological Rehabilitation* (Eds. M. P. B. R. Greenwood, T. M. McMillan & C. D. Ward). New York: Churchill Livingstone, pp. 423–436.

Oddy, M., Bonham, E., McMillan, T., Stroud, A. & Rickard, S. (1989). A comprehensive service for the rehabilitation and long-term care of head injury survivors. *Clinical Rehabilitation*, **3**, 253–259.

Oddy, M., Coughlan, T., Tyerman, A. & Jenkins, D. (1985). Social adjustment after closed head injury: a further follow-up seven years after injury. *Journal of Neurology, Neurosurgery and Psychiatry*, **48**, 564–568.

Ponsford, J. L. & Kinsella, G. (1988). Evaluation of a remedial programme for the attentional deficits following brain injury. *Journal of Clinical and Experimental Neuropsychology*, **10**, 693–708.

Prigatano, G., Fordyce, D. J., Zeiner, H. K., Roueche, J. R., Pepping, H. & Wood, B. C.

(1984). Neuropsychological rehabilitation after closed head injury in young adults. *Journal of Neurology, Neurosurgery and Psychiatry*, **47**, 505–513.

Prigatano, G. (1986). Neuropsychological Rehabilitation after Brain Injury. Baltimore: Johns Hopkins University Press.

Prigatano, G. & Klonoff, P. S. (1988). Psychotherapy and neuropsychological assessment after brain injury. *Journal of Head Trauma Rehabilitation*, **3**, 45–56.

Prigatano, G. P. (1991). Disordered mind, wounded soul: the emerging role of psychotherapy in rehabilitation after brain injury. *Journal of Head Trauma Rehabilitation*, **6**(4), 1–10.

Prigatano, G. P. & Altman, I. M. (1990). Impaired awareness of behavioral limitations after traumatic brain injury. *Arch. Phys. Med. Rehabil.*, **71**(Dec.), 1058–1064.

Prigatano, G. P., Klonoff, P. S., O'Brien, K. P., Altman, I. M., Amin, K., Chiapello, D., Shepherd, J., Cunningham, M. & Mira, M. (1994). Productivity after neuropsychologically oriented milieu rehabilitation. *Journal of Head Trauma Rehabilitation*, **9**(1), 91–103.

Ragnarsson, K. T, Thomas, J. P. & Zasler, N. D. (1993). Model systems of care for individuals with traumatic brain injury. *Journal of Head Trauma Rehabilitation*, **8**(2), 1–11.

Robertson, I. (1994). Methodology in neuropsychological rehabilitation research. *Neuropsychological Rehabilitation*, **4**(1), 1–6.

Ruff, R., Mahaffey, R., Engel, J., Farrow, C., Cox, D. & Karzmark, P. (1994). Efficacy study of THINKable in the attention and memory retraining of traumatically head-injured patients. *Brain Injury*, **8**(1), 3–14.

Ruff, R. M., Baser, C. A., Johnston, J. W., Marshall, L. F., Klauber, S. K., Klauber, M. R. & Minteer, M. (1989). Neuropsychological rehabilitation: an experimental study with head injured patients. *Journal of Head Trauma Rehabilitation*, **4**(3), 20–36.

Sale, P., West, M., Sherron, P. & Wehman, P. H. (1991). Exploratory analysis of job separations from supported employment for persons with traumatic brain injury. *Journal of Head Trauma Rehabilitation*, **6**(3), 1–11.

Sohlberg, M. M., Mateer, C. A. & Stuss, D. T. (1993). Contemporary approaches to the management of executive control dysfunction. *J. Head Trauma Rehabil.*, **8**(1), 45–58.

Spivack, G., Spettell, C. M., & Ellis, D. W. (1992) Effects of intensity of treatment and length of stay on rehahilitation outcomes. *Brain Injury*, **6**, 419–434.

Teasdale, T. W., Chrislensen, A.-L. & Pinner, E. V. (1993). Psychosocial rehabilitation of cranial trauma and stroke patients. *Brain Injury*, **7**(6), 535–542.

Tuel, S. M., Presly, S. K., Meythaler, J. M., Heinemann, A. W. & Katz, R. T. (1992). Functional improvement in severe head injury after readmission for rehabilitation. *Brain Injury*, **6**(4), 363–372.

Voganthaler, D. R., Smith, K. R. & Goldfader, P. (1989). Head injury: a multivariate study: predicting long-term productivity and independent living outcome. *Brain Injury*, **3**, 369–385.

Ward, C. V. & McIntosh, S. (1993). The rehabilitation process: a neurological perspective. In *Neurological Rehabilitation* (Eds R. Greenwood, M. Barnes, T. McMillan & C. D. Ward),. Edinburgh: Churchill Livingstone, pp. 13–28.

Wehman, P., Kreutzer, J., Wood, W. & Stonnington, H. H. (1988). Supported employment for persons with traumatic brain injury: a preliminary report. *Journal of Head Trauma Rehabilitation*, **3**(4), 82–93.

Wehman, P., Kreutzer, J. S., West, M. D., Sherron, P. D., Diambra, J., Fry, R., Groah, C., Sale, P. & Killan, S. (1989a). Employment outcomes of persons following traumatic brain injury: pre-injury, post-injury and supportive employment. *Brain*

Injury, **3**(4), 397–412.

Wehman, P., West, M., Fry, R., Sherron, P., Groah, C., Kreutzer, J. & Sale, P. (1989b). Effect of supported employment on the vocational outcomes of persons with traumatic brain injury. *Journal of Applied Behaviour Analysis*, **22**(4), 395–405.

Wehman, P. H., Kreutzer, J. S., West, M. D., Sherron, P. D., Zasler, N. D., Groah, C. H., Stonnington, H. H., Burns, C. T. & Sale, P. R. (1990). Return to work for person with traumatic brain injury: a supported employment approach. *Archives of Physical Medicine and Rehabilitation*, **71**, 1047–1052.

Wilson, B. (1992). Recovery and compensatory strategies in head-injured memory-impaired people several years after insult. *Journal of Neurology, Neurosurgery and Psychiatry*, **55**, 177–180.

Wilson, C. & Robertson, I. (1992). A home-based intervention for attentional slips during reading following head injury: a single case study. *Neuropsychological Rehabilitation*, **2**(3), 193–206.

Wilson, S. L. & McMillan, T. M. (1993). A review of the evidence for the effectiveness of sensory stimulation treatment for coma and vegetative states. *Neuropsychological Rehabilitation*, **3**(9), 149–160.

Wood, R. L. (1993). The rehabilitation team. In *Neurological Rehabilitation* (Eds. R. Greenwood, M. Barnes, T. McMillan & C. D. Ward). Edinburgh: Churchill Livingstone, pp. 41–50.

Wood, R. L., Winkowski, T. B. & Miller, J. L. (1992). Evaluating sensory regulation as a method to improve awareness in patients with altered states of consciousness: a pilot study. *Brain Injury*, **6**, 411–418.

World Health Organisation (1980). *The International Classification of Impairments, Disabilities and Handicaps — a Manual of Classification Relating to the Consequence of Disease*. Geneva: World Health Organisation.

Wrightson, P. (1989). Management of disability and rehabilitation services after mild head injury. In *Mild Head Injury* (Eds. H. S. Levin, H. M. Eisenberg & A. L. Benton). New York: Oxford University Press, pp. 245–256.

Zasler, N. D. (1992). Advances in neuropharmacological rehabilitation for brain dysfunction. *Brain Injury*, **6**(1), 1–14.

Zencius, A., Wesolowski, M. D., Krankowski, T. & Burke, W. H. (1991). Memory notebook training with traumatically brain-injured clients. *Brain Injury*, **5**(3), 321–326.

5

THE SOCIAL CONTEXT

ANDY TYERMAN

Head Injury Service, Aylesbury

INTRODUCTION

The social impact of severe head injury can be far-reaching, affecting both the person with the injury and members of the family. Whilst those with minor head injuries will generally resume their former lifestyle, those with more severe injuries will face restrictions in their work, leisure, social and family life. These restrictions are often shared by other members of the family who may experience considerable stress in caring for the person with the injury, often amidst marked changes in family relationships, roles and functioning. Family and broader social circumstances at the time of injury often have a major bearing on the course of rehabilitation, resettlement and reintegration. The family in particular plays a vital role in reinforcing progress in rehabilitation and supporting the person in long-term readjustment.

This chapter will review the social, occupational and family impact of head injury in adults, focusing on those with severe head injury (i.e. those unconscious more than 6 hours and/or with a post-traumatic amnesia (PTA) of at least 24 hours), for whom the social effects are often extensive and long-term. The generally disappointing social outcome will be viewed in the context of health, social and vocational services, which are often inappropriate or inadequate to meet the complex needs of persons with severe head injury and their families. The review will then consider recent initiatives in community and vocational rehabilitation which seek to address such needs and offer some hope of improved social outcome.

Brain Injury and After: Towards Improved Outcome. Edited by F.D. Rose and D.A. Johnson.
© 1996 John Wiley & Sons Ltd.

SOCIAL OUTCOME

The complex array of physical, cognitive and personality changes resulting from severe head injury have a marked impact on the person and his/her life. As the majority are under 25 years at the time of injury, many will live with the effects of their injuries for 50 years or more. They are often enjoying their newfound personal and financial independence, developing new roles and relationships and living a full leisure and social life, all of which may be threatened by the effects of head injury. Those injured at an older age will of course have greater responsibilities both at home and at work.

Many will recover full independence after severe head injury or require occasional help with more complex tasks. Loss of independence stems from a combination of physical, sensory, cognitive and personality changes. An indication of the level of dependence is provided by a 3–10 year rehabilitation follow-up of 100 persons after very severe head injury (PTA > 4 days, mean 11.6 weeks) in Australia: 53% were judged as able to live independently (with emotional support if required); 29% as independent only with support services and/or in sheltered accommodation; and 18% as fully dependent upon the family or an institution (Tate et al., 1989).

Loss of independence of course impacts both on the person and the family. For the minority who require help for personal care there may the cost of aids and adaptations as well as the time and cost for the family in providing or arranging care. Others with marked cognitive impairment will need constant supervision or the ready availability of assistance. For those unable to travel alone there are obvious restrictions for the person and possibly additional costs and inconvenience for the family. Others may be independent in daily activities but need help in managing the home or their financial affairs. However, for many the major loss is that of employment.

Occupation

Return to productive occupation represents a major challenge after head injury. Successful return to education or work represents a major step which can restore a sense of direction and self-worth and provide the foundation for long-term personal, family and social readjustment. Head injury poses many obstacles to return to work, not least because it commonly affects teenagers or young adults who are either still in training or just establishing themselves in their chosen careers, with most of their working lives ahead of them. Loss of employment of course has a major bearing on the financial resources of both the individual and the family, particularly where the person is living with a spouse and is, as such, a major breadwinner (McMordie & Barker, 1988)

For those with mild or moderate injuries, most will return to work. However, in the absence of specialist assessment many return too soon and struggle with post-concussional symptoms such as headaches, fatigue, poor memory and concentration, and irritability. Where these persist the person may enter a downward spiral of self-doubt, anxiety and lost confidence.

For those with severe injuries return to former duties is in doubt. Without guidance, and sometimes contrary to advice, some with limited insight insist on an early return, inadvertently jeopardising the future of their jobs. For those with very severe injuries (i.e. unconscious > 48 hours and/or a PTA > 7 days) only a minority will return to previous education, training or employment.

Whilst varying enormously in specialist knowledge and skills, most jobs require integrated physical, cognitive and social skills. Slow speed, poor concentration and fatigue render many persons uncompetitive after head injury. Some also face specific restrictions: those with physical disability may be prevented from returning to manual work; those with visual field deficits will be precluded from driving; those with poor memory will require supervision; those lacking in initiative, problem-solving and decision-making skills will struggle to cope with managerial positions; those with emotional changes may not feel able to cope with pressure or responsibility; and those with poor behavioural control, especially disinhibition and aggression, are unlikely to be tolerated in the workplace. A minority also face the practical restrictions and social stigma of epilepsy. However, re-employment prospects are also compromised by the lack of knowledge of employers, who have little conception of the subtleties of acquired brain damage and may equate head injury with learning disability. The lack of adequate equal opportunities legislation and specialist vocational services also means that the misperceptions and prejudices of employers go largely unchallenged.

Reported return to employment or education varies markedly from 12% to 100% (Crisp, 1992). In a large-scale follow-up of 485 persons with mainly mild injuries in Norway, 73% were employed at 3–5 years post-injury (Edna & Cappelin, 1987). Similarly, 73% of 102 persons with mostly moderate injuries in Washington returned to work within a year, although 40% were still reporting difficulties (Fraser et al., 1988). In contrast, of 134 persons with mainly very severe injuries in Glasgow, only 29% were employed at 2–7 years (Brooks et al., 1987). However, few had received much rehabilitation.

Outcome from rehabilitation centres in the UK is, however, also disappointing. In a very severe group (median PTA 6 weeks) from

Addenbrooke's Hospital, Cambridge, a return to work was achieved by 38% with another 28% trying but failing to do so (Johnson, 1987). Of 44 persons admitted to the Wolfson Medical Rehabilitation Centre, London, after very severe injuries (PTA > 7 days) only 36% were in full-time employment at 2 years follow-up, with the majority working at a reduced level (Weddell, Oddy & Jenkins, 1980). By 7 years four had progressed from working in a reduced capacity to jobs comparable to pre-injury, but no-one unemployed at 2 years had since found employment, leaving just 35% in work (Oddy et al., 1985). A meta-analysis of 41 studies suggested that the highest and most reliable correlations were between unemployment and executive dysfunction, emotional disturbance, reduced activities of daily living and lack of vocational rehabilitation (Crepeau & Scherzer, 1993).

Leisure and Social Life

Many persons with less severe head injury will resume former leisure activities, but may find that they have lost the edge in performance in sports or other skilled activities due to poor coordination or slowed reactions, or may feel that they no longer fit in socially due to subtle changes in personality. Those with more severe injuries may find that activities such as sport, cycling, walking and keep-fit are precluded by physical disabilities, or may be impeded by the inability to drive. Less physical pursuits, such as photography, art, model-making, etc. may be less rewarding due to loss of concentration or dexterity; whilst activities such as chess or bridge may be limited by poor memory, reasoning and planning. Reading is a common casualty, affected both by visual/perceptual deficits and by poor concentra-tion and memory. Furthermore, unable to pursue previous activities, the person with head injury may no longer have the imagination or initiative to explore alternatives, or may be resistant to such suggestions due to depression or unrealistic expectations of further recovery, which it is hoped will allow a return to previous activities.

The impact on leisure activities is often paralleled by social isolation. The person with the injury may feel less inclined to pursue an active social life due to lack of confidence, low mood, intolerance to noise or difficulty in participating fully in conversations. In addition, friends tend to fade away gradually in the realisation that the person is no longer as before. They may find it hard to handle the irritability, impatience and aggression. They may find the person's conversation less rewarding due to repetition, preoccupation with a few topics or impoverished content. They may be embarrassed by the person's physical disability, cognitive failures or lack of refinement in social skills, e.g. their bluntness, over-familiarity, inappropriate sexual remarks or uncontrolled laughter. In response, a few friends or acquaintances may naturally grasp and adapt to such changes, providing vital support and companionship. However, many others, including boy/girlfriends, will find such changes too great and gradually fall by the wayside.

An overall indication of social outcome is again provided by the rehabilitation follow-up study reported by Tate et al. (1989): 24% were rated as 'good' in psychosocial outcome; 43% as 'substantially limited' and 33% as 'poor', the life of this latter group being described as 'impoverished in the extreme'. In a controlled study of 50 persons after severe injuries (PTA > 24 hours), 50% reported impaired leisure activities at 2 years post-injury, enjoying fewer social outings than an orthopaedic control group (Oddy, Humphrey & Uttley, 1978; Oddy & Humphrey, 1980). In a rehabilitation follow-up at 2 years post-injury, 44 persons with very severe injuries reported fewer interests and hobbies, fewer friends, less social and sexual activity and a more lonely life than those with less severe injury (Weddell, Oddy & Jenkins, 1980). In the further 7-year follow-up the dearth of leisure and social activities remained, with half the group having very limited contact with friends and 60% with no boy- or girl-friend (Oddy et al., 1985). Whilst such a low level of leisure and social activity at follow-up has been found to be to be associated with the extent of personality disability (Tyerman, 1987), few reported a loss of interest in such activities and the lack of opportunity due to lack of work and/ or an inability to drive post-injury was clearly a contributory factor.

It is clear that a reduction in leisure and social life is common after severe head injury, with about one-third reporting marked isolation with very few activities outside the family. Whilst there are a number of leisure and social activities provided for persons with a physical disability (for example PHAB clubs for the 'Physically Handicapped and Able Bodied', riding for the disabled, etc.), persons with head injury rarely identify with those with a physical disability and clearly state their preference for 'normal' activities with 'normal' people. Some in the UK are fortunate to be able to attend the expanding network of local Headway Houses, day activities run by local groups of the National Head Injuries Association, some with a Coordinator and professional sessions funded by statutory bodies, others remaining reliant on fund-raising and volunteers. Others take refuge in watching television and videos, in listening to music, in reading magazines (rather than books), in pottering around the garden or into town and possibly in helping out around the home. However, many remain overly dependent on partners, parents and siblings for their leisure and social life, the quality of which often remains poor in spite of the efforts of the family to compensate for the loss of former leisure and social activities.

Sexual Relationships

Sexual relationships are often a casualty for the person with severe head injury, many of whom are single but with boy- or girl-friends at the time of injury. Relationships may fail amidst the strain and uncertainty of acute care, particularly where the relationship is not yet well established and the person requires lengthy in-patient treatment. Others fail in the months or years after discharge, the boy/girlfriend being worn down by the physical, cognitive and emotional dependency, confused and hurt by erratic, rude or aggressive behaviour, or gradually coming to realise that the person has changed too much for the relationship to have a long-term future. The impact of such break-ups is all the greater as persons with head injury often find it difficult to make new relationships.

In the author's rehabilitation follow-up study, of eight couples still together at follow-up, only three had resumed former sexual relations, with four reporting less satisfaction and one couple yet to resume an active sexual life. Furthermore, only three of the other 45 young adults were in established relationships, with many blaming the head injury for the breakup of past relationships (Tyerman, 1987). However, perhaps the most worrying feature was that only one new boy–girl relationship was reported by follow-up at on average 20 months post-injury. As such, the majority of the group had no partner with whom to enjoy sexual relations. A lower level of sexual activity and satisfaction was correlated with the extent of physical, cognitive and personality disability.

It might be assumed that the problem is situational and social rather than sexual, with few in the above studies reporting specific sexual dysfunction. Clinically, however, it is evident that some individuals do experience difficulties with sexual interest, arousal and performance. This is supported by studies of psychosexual functioning. In a follow-up of 21 sexually active males with mild, moderate and severe head injury, Kreutzer & Zasler (1989) found that over half reported reduced sexual drive and difficulties in sustaining erections, with a quarter having difficulties reaching orgasm.

Sexual difficulties are therefore common after head injury, probably reflecting a combination of physical, interpersonal and social factors. The full extent of sexual dysfunction is probably obscured by the fact that many are without partners. As such, the presence of sexual dysfunction may go unrecognised for months or years post-injury pending an opportunity for sexual expression. For those aware of some sexual dysfunction this is likely to prove an additional barrier to forming new intimate relationships. For those with partners, sexual difficulties must be viewed in the context of the impact of head injury upon marriage as a whole.

Marital Relationships

Spouses often fulfil a vital caring and/or therapy role for an injured partner during the course of recovery. However, faced with the task of adapting to long-term changes in the injured person as expectations of further recovery recede, spouses may review their role and the future of the relationship. The position of the spouse is uniquely difficult, having selected the injured person as their mate. Where that person changes not just in physical and cognitive skills but also in his/her personality, this may alter the relationship and threaten the viability of the marriage. This may be exacerbated by tension or conflict with the injured person's family who may be unsupportive, critical of the spouse's management of the situation and unaware or unsympathetic to the needs of the spouse.

Where there is physical disability the couple may have lost shared activities (e.g. walking, sport, dancing); where there is cognitive impairment the spouse may miss former stimulating conversation, companionship and partnership; where there are behavioural difficulties there may be embarrassment socially and tension or aggression within the relationship, particularly where the person lacks awareness and disputes difficult behaviour. Spouses may also find their caring role incompatible with that of a sexual partner, whilst crude language, socially inappropriate behaviour and poor personal hygiene are a major obstacle to reactivating sexual relations. Just as the injured person may feel dependent on and closer to his/her partner, the spouse may feel trapped in a relationship which he/she no longer finds rewarding.

Spouses often struggle to cope with the competing needs of work, their partners and the children. They may have little if any time for their own leisure and social needs, especially where the injured partner is not able to share responsibility for the children due to his/her cognitive impairment (e.g. lack of vigilance, forgetfulness or poor judgement) or behaviour (e.g. intolerance or aggression). Isolation and loneliness amongst wives of 10 husbands with severe injuries was found at 1 year post-injury (Rosenbaum & Najenson, 1976). Husbands were reported to be less involved in child-rearing and the wives reported less leisure and social activities than wives of persons with spinal cord injuries and non-injured controls.

The impact on marriage appears to increase with severity and time since injury. Oddy & Humphrey (1980) for example, found that of 12 married men only one spouse and two patients reported an appreciably worse relationship at 12 months. However, in his very severe rehabilitation group, Tyerman (1987) found that two of nine couples had separated by 2 years post-injury and, of the others, only two reported 'normal' sexual relations. Furthermore, in a 10–15-year follow-up of 40 people with extremely severe head injuries

(PTA > 1 month), Thomsen (1984) found that five women and two men of nine that were married when seen at 2 years had since divorced.

Whilst high marital breakdown is reported, less is known about the quality of marriage after head injury. In two of few reported studies Peters et al. (1990; 1992) found that wives of husbands with severe head injury rated their marital relationship less positively than wives of husbands with moderate or mild head injury or with spinal cord injury, scoring lower in expression of affection, satisfaction and cohesion. In an exploratory study Young (1994) compared the perceptions of persons with severe injuries and their spouses. This confirmed a marked impact upon marriage but also revealed a tendency for the injured persons both to overestimate the state of the marriage compared with their spouse in terms of satisfaction, communication and intimacy and to underestimate the changes desired of them by their partner. This discrepancy in perceptions was dramatic in some cases.

Severe head injury clearly has a major impact on marriage: some couples remain close but with increased strain on the spouse and less fun and relaxation in their relationship; some spouses remain caring and supportive but no longer reciprocate the intimacy of their partner; in other cases the severity of cognitive and/or behavioural problem may be such that the spouse is unable to cope and the marriage fails.

Family Effects

Head injury has a major impact upon the family. As the family routine is tailored to meet the needs of the injured person, the leisure and social lives of family members often falters. For the highly dependent, family members may need to cut back or give up their employment as statutory services are seldom sufficient to provide adequate home care and few families can afford to employ professional carers. Even where employment is maintained, carers may be too preoccupied or drained to apply themselves effectively. Families are generally left to cope with little support, especially where the person is left with subtle changes in cognition and personality which may not be apparent to the extended family and friends. For ageing parents there is the added worry about the person's long-term needs.

The stress on relatives is well established. Oddy, Humphrey & Uttley (1978), for example, found that just over half the relatives of carers of 54 men with severe head injury reported stress at 6 and 12 months post-injury. Similarly, in a longitudinal study of 54 close relatives of persons with severe head injury (PTA > 2 days) the 'moderate' level of 'subjective burden' at 3 months post-injury had not diminished by 12 months. Higher subjective burden was found to be related to mental and behavioural changes but not physical or speech/language changes (McKinlay et al., 1981). In a 5-year follow-up, increased personality change and disturbed behaviour reported in the injured person was accompanied by a marked increase in relatives' stress: the number of relatives in the "high" subjective burden category rose from 24% at 1 year to 54% at 5 years post-injury (Brooks et al., 1986).

The psychological health of family members is also affected. Significant psychiatric disturbance was found in 57 relatives 3 months after severe head injury (PTA > 2 days) (Livingston, Brooks & Bond, 1985a). Whilst there was some improvement in general health by 12 months, there was no reduction in anxiety (37%) and a modest increase in depression (26%) (Livingston, Brooks & Bond, 1985b). Higher levels of distress (44% anxious, 60% depressed) were found by Tyerman (1987) in his rehabilitation group at on average 20 months post-injury.

Less is known about the impact upon family members other than primary carers in spite of the clinical experience that there is, in some families, a major impact upon parent–child or sibling relationships. In one of few studies Pessar et al. (1993) found that in 22 of 24 families, the children were reported by the uninjured parent to have a poor relationship with the injured parent, or to exhibit acting-out behaviour or emotional problems, with significant problems in about 10 families. However spouses strive to protect children from the impact of their partner's behaviour and fears about the long-term effect on the children is often a primary factor where spouses decide to separate.

There have also been very few studies of family functioning. In his rehabilitation follow-up Tyerman (1987) found that families were rated by primary carers as just as friendly, caring and close, but more worried and dissatisfied, and less outgoing, relaxed, interested, active, happy, enthusiastic, hopeful, productive, sociable and independent than prior to injury. Substantial difficulties were also found in a study of 62 persons with head injuries of variable severity at 1–60 months post-injury (median 8 months), with over half in the 'unhealthy' range in communication, affective involvement and general functioning (Keutzer, Gervasio & Camplair, 1994).

In a recent follow-up of 41 persons with very severe injuries, primary carers rated families as less cohesive, to have more conflict, to be less active socially, to have a more external locus of control, to be less like the ideal family and to have increased enmeshment and decreased disengagement post-injury. Marked changes in family roles were reported for the injured person living with a partner: the injured persons contribute much less to practical, social and parenting roles; spouses increase in some practical roles (such as DIY, driving), but struggle to compensate for their partners reduced parenting and social roles; and the couples' marital roles of lover and friend were much reduced. The impact on children was very variable with no overall pattern. Parents reported stress and worry with fathers contributing more to practical roles, but there was generally less change for parents and no significant change for siblings (Tyerman, Young & Booth, 1994).

In response to the reduced role of the injured person, other family members may assume additional roles: parents may revert to a familiar parental role but struggle under the additional strain; spouses may have to take on a caring role for their partner and sole responsibility for the children; in turn the children may have to take more responsibility for themselves. Such changes may evolve naturally and help the family in coping short-term with the effects of the injury. However, they may also alter further family functioning and prove difficult to reverse in line with the person's progress. At present families are left to make such adaptations with little if any guidance or support.

COMMUNITY REHABILITATION

The social consequences of brain injury can therefore be quite devastating for persons with major restrictions on their occupational, leisure, social and sexual lives. This is often mirrored by substantial psychological and social impact upon the family, especially the primary carer, with couples also experiencing marital and sexual difficulties. However, this depressing catalogue of social restrictions does not of course occur in a vacuum and must be viewed in the context of available health, social and vocational services.

Service provision in the UK has been sharply concentrated on acute care (British Psychological Society, 1989), with virtually no rehabilitation and retraining to assist the individual in returning to an independent and productive role in society (Greenwood & McMillan, 1993). Typically, persons with head injuries are admitted to a general hospital, with a small proportion transferred to a regional or subregional neurosurgical unit for further investigation, management and intervention. Once stable neurologically they return to their local general hospital for further care, typically on an orthopaedic ward with some left languishing on surgical or geriatric wards. Rehabilitation in general hospitals varies widely, with patchy implementation of recommendations such as a rehabilitation ward, as advocated by the Medical Disability Society (1988).

Rehabilitation after discharge is, if anything, even more haphazard. In a study in north London, Murphy et al. (1990) found little evidence of ongoing rehabilitation: of 40 persons with severe injuries admitted to 11 general hospitals, 80% had received some physiotherapy but only 30% occupational therapy, 12% speech therapy, 12% social work and less than 5% had been seen by a clinical psychologist. Furthermore, all treatment was found to diminish dramatically after 6 months.

The contribution of vocational rehabilitation has also been very limited. In the follow-up study of Brooks et al. (1987), for example, only eight of 134 persons with severe injuries had attended an employment rehabilitation centre, of whom just two returned to work. Similarly, in a follow-up study from Addenbrooke's Hospital, Cambridge, most of those with very severe injuries who returned to work did so without employment rehabilitation schemes and 12 of 16 completing such schemes remained unemployed (Johnson, 1989). The difficulty that employment rehabilitation services have in meeting the needs of persons with severe head injury was also illustrated in the author's rehabilitation group, of whom only one of 13 referred to such centres progressed to any form of work or training (Tyerman, 1987) Furthermore, the common recommendation that the person returns in a further year for reassessment in the vain hope of further recovery, often condemns the person to a year of frustration and despair, which is more likely to lead to deterioration than improvement.

In spite of mounting evidence of the human and social cost of head injury, there was little development of services in the UK during the 1980s, with the few specialist brain injury rehabilitation centres accommodating only a small proportion of the most severely injured. This contrasts with the growth in the USA, which witnessed an enormous growth in specialist 'comprehensive' head injury rehabilitation centres, with one company increasing rehabilitation places from 15 to 564 over just 4 years (McKinlay & Pentland, 1987). Whilst recommended staffing levels (Medical Disability Society, 1988) are rarely achieved in the UK, these are often exceeded two- or threefold in the USA (McMillan & Greenwood, 1993).

It would however be a mistake to believe that intensive early rehabilitation automatically results in social reintegration, as indicated by the disappointing outcome in the follow-up studies from the Wolfson Medical Rehabilitation Centre (Weddell, Oddy & Jenkins, 1980; Oddy et al., 1985). However, the focus of such regional/supraregional units is on the restoration of functional independence rather than on long-term social reintegration. This is illustrated in the author's own study of 60 persons with very severe injuries admitted both to the Wolfson and to the Joint Service Medical Rehabilitation Unit (RAF Chesington): marked progress in mobility, self-care and performance was evident on discharge, but this was insufficient to allow a return to former occupational, leisure and social lives with over half the group languishing at home at follow-up with no regular occupation or social life (Tyerman, 1987). However, few had received any further rehabilitation, guidance or support from local health, social or employment services. Such support is critical, as most left rehabilitation confident of a return to previous work, etc. and were not ready to accept the need to consider alternatives. With a gradual realisation of the extent and implications of their injuries and with no ongoing advice and support, the number clinically depressed or anxious increased from 32% at discharge to 44% at follow-up.

This study highlighted many service needs: a lack of district rehabilitation and community support services; poor liaison between regional and local services; a need for specialist vocational services and supported work opportunities; and psychotherapeutic initiatives to promote personal, family and social adaptation (Tyerman & Humphrey, 1988). Some of these needs have been addressed by developments abroad, in the form of post-acute and vocational rehabilitation programmes.

Post-acute Rehabilitation

In the late 1970s a community-based rehabilitation programme (5 hours per day, 4 days per week) was developed at the Santa Clara Valley Medical Center, California. The goals of the programme were to provide a highly structured, supportive environment to maximise work and study habits, cognitive and academic skills, social and behavioural awareness. Of 95 students joining the programme at a median of 14 months post-injury, 47% attained an improved level of function enabling referral on to college, vocational rehabilitation or sheltered workshops, etc. (Cole, Cope & Cervelli, 1985).

Similarly, a Neuropsychological Rehabilitation Program (4 days per week for 6 months) was developed in Oklahoma in the early 1980s focusing on awareness, acceptance and understanding; cognitive retraining; compensation skills; and vocational counselling. Compared with matched controls, 18 persons with severe injuries (admitted at on average 22 months post-injury) showed gains in cognitive skills and personality ratings, with 50% productively employed compared with 34% of controls (Prigatano et al., 1984). However, fewer returned to work than was hoped and the need for job placement and maintenance skills was stressed.

A European example is provided by the Centre for Hjerneskade, Copenhagen, where groups of 10–12 persons with brain injury undergo a programme of 'psychosocial rehabilitation' 6 hours per day, four days per week for 4.5 months. This comprises sessions of cognitive therapy, speech and language therapy and special education (where required), individual and group psychotherapy, physical exercise, family meetings and follow-up support. Teasdale, Christensen & Pinner (1993) report on 22 persons with head injury admitted at on average 3.21 years post-injury: those married/cohabiting increased from 18% on admission to 32% at follow-up; those requiring home services decreased from 36% to 14%; those in work or education rose from 18% to 32%; and those participating in social activities outside the home rose from 27% to 55%. An independent study reportedly found that the savings in public sector costs exceeded the cost of the programme itself.

In the USA there is now an impressive network of post-acute rehabilitation programmes. Cope et al. (1991a), for example, report upon a coordinated system comprising a continuum of treatment options including residential, community and home programmes. Treatment approaches include: medical/rehabilitation care; behavioural contingency management; activities of daily living; self-management, substance abuse, social, academic and social skills training; counselling and family education. Results for 115 persons with head injury admitted on average 15 months post-injury and receiving on average 6 months' treatment (range 46–485 days) are reported: those living at home rose from 44% on admission to 69% at follow-up; those in active treatment reduced from 50% to 17%; those totally independent in daily care rose from 27% to 76%; and those in competitive employment or academic study rose from 6% to 36% (Cope et al., 1991b). These improvements were achieved at an average cost of $50 000 per person.

Comparable results are reported by Johnson & Lewis (1991) for 82 persons (71% closed head injury) admitted on average 15 months post-injury to nine residential community re-entry programmes in the USA. After an average of 8.8 months rehabilitation, those living in institutions fell from 45% on admission to 7% at 1 year follow-up; those requiring constant supervision fell from 72% to 16%; and 82% improved in their productive paid or unpaid occupational activities. Overall, 92.5% of cases were reported to have improved either in independent living or occupational activity.

Johnston (1991), however, draws attention to the high cost of these residential programmes, i.e. $108 000 per person, especially as the majority did not make it back to gainful employment. As such, specialist vocational rehabilitation programmes for persons with brain injury will now be reviewed.

Vocational Rehabilitation

Recognising the difficulties of vocational services in meeting the complex needs of persons with severe head injury, a number of specialist vocational rehabilitation programmes have been developed. The New York University Head Trauma Program for example has three phases: remedial intervention; guided occupational trials; and vocational placement. The first phase comprises intensive individual and group intervention 5 hours per day, 4 days per week for 20 weeks, focusing on cognitive remediation, self-awareness and social skills. The second phase is voluntary occupational trials for up to 9 months prior to progressing to suitable work placements. Ben Yishay et al. (1987) report on 94 persons with very severe injuries (average coma 34 days). At 6 months follow-up, 56% were in competitive and 23% sheltered work with outcome holding up well at 3 years (50% competitive, 22% sheltered work). Given that the group were previously regarded as unemployable, the figures are impressive, although this was a selected group: including only those with IQ of at least 80, ambulatory, manageable without constraints and able to communicate reliably; and excluding any with previous brain damage or with a significant history of psychiatric problems or drug/alcohol abuse.

An alternative to the year's work preparation in the New York programme is the supported placement model, characterised by: intense one-to-one training, counselling and advocacy services by a skilled employment specialist; training and support services directly at the job site; ongoing support throughout the individual's employment (Wehman et al., 1993). The 'job coach' also assists with job matching, applications, interviews, practicalities such as transport, as well as communication with the employer. Of 43 persons with severe injuries, over 70% were competitively placed in employment at 6 months but this required an average of 290 hours of specialist intervention. Costs ranged from about $6 000 for the least difficult to place to around $12 000 for the most difficult. At an average cost of up to even $10 000 per placement this would seem a sound economic investment when set against the cumulative cost of state benefits over many years.

A detailed cost–benefit analysis has been made of the Work Re-entry Program for persons with traumatic brain injury at the Sharp Memorial Rehabilitation Center, San Diego. This programme combines elements of work rehabilitation (i.e. simulated work, work hardening placements, vocational counselling, job seeking/keeping skills) with a supported placement, for which ongoing on-site support was limited to 60 days on-site, plus an adjustment/support group and 6-monthly follow-ups. Of 142 participants (mean coma 12 days), 65% were back in employment within a year and 75% within 3–5 years, with 55% remaining employed at the last follow-up. The total operational costs of the project over 5 years works out at $4 377 per person. However, taking into account taxes paid in employment and savings in state benefits (totally around $222 per month), the average payback period of just 20 months was claimed to reveal unequivocally the value of the Work Re-entry Program (Abrams et al., 1993).

The above initiatives focus on the injured person. As their primary source of support, there is a parallel need to address the needs of the family. It is vital to involve the family fully in assessment, feedback, and rehabilitation planning, implementation and monitoring. However, there is also a need to address family needs more directly through family education, counselling and support. There are now many examples of family intervention programme (e.g. Jacobs, 1989; Rosenthal & Young, 1988). In a detailed discussion Sachs (1991) sets out a framework for assessment and treatment of families and a number of general principles. The practitioner must:

1. Be knowledgeable in traumatic brain injury rehabilitation.
2. Consider the family's structure and development.
3. Be flexible (both in modifying treatment techniques and his/her own role in meeting the needs of these families).
4. Establish a close working relationship with the family.
5. Be a member of the rehabilitation team.
6. Be mindful of his/her own personal values as they affect treatment.

Such accounts are helpful for the clinician. However, there have as yet been very few studies evaluating the effectiveness of such family interventions.

Service Requirements

In summary, whilst there is a need to identify the effective programme components, there is accumulating evidence of the benefits of post-acute and vocational rehabilitation in enhancing independence, reducing care requirements and enhancing work prospects. Sadly, the UK has to date been slow to adopt such developments with, until recently, most of the development coming in the independent sector, catering for only a small and selective population with access to funding.

However, the climate in the UK is changing. This is fuelled by the current Brain Injury Rehabilitation Initiative of the Department of Health (in press), with 12 projects funded for 5 years (1992–97) and evaluated independently within a National Traumatic Brain Injury Study. In addition to the individual service contributions, the initiative has raised the profile of brain injury. Furthermore, the need to address the rehabilitation of persons with brain injury is a current NHS purchasing priority. This provides a welcome opportunity for providers units to secure contracts. Implementation of the Community Care Act in the UK similarly offers an opportunity for providers to secure contracts for both day and residential provision, which needs to address the particular care and occupational needs of this young adult population. Recent changes in employment services, with employment rehabilitation now contracted out to independent agencies, similarly offers an opportunity to secure contracts for specialist brain injury vocational rehabilitation programmes.

Development opportunities do therefore exist, but what form should these take to promote long-term social reintegration? There have been numerous national, regional and district policy documents. However, these have tended to focus on acute care rather than community reintegration, which demands continuity of rehabilitation across health, social and employment services. The British Psychological Society (1989) provides a model of services for young adults with acquired brain damage which includes elements of such a service.

This model acknowledges the need for active rehabilitation in the acute hospital, specialist (regional) in-patient rehabilitation facilities for those with the most severe injuries, and behavioural treatment units for the small number with severe behavioural disturbance. However, the heart of the envisaged service is a local day rehabilitation facility. This would be the base for a rehabilitation team comprising clinical psychology, occupational therapy, physiotherapy, speech and language therapy and social work, with sessional input from various medical specialties. The team would provide: an out-patient assessment and advisory service; a coordinating role for rehabilitation services; a treatment/retraining function; an occupational/social outlet; and advice, training and support for both families and professionals. However, the need for a range of other services is stressed: respite care for both emergencies and carer breaks; supported living facilities (high, medium and low dependence) for those who need or wish to live independently; and work centres to provide for those unable to return to previous work/training.

It would of course be fanciful to imagine that such a model could readily be adopted in all districts, even if there were the required professional expertise. However, our experience at Rayners Hedge is that such a service can be achieved. Rayners Hedge is home to a physical rehabilitation service within a community healthcare NHS trust. When the needs of persons with head injury and their families were highlighted in 1988, we had no specialist services. We have since been building a community head injury service. This currently comprises: a head injury clinic; individual treatment programmes; cognitive and communication group; individual family support; relatives' group; 'Working Out' — a specialist vocational rehabilitation project; and marital/family counselling. Whilst most of our work is on an out-patient basis, we offer relief care and a limited amount of in-patient assessment and rehabilitation.

The current service reflects four phases of development, each requiring additional funding: the development of our cognitive rehabilitation programme was made possible by redeployment of resources within the clinical psychology service in 1990; the establishment of the Head Injury Clinic was funded by Joint Finance in 1992; 'Working Out' was funded in 1992 by the Department of Health Brain Injury Rehabilitation Initiative; and the relatives' group and marital/family counselling was made possible by redeployment in the physical rehabilitation services. Funding has also just been secured from the Employment Service for joint research and development with our regional Ability Development Centre on the 'Working Out' project.

Whilst the service has been health-service led, collaboration with other agencies is essential: with our regional in-patient rehabilitation facility to ensure smooth transfer of care; with the independent sector to ensure specialist treatment for the more behaviourally disturbed; with Social Services to set up appropriate home care and residential care placement; with our local Headway group who provide some day centre provision; with our local college for both special needs and mainstream courses, and with employment services for the development of the specialist vocational assessment and rehabilitation programme.

We recognise that we were fortunate to start from the base of a community physical rehabilitation service. Where there has been no local rehabilitation service on which to build, the local Headway group may already provide day care provision, often with some rehabilitation input from professional staff. Local circumstances will therefore lead to various patterns of services that may prove equally or possibly more effective than our own. However, our experience demonstrates that statutory services working in partnership are able to develop a range of services that offer persons with head injury and their families opportunities for improved social outcome.

CONCLUSIONS

To summarise, previous research has catalogued a depressing array of social problems for the person with head injury and his/her family. However, in the UK this disappointment has to be seen in the context of patchy acute and scarce post-acute rehabilitation, inadequate vocational rehabilitation and very limited specialist social services provision. This is reinforced repeatedly to us in the number of referrals to our community-based service of persons with injuries of 5 or 10 years' standing, who have generally struggled alone without the benefit of appropriate assessment and/or rehabilitation.

The evidence accumulating from post-acute and specialist vocational rehabilitation suggests that social outcome can be improved for the person, thereby reducing the stress on the family. There will remain a need for long-term community support, both to respond to problems that emerge late post-injury, such as marital and sexual problems, and in assisting the person as they take further steps in rebuilding their lives, such as starting a new job or relationship. Whilst such a commitment of community support is costly, this needs to be offset against the cost of family stress and breakdown, the substantial potential savings in service provision and state benefits, as well as the prospect of some additional tax revenues for those who make it back to open employment. Changes in health, employment and social service provision in the UK provide opportunities to secure contracts to address the needs of persons with head injuries and their families.

To be maximally effective in long-term social reintegration requires a network of health, social, employment, educational and voluntary services, working in partnership with the person and the family. Health services need to provide acute care, short-term in-patient rehabilitation (including provision for those with severe behavioural disturbance), and longer-term community rehabilitation to build upon earlier recovery, meet ongoing needs and promote social reintegration. The latter needs to include provision for education and support for employers, tutors and providers of occupational provision, as well as initiatives to promote social and family adaptation.

For those unable to return to former activities, health services need to work with a range of other services: with Social Services to identify appropriate day care and residential care that can meet the care, occupational and social needs of persons with head injury; with Employment Services to address the specialist vocational assessment and rehabilitation needs of persons with head injury; with the Education service not just for those who wish to continue with their studies but also in identifying suitable courses for those who wish to retrain and constructive leisure for those unable to return to work; with the voluntary organisations, principally Headway in the UK, in disseminating information about head injury, in providing suitable daycare facilities and leisure pursuits, and in supporting families. All agencies also need to educate colleagues, employers, teachers, politicians and the general public about not only the needs but also the as yet unrealised potential of persons with head injury.

The complex needs arising from head injury are such that no one agency can hope to develop an all-embracing service. Implementation of the required components of the service will depend largely on the pattern of existing regional and local services. However, an essential first step is a clear referral and assessment policy for persons with head injury. Whilst a case manager may help to ensure persons are referred on for further assistance from existing services, a vital component is the formation of a specialist head injury team to develop specialist acute and post-acute rehabilitation programmes. Whereas medical and nursing care, physiotherapy and in some cases speech and language therapy have the major role in acute rehabilitation, clinical psychology, occupational therapy and social work provide the key personnel in community rehabilitation. Whilst rehabilitation is naturally a health responsibility, community reintegration requires close collaboration with other agencies. The head injury team will be required to provide training and support for those from other agencies with limited experience of head injury, whilst representatives of social, employment, education and voluntary services will need to be involved in joint service planning and monitoring.

Large-scale multicentre research will be required to evaluate the most effective model of service provision. However, our experience within a specialist community service is that it is possible to build a network of services which offer persons with severe head injury and their families the opportunity and support to start to rebuild their shattered lives.

REFERENCES

Abrams, D., Barker, L. T., Haffey, W. & Nelson, H. (1993). The economics of return to work for survivors of traumatic brain injury: vocational services are worth the investment. *Journal of Head Trauma Rehabilitation*, **8**, 59–76.

Ben-Yishay, Y., Silver, S. M., Piasetsky, E. & Rattok, J. (1987). Relationship between employability and vocational outcome after intensive holistic cognitive rehabilitation. *Journal of Head Trauma Rehabilitation*, **2**, 35–48.

British Psychological Society (1989). *Working Party Report. Services for Young Adult Patients with Acquired Brain Damage*. Leicester: British Psychological Society.

Brooks, N., Campsie, L., Symington, C., Beattie, A. & McKinlay, W. (1986). The five year outcome of severe blunt head injury: a relative's view. *Journal of Neurology, Neurosurgery and Psychiatry*, **49**, 464–470.

Brooks, N., McKinlay, W., Symington, C., Beattie, A. & Campsie, L. (1987). Return to work within the first seven years of severe head injury. *Brain Injury*, **1**, 5–19.

Cole, J. R., Cope, D. N. & Cervelli, L. (1985). Rehabilitation of the severely brain injured patient: a community-based, low-cost model program. *Archives of Physical Medicine and Rehabilitation*, **66**, 38–40.

Cope, D. N., Cole, J. R., Hall, K. M. & Barkan H. (1991a): Brain injury: analysis of outcome in a post-acute rehabilitation system. Part 1. General Analysis. *Brain Injury*, **5**, 111–125.

Cope, D. N., Cole, J. R., Hall, K. M. & Barkan H. (1991b): Brain injury: analysis of outcome in a post-acute rehabilitation system. Part 2. Subanalysis. *Brain Injury*, **5**, 127–139.

Crepeau, F. & Scherzer, P.(1993). Predictors and indicators of work status after traumatic brain injury: a meta-analysis. *Neuropsychological Rehabilitation*, **3**, 5–35.

Crisp, R. (1992). Return to work after traumatic brain injury. *Journal of Rehabilitation*,

58, 27–33.

Department of Health (in press). *Report of the Brain Iniury Rehabilitation Conference,* Peterborough, March 1994.

Edna, T. H. & Cappelen, J. (1987). Return to work and social adjustment after traumatic head injury. *Acta Neurochirugica,* **85**, 40–43.

Fraser, R., Dikmen, S., McLean, A., Miller, B. & Temkin, N. (1988). Employability of head injury survivors: first year post-injury. *Rehabilitation Counselling Bulletin,* **31**, 276–288.

Greenwood, R. J. & McMillan, T. M. (1993). Models of rehabilitation programmes for the brain-injured adult. 1. Current provision, efficacy and good practice. *Clinical Rehabilitation,* **7**, 248–255.

Jacobs, H. E. (1989). Long-term family intervention. In *Neuropsychological Treatment After Brain Injury* (Eds. D. W. Ellis & A. L. Christensen). Boston: Kluwer Academic.

Johnson, R. (1987). Return to work after severe head injury. *International Disability Studies,* **9**, 49–54.

Johnson, R. (1989). Employment after severe head injury: do Manpower Services Commission schemes work? *Injury,* **20**, 5–9.

Johnston, M. V. (1991). Outcomes of community re-entry programmes for brain injury survivors: Part 2. Further investigations. *Brain Injury,* **5**, 155–168.

Johnston, M. V. & Lewis, F. D. (1991). Outcomes of community re-entry programmes for brain injury survivors: Part 1. Independent living and productive activities. *Brain Injury,* **5**, 141–154.

Kreutzer, J. S., Gervasio, A. H. & Camplair, P. S. (1994). Primary caregivers' psychological status and family functioning after traumatic brain injury. *Brain Injury,* **8**, 197–210.

Kreutzer, J. S. & Zasler, N. D. (1989). Psychosexual consequences of traumatic brain injury: methodology and preliminary findings. *Brain Injury,* **3**, 177–186.

Livingston, M. G., Brooks, D. N. & Bond, M. R. (1985a). Three months after severe head injury: psychiatric and social impact on relatives. *Journal of Neurology, Neurosurgery and Psychiatry,* **48**, 870–875.

Livingston, M. G., Brooks, D. N. & Bond, M. R. (1985b). Patient outcome in the year following severe head injury and relatives' psychiatric and social functioning. *Journal of Neurology, Neurosurgery and Psychiatry,* **48**, 876–881.

McKinlay, W. W., Brooks, D. N., Bond, M. R., Martinage, D. P. & Marshall, M. M. (1981). The short-term outcome of severe blunt head injury as reported by relatives of the injured persons. *Journal of Neurology, Neurosurgery and Psychiatry,* **44**, 527–533.

McKinlay W. W. & Pentland, B. (1987). Developing rehabilitation services for the head-injured: a UK perspective. *Brain Injury,* **1**, 3–4.

McMillan, T. M. & Greenwood, R. J. (1993). Models of rehabilitation programmes for the brain-injured adult. II. Model services and suggestions for change in the UK. *Clinical Rehabilitation,* **7**, 346–355.

McMordie, W. R. & Barker, S. L. (1988). The financial trauma of head injury. *Brain Injury,* **2**, 357–364.

Medical Disability Society (1988). *The Management of Traumatic Brain Injury.* London: Medical Disability Society.

Murphy, L. D., McMillan T. M., Greenwood, R. J., Brooks, D. N., Morris, J. R. & Dunn, G. (1990). Services for severely head injured patients in North London and environs. *Brain Injury,* **4**, 95–100.

Oddy, M., Coughlan, A., Tyerman, A. & Jenkins, D. (1985). Social adjustment after closed head injury: a further follow-up severe years after injury. *Journal of*

Neurology, Neurosurgery and Psychiatry, **48**, 564–468.

Oddy, M. & Humphrey, M. (1980). Social recovery during the year following severe head injury. *Journal of Neurology, Neurosurgery and Psychiatry*, **43**, 798–802.

Oddy M., Humphrey, M. & Uttley, D. (1978). Subjective impairment and social recovery after closed head injury. *Journal of Neurology, Neurosurgery and Psychiatry*, **41**, 611–616.

Pessar, L. F., Coad, M. L., Linn, R. T. & Willer, B. S. (1993). The effects of parental traumatic brain injury on the behaviour of parents and children. *Brain Injury*, **7**, 231–240.

Peters, L. C., Stambrook, M., Moore, A. D. and Esses, L (1990). Psychosocial sequelae of closed head injury: effects on the marital relationship. *Brain Injury*, **4**, 39–47.

Peters, L. C., Stambrook, M., Moore, A. D., Zubek, E., Dubo, H. & Blumenschein, S. (1992). Differential effects of spinal cord injury and head injury on marital adjustment. *Brain Injury*, **6**, 461–467.

Prigatano, G. P., Fordyce, D. J., Zeiner, H. K., Roueche, J. R., Pepping, M. & Wood, B. C. (1984). Neuropsychological rehabilitation after closed head injury in young adults. *Journal of Neurology, Neurosurgery and Psychiatry*, **47**, 505–513.

Rosenbaum, M. & Najenson, T. (1976). Changes in life patterns and symptoms of low mood as reported by wives of severely brain injured soldiers. *Journal of Consulting and Clinical Psychology*, **44**, 881–888.

Rosenthal, M. & Young T. (1988). Effective family intervention after traumatic brain injury: theory and practice. *Journal of Head Trauma Rehabilitation*, **4**, 42–50.

Sachs, P. R. (1991). *Treating Families of Brain Injury Survivors*. New York: Springer.

Tate, R. L., Lulham, J. M., Broe, G. A., Strettles, B. & Pfaff, A. (1989). Psychosocial outcome for the survivors of severe blunt head injury the results of a consecutive series of 100 patients. *Journal of Neurology, Neurosurgery and Psychiatry*, **52**, 1128–1134.

Teasdale, T. W., Christensen, A.-L. & Pinner, E. M. (1993). Psychosocial rehabilitation of cranial trauma and stroke patients. *Brain Injury*, **7**, 535–542.

Thomsen, I. V. (1984). Late outcome of very severe blunt head trauma: a 10–15 year second follow-up. *Journal of Neurology, Neurosurgery and Psychiatry*, **47**, 260–268.

Tyerman, A. D. (1987). Self-concept and psychological change in the rehabilitation of the severely head-injured person. Unpublished doctoral thesis. London: University of London.

Tyerman, A. & Humphrey M. (1988). Personal and social rehabilitation after severe head injury. In *New Developments in Clinical Psychology*, Vol. 2 (Ed. F. N. Watts). Chichester: Wiley.

Tyerman, A., Young K. & Booth, J. (1994). Change in family roles after severe traumatic brain injury. Paper presented at *The Fourth Conference of the International Association for the Study of Traumatic Brain Injury*. St. Louis, September.

Weddell, R., Oddy, M. & Jenkins, D. (1980). Social adjustment after rehabilitation: a two-year follow-up of patients with severe head injury. *Psychological Medicine*, **10**, 257–263.

Wehman, P., Kregel, J., Sherron, P., Nguyen, S., Kreutzer, J., Fry, R. & Zasler, N. (1993). Critical factors associated with the successful supported employment placement of patients with severe traumatic brain injury. *Brain Injury*, **7**, 31–34.

Young, K. (1994). The quality of marriage after head injury: Investigating both partners views. Unpublished Dissertation. Leicester: British Psychological Society.

$$\boxed{6}$$

LONG-TERM MANAGEMENT

WILLIAM W. MCKINLAY*† AND ANNA J. WATKISS*

*Case Management Services Ltd, Edinburgh and †Scotcare National Brain Injury Rehabilitation Unit, Lanarkshire

INTRODUCTION

Although traumatic brain injury (TBI) is a major cause of death and disability, especially in the first half of life, the development of specialist services has been patchy and in some places slow. However, studies of outcome have identified the sequelae of brain injury in increasing detail, and there have been considerable developments in both acute and rehabilitation services. Good quality acute care was, in the past, all too often not followed up with rehabilitation, and individuals with TBI were often discharged into the care of family members, who struggled to cope. Now, as rehabilitation services develop, the challenge for them is to develop effective community re-entry strategies for individuals with TBI with the aim of achieving stable and sustainable long-term outcomes, without unrealistic demands on health and social services.

In this chapter, after briefly reviewing evidence on late outcome, we shall consider some of the approaches to long-term management, and consider what evidence is relevant to evaluating these approaches.

WHAT ARE THE LONG-TERM SEQUELAE?

Persisting Emotional and Behavioural Problems

It is well established that serious physical disability is comparatively rare in those with even severe head injury, but that so-called 'psychosocial' problems are much more common (e.g. McKinlay et al., 1981). A variety of studies in

Brain Injury and After: Towards Improved Outcome. Edited by F.D. Rose and D.A. Johnson.
© 1996 John Wiley & Sons Ltd.

Table 6.1: The six problems most frequently reported by relatives of individuals with traumatic brain injury (n = 42).

Problem	Relatives reporting (%)	
	1 year	5 years
Personality change	60	74
Slowness	65	67
Poor memory	67	67
Irritability	67	64
Bad temper	64	64
Tiredness	69	62

From Brooks et al. (1986b), with permission.

the 1980s reported continuing problems at long-term follow-up of those with TBI. Table 6.1 shows the most common problems reported by relatives of the brain-injured at 1 and 5 years post-injury from a study by Brooks and his group in Glasgow (Brooks et al., 1986). It can be seen from this, firstly, that persisting problems are common and, secondly, that far from showing a decline between 1 and 5 years some of them become increasingly common.

Findings from follow-up studies at 7 years (Oddy et al., 1985) and at 10–15 years (Thomsen, 1984) have shown considerable similarity with poor memory and concentration, poor control of temper and tiredness amongst the most common problems reported. That these fail to resolve and some reportedly increase has prompted discussion, and has led McKinlay & Brooks (1984) to suggest that this increased reporting may reflect either a secondary psychological disorder in reaction to the limitations imposed by TBI, or decreased tolerance by relatives as problems persist.

Studies continue to appear which reinforce and expand upon these earlier findings. For example, Dikmen, Machamaer & Temkin (1993) reported on subjects with severe head injury which had a significant long-term impact on psychosocial functioning. Many patients were unable to return to work, support themselves financially, live independently, or participate in previously enjoyed leisure activities in the years following injury. Initially the patients' self-reports had focused on physical limitations, but as these problems began to resolve there was a heightened awareness of psychosocial limitations. Whereas fatigue, headaches, dizziness and insomnia were amongst symptoms showing decline from 1 month to 2 years post-injury, complaints of memory difficulties and irritability showed the clearest increases over the same period. Linn, Allen & Willer (1994) also suggest that there is an increase in either awareness or incidence of problems over time. In their sample population of 60 individuals with TBI (averaging 6 years post-injury) and their spouses, they found that *both* individuals with TBI *and* their spouses showed elements of depression and anxiety: 70% or more in each group had at least mild depression, while 50% or more showed at least mildly elevated anxiety.

Cognitive Impairments

Although emotional and behavioural changes have received the greatest attention, and have shown the closest apparent relationship to distress in both patients and families, cognitive changes have also been widely reported. Again there is a well established literature on cognitive deficits following brain injury (Oddy et al., 1985; Thomsen, 1984; Brooks et al., 1986b; Brooks, 1984; Arcia & Gualtieri, 1994). This literature demonstrates the deficits that have consistently been found in the areas of memory and learning, and attention and concentration. For example, Scherzer et al. (1993) followed up patients with a mean coma duration of 1.6 months who were seen between 10 months and 22 years (average 4 years) post-injury. Deficits were found in tasks requiring information processing, the use of categories, and the establishing of new concepts.

A number of studies have shown the implications for returning to work of the major and chronic difficulties experienced by those who have suffered severe brain injury. In a study of 134 patients in the West of Scotland, Brooks and his associates (1987) found that the percentage in employment fell from 86% pre-injury to 29% post-injury. This figure of 29% was the average number in employment at various times between 2 and 7 years during the period. There was no overall increase in the numbers working over this period. Verbal memory, and mental speed or sustained concentration were the main cognitive predictors of failure to return to work.

In a recent study Ruff et al. (1993) reported on employment status at 6 and 12 months from data at the US National Traumatic Coma Data Bank. The two most important cognitive predictors were the patient's verbal intellectual power and speed of information processing on neuropsychological tests.

Family Distress

It is mentioned above that it not just the individual with TBI who suffers from these long-term problems, but also that the family have to bear some of the impact of the brain injury. They are frequently under considerable strain and can experience extreme stress.

Lezak (1988) carried out a comprehensive review of emotional and behavioural changes after brain injury and the effect they have on family members. She explains the particular problems for various family members. If the brain-injured individual is the child and one of the parents (usually the mother) is the main carer, marital conflict may result from competition for the carer's attention between the TBI child and the other parent and children, which can end in the marriage dissolving. If the person who suffered TBI has a sibling then there may well be a reduction in parental attention, and an increase in responsibilities for the members of the family without TBI. Shame and guilt along with frustration and anger are all felt from having a 'different' family. If the spouse is injured, a main source of emotional support, affection and companionship is lost. Deteriorated sexual relations are often experienced, and social contacts are often lost as they are no longer a 'couple'. If the spouse is also the caregiver, he/she may even receive verbal and sometimes physical abuse.

Gainotti (1993) has also observed that the problems do not get easier over time but rather increase as the family have to accept and adjust to these changes. Kreutzer et al. (1994a, b), studying carers of brain-injured individuals (whose injuries ranged from mild to severe, and who were assessed at a mean time post-injury of 16 months) found reports of elevated distress in approximately 50% of carers. Feelings of burden and alienation were common, with spouses significantly more likely than parents to report elevated distress (a point previously raised by Thomsen, 1974).

The picture which emerges is that physical problems, although they are present and may be severe in some TBI cases, are not the main issue for long-term management. Rather, the difficulties reside primarily in the emotional and behavioural changes which follow brain injury and which are a particular source of distress to relatives. These together with cognitive deficits present difficulties in terms of return to work. Moreover, caregiving relatives usually show increasing rather than decreasing distress over time.

REHABILITATION

In spite of this seeming litany of difficulties, there is a growing body of evidence to suggest that worthwhile gains can be made through rehabilitation and skilled management. Whilst it is virtually never possible to restore the individual with severe TBI to premorbid status, rehabilitation can give such individuals skills (including both re-learned 'old' skills and new 'compensatory' skills) and contacts (both formal and informal) which improve quality of life and allow survival in the community with the least possible degree of dependence. Gains can be made and in the previous chapter there is a discussion of studies both of specific rehabilitation areas (e.g. memory, social skills, control of anger) and also overall rehabilitation outcome. A good deal of research is rightly devoted to building coherent theoretical bases for interventions, analysing constituent parts of rehabilitation packages, evaluating their effectiveness, and trying to improve on them. In the short term, however, it is studies of overall outcome which are likely to have the most immediate impact in terms of securing funding. Clear and strong evidence is needed that dependence can be reduced and quality of life improved, given the inevitable pressure for funds from limited resources in the whole arena of health care, and also given the costs of rehabilitation.

Costs and Savings

Against the short-term costs of rehabilitation, one has to set the long-term savings that may be realised. For example, an individual with TBI may be unsafe at home, and therefore require 24 hour attendance. Teaching such a person to follow some memory routines, so as to be able safely to lock up the house at night and switch off appliances, may reduce the need for care from 24 hour to only day-time care. The savings in costs of such a gain would be significant and need to be borne in mind in assessing the costs of rehabilitation. Table 6.2 presents a real example of financial savings following a period of rehabilitation. In addition to the immediate financial savings, it also has to be borne in mind that before rehabilitation there was a danger that the care arrangements would break down altogether: in this case, the carers were intimidated and unable to cope, and were considering leaving the care

Table 6.2: Case example of financial savings after appropriate rehabilitation.

A 50-year-old male, divorced, former manual worker, had fallen 30 feet at his work and sustained severe brain injury. Six years post-injury, he was being cared for in his own home by a team of carers. The regime of care had increased from two day-time shifts initially, to a 24-hour schedule of waking carers. The carers were intimidated by his aggressive outbursts. Lacking access to suitably experienced advice, they had been unable to prevent his behaviour from deteriorating.

The prices quoted in this example are taken from the actual hourly rates which were being charged. These are comparable with rates charged by other agencies. At 1995 prices, the 24-hour schedule of waking care would cost £54 960 per annum. After 10 weeks of rehabilitation at a cost of £9 000, a less intensive regime was put in place and proved to be sustainable. This would cost on the same basis £44 170. This represents an annual saving of £10 790. It would therefore take, in this example, 10 months to recoup the cost of rehabilitation.

package. As a result of the rehabilitation, the person with TBI became manageable, reducing the considerable strain on his carers.

While there are examples of cases where worthwhile gains and cost savings are made, nevertheless rehabilitation and other health professionals know that all rehabilitation programmes are not always keenly focused on practical gains, and it is not unknown for individuals to enter rehabilitation very disabled and to emerge months or even years later still very disabled, but at vast expense. It is therefore not surprising that attempts to evaluate effectiveness of rehabilitation have, in recent years, come to concentrate increasingly on such overall measures as the extent of attendant care and the extent to which the individual can engage in productive activity.

An example of such studies is the work of Cope and his associates (1991a, b), which included single-blind telephone follow-ups of individuals with TBI who had been through post-acute rehabilitation programmes. High response rates were achieved, and the authors reported improvements in rates of productive activity (broadly defined) and reductions in the amount of care and supervision needed.

Despite these improvements, the studies of Kreutzer (1994b), mentioned above, have shown that, even in the United States where there is allegedly greater access to rehabilitation, families of individuals with TBI still reported difficulties. Such findings, together with the difficulty often experienced by rehabilitation staff in securing suitable post-rehabilitation support for the individual with TBI, make it clear that achieving community reintegration remains a key challenge for rehabilitation professionals. Without successful rehabilitation and reintegration, many survivors will lead lives of long-term unemployment and will be highly dependent, consuming services or preventing relatives from working. Key questions are to what extent individuals with TBI have access to rehabilitation and other services, as well as how effective these services are.

Development of Services

Despite the extent of the late problems after brain injury, and the growing evidence that something worthwhile may be done about them, at least in some cases, there has been a lack of facilities and even of a coherent approach to their management in the UK.

The Royal College of Physicians' 1986 report on physical disability noted that:

> In our experience, head injury services are frequently not well organised and

there is considerable scope for improvement. This is occurring despite the obvious heavy economic cost, both to the state, and for individuals. ... The majority of Health Districts do not appear to have developed specific facilities for the management of disabled head-injured patients. (p. 177).

This general view was consistent with data obtained in follow-up studies. Brooks et al (1986a) had found that in the West of Scotland there was little or no rehabilitation provided after 6 months post-injury, whilst the rehabilitation provided within the first six months was by no means coordinated specialist rehabilitation but rather was mainly physiotherapy with small amounts of other therapies. Murphy et al. (1990) reported on services for the head injured in North London and found a picture which was broadly similar. Of 40 patients in the sample, 82.5% received physiotherapy, 30% occupational therapy, 12.5% speech therapy, 12.5% social work and 5% clinical psychology. However, the amounts of therapy received, in terms of actual hours, appear to have been modest at best. For example, each physiotherapist in the study provided on average 3–4 hours of therapy a week to head-injured patients referred, whilst the six clinical psychologists who supplied services to the hospitals involved spent on average less than half an hour per week working with individuals with a TBI (their main caseload being in the mental illness field). The same paper shows virtually no contact between these professionals and head-injured patients more than 6 months post-injury. It is clear from studies outlined above and in other chapters that recovery of the individual with TBI is by no means complete at 6 months. Indeed, some problems will only just be surfacing at this time.

The level of service provision in the UK has received further attention from Greenwood et al. (1994) who carried out a study to investigate the effects of early case management in a population of severely head-injured patients. Their aim was to examine the effects of case management on outcome, family function and provision of rehabilitation services. What is of interest in the present context is their control group, who were not case-managed but progressed through the usual National Health Service care system. Although these patients had an average post-traumatic amnesia of 40.8 days (well into the 'extremely severe' category of Teasdale & Jennett, 1974, virtually guaranteeing long-term problems), only 21% were referred to a rehabilitation unit, 33% to out-patient services, and 5% to a day centre. These figures suggest bleak prospects for these individuals. The problem is further compounded given the observations by Greenwood et al. about the (modest) amounts of rehabilitation provided to those who do receive it.

Many other authors have noted the paucity of services, especially as regards long-term follow-up and care. For example, Gloag (1985) referred to after-care being 'generally poor' and Evans (1987) referred to 'wide-areas of neglect'. Livingston (1986) found that at 3, 6 and 12 months after severe head injury, the majority of patients (between 75 and 84% depending on follow-up time) were receiving no rehabilitation services. A multidisciplinary group in Yorkshire Regional Health Authority (1989) also reported that there was a lack of pattern to care, with what input there was being provided on a sporadic and *ad hoc* basis, but with no observable logic as to who received care and who did not. Professional staff expressed dissatisfaction about the lack of possibilities available for continuing care. Wade (1991) highlighted the shortfall, stating that specialist services for head-injured patients are not available to most patients in Britain as local policies on numbers referred for rehabilitation did not bear a relationship to severity of injury, or rehabilitation prospects, or even the number injured. Rather, financial resources available seemed to determine supposed need:

> It is difficult to give specific guidance on who should be referred to a Regional Unit. It will depend upon the resources available within the district. (p. 150)

There have been other studies which have attempted to quantify the proportion of the population who have been brain-injured as well as identifying the services available for them. The British Psychological Society's (1989) report found the UK national picture of resources to be dismal, with only 200 specialist brain-injured beds in the whole UK at that time (with a population of approximately 56 million). They estimated that 8 places per annum are needed for head injury rehabilitation to serve a population of 0.25 million, plus a further 24 community support and daycare places per annum for that same population. Multiplied to cover the UK, on the basis of 56 million population, this would give a total requirement for residential places of 1792 plus 5376 community/day centres. The BPS estimates were based on epidemiological figures and took into account the likely needs of patients with different severities of injury.

The BPS figures produced appear to be of the correct order of magnitude in the light of other studies. Miller & Jones (1985) reported on various aspects of head injury in a population of 1.2 million in the Edinburgh area. In this study there were 116 survivors of brain injury who were classified as Severely Disabled or Vegetative using the Glasgow Outcome Scale (Jennett & Bond, 1975) 1 month post-injury. Others, whilst not so disabled, would also need long-term help. The BPS figures, multiplied for 1.2 million population, would give an estimated 154 cases needing long-term help, a figure not dissimilar to the 116 plus from the Miller & Jones study.

This lack of provision for the brain-injured does not reflect a general national shortfall in health care. The Medical Disability Society's report (1988) on the management of traumatic brain injury includes the comment that brain injury is 40 times more common than spinal injury. However, while there is excellent NHS provision of special units for spinal injury, at the time of their report there was no NHS rehabilitation unit specifically designated for brain injury. They noted that it was very difficult to obtain daycare for those with little or no physical disability but where behaviour was disturbed: individuals with TBI were often left on surgical wards where no-one was qualified to provide rehabilitation, and there was no standardised follow-up procedure. They provide detailed recommendations on services needed, but above all, there is a need for someone to take responsibility.

In spite of this, it would be wrong to be entirely pessimistic about the position in the UK, or indeed in other countries. A wide range of facilities for individuals with TBI has developed in North America and in parts of Europe. There has, over recent years, been a gradual development of services in the UK, albeit on a piecemeal basis whereby a small proportion of individuals do receive good services, despite the fact that many others fail to get any or adequate services.

Rehabilitation Effectiveness

A primary problem in convincing health care professionals that rehabilitation is worth trying lies in lack of education about brain injury outcome. Another problem is the lack of double-blind controlled studies of brain injury rehabilitation, given that the double-blind controlled trial is the 'gold standard' in treatment research.

Cope (1995) explains the scepticism of TBI rehabilitation as a direct result of its nature. It encompasses so many disciplines, requiring different therapies from many professionals, that it is hard to assess and the continual monitoring of the service is a difficult procedure. In terms of rehabilitation outcome, its success must be measured not only by underlying improvement in an impairment, but also improvement in tasks of daily living, and in the 'quality of life'. Cope then sets out to investigate if rehabilitation, quite simply, 'works'.

In considering the efficacy of TBI rehabilitation Cope states that 'the ultimate design' for strong clinical evidence is 'the double-blinded, randomly assigned, matched (if necessary), prospective study'. He also notes that 'no studies of (this) type are yet available on the efficacy of rehabilitation'. He assesses the different stages of rehabilitation, based on research that comes as close as possible to the ideal conditions stated above, breaking them down into the following sections:

- *ICU/Acute Neurosurgical Setting*, where he compares early versus late intervention, and rehabilitation versus no rehabilitation in the acute stage, that is whilst still in a centre providing medical/surgical attention.

- *Acute Inpatient Hospital Rehabilitation*, where Cope explores the benefit gained in terms of receiving rehabilitation, the intensity of rehabilitation received, and at what point the patients were referred to an inpatient rehabilitation programme. Better outcomes were found in those receiving than those not receiving such rehabilitation.

- *Post-acute Rehabilitation* in Outpatient and Residential settings, both shown to be beneficial and, with the inclusion of follow-ups, shown to have lasting effects.

- *Specialised Rehabilitation*, that is Vocational/Cognitive Retraining.

- *Neurobehavioural*, where he looks at the successful rehabilitation of TBI victims with behavioural problems.

Cope reaches the conclusion that:

> ... it now has become very difficult to hold the view that the rehabilitation of neurologically damaged patients may be ineffective or reflect only placebo action. Ethical considerations, with the accumulation of evidence of efficacy, have now become fairly prohibitive of denying rehabilitation to any control group for research purposes.

He supports this statement not only with the evidence of improvement in disabilities and impairments, but also with the financial implications from the savings made, compared to the on-going costs of care and financial support required by those denied access to rehabilitative intervention.

In summary, the evidence is that after TBI many of the problems persist over time, but they can be ameliorated by rehabilitation. However, it also seems that too few individuals have access to rehabilitation (although the position may be improving).

LONG-TERM MANAGEMENT

The achievement of adequate long-term management is indivisible from the availability of and access to adequate rehabilitation, and also having adequate financial resources to meet reasonable needs for long-term support. However, in order that individuals with TBI, their families, and the health professionals working with them even try to access the help needed, it is necessary that they know what is available and what gains may be achievable.

Information and Support

One of the first and most easily implemented contributions to good long-term management would be the availability of reliable and appropriate information. Many countries have patients' and relatives' groups (the National Head Injury Association or Headway in the UK) as well as other voluntary sector groups who provide general information about the brain-injured. It would be of great value if the staff in acute neurosurgical units, admittedly often hard-pressed, developed a tradition of thinking more carefully about the long-term needs of their patients, and providing them with reasonable information.

The need for this is brought out by McMordie, Rogers & Barker, (1991), who describe the views of patients and families towards professional health care services. Their findings do not make happy reading in terms of the quality of information provided in acute units. A survey questionnaire containing questions on adjustment issues after head injury was sent out to members of the Iowa Head Injury Association. McMordie and his colleagues state that his population will over-represent severe head injuries where there has been poor outcome and poor prognoses. If this is the case then it would be anticipated that they would be less satisfied with the health care provision than a random sample of head-injured patients. However, over 70% of respondents stated that they were not given adequate information on where they could find out more about head injury, where there were available resources for themselves and the brain-injured patients, and were not given adequate information about long-term outcome. The authors recommend that a family member be present during neuropsychological testing and should be part of any cognitive rehabilitation intervention.

The first requirement therefore seems to be one of better education of all involved, a matter increasingly addressed by family and other organizations. Lezak (1988) also raises this point stating that specific family problems may be relieved through education, counselling and emotional support. However, she observed that this is seldom received and families are too often left to cope with persisting problems they do not understand. Indeed, Lezak (1978) previously set out detailed recommendations for counselling and dealing with family problems after brain injury. Others have also stressed the importance of family support (e.g. McMordie, Rogers & Barker, 1991; Mauss-Clum & Ryan, 1981), and it would seem that social support within a family is associated with less depression in the TBI individual (Leach et al., 1994).

In the UK, in the context of the NHS, the problem of getting patients into rehabilitation has arisen from a number of sources. One is the lack of knowledge of what may be available on the part of physicians, surgeons and others in acute settings who *should* be referring their patients. Another is the lack of resources. Reference to lack of services has already been made, and lack of knowledge is also relevant here: an example was the statement of a health care planner to one of the authors that only two patients per annum required rehabilitation in his district (which had a population of 500 000). Using the figures from the Miller & Jones (1985) study, in a population of 1.2 million, 116 patients remained severely disabled or vegetative (in terms of GOS) at 1 month post-injury. It seems likely that these patients as well as some not so seriously injured would be likely to need rehabilitation. For a population of 500 000, this would translate to an estimated 48 or more patients requiring rehabilitation.

In other health care systems, access is also a potential problem. Where there is litigation for personal injury, the sum needed to fund rehabilitation may be obtained, but this is a slow process and settlement of litigation may not take place for many years after injury. Availability of adequate insurance cover may be a key consideration. Those injured parties with adequate insurance may claim from their own private medical insurance and some insurers are proactive in accessing good initial services to reduce the costs at a later stage. The rationality of such an approach is in contrast to the position of many UK health planners who see rehabilitation as something that is too expensive but who fail to reckon the long-term costs of not providing it. However, Eames (1994) highlights one particular drawback with the American system being that insurers demand such high levels of justification, to the extent that a quarter of professionals' time is taken up with filling in forms detailing the hours of their time spent with clients and what exactly they did during this time. However, according to Eames, American centres view rehabilitation as a long process (periods as long as 2 years would be unremarkable), with a realisation that in general, the more rehabilitation the better the improvement.

Financial Compensation

As regards the later stages of management, it is probably those who have funds available as the result of financial compensation who are in the best position, inasmuch as it is possible to assess their reasonable needs without being constantly limited by availability of resources locally. Deutsch and his associates have developed a needs-based approach to assessment in this area (e.g. Deutsch et al., 1989). Their plans are used in the first instance to allow the courts to estimate the quantum of damages required to meet the individual's needs but they are also used, and indeed it is a test of their realism that they are used, as the basis for the actual long-term management of the individual with TBI. It is a key element of their approach that needs are assessed independently of funding and availability of services. When needs are established, choices may include moving to an area with better resources. An approach which has one eye on funding, and only identifies as 'needs' those which can be funded, will be misleading and may inhibit the development of necessary services.

The problem still remains that although the reports may make adequate provision for long-term care, this is not necessarily what is received in a settlement. A recent survey looking at the compensation received through personal injury litigation has raised issues. This survey, which received financial support from the insurance industry in the UK, described the uptake of services by those receiving settlements in excess of £150 000 and documented their (then current) socio-economic, functional and medical status (Cornes, 1993). This report does raise a number of interesting observations, although it also raises a number of points that beg discussion. Cornes highlights several areas where recommendations from professionals have not been acted upon. The implication is that some professionals in their reports may have overstated the required levels of support and supply of equipment. In particular, where paid carers were recommended, few took up the suggestion, seemingly preferring to use informal support, if any. However, it may not be a matter of whether or not a particular option is a reasonable need but whether the award provided enough funding for all the needs which were identified. Did assessment of contributory negligence, for example, reduce the final sum awarded? Did families worry about the award lasting and economise in the early stages of providing care while they remained reasonably fit? Cornes does note that there is evidence of some detriment to the health of carers and this may very well be as a consequence of them being unwilling or unable to follow the advice provided about obtaining help with future care.

As an aside, what is more disturbing in Cornes' report — which received serious consideration in some quarters — is the picture painted of long-term outcome of brain injury. It is claimed that the cognitive and behavioural problems were generally overstated by those who assessed them, but Cornes gives no sensible basis for this conclusion. The persistence and significance of these cognitive and behavioural changes is widely accepted through a large established literature in reputable peer-refereed journals. No comment is made by Cornes on this seeming contradiction. Reports such as Cornes's are unfortunate: head injury is sometimes said to be a silent epidemic — survivors often can walk and talk and it is only on careful assessment that the full extent and implications of their deficits are identified. It is important that non-clinicians, including lawyers and insurers, are educated in the nature and implication of these sometimes invisible deficits. Fortunately, the general standard of debate in the medico-legal arena has been rising with the development of the field of neurolaw, through such publications as *The Neurolaw Letter* and a variety of published papers (e.g. Taylor, Harp & Elliott, 1990; Taylor, 1994).

Financial compensation does potentially give access to rehabilitation and adequate long-term support, and in some cases it certainly does so. However, further research on what levels of compensation are adequate, and what services are actually put in place after settlement, remains to be done.

Community Reintegration

The long-term management of individuals with TBI would be likely to be easier with good information, a coordinated and rational approach to referral and early intervention before problems become established. However, reintegration after severe brain injury requires careful planning. For those TBI individuals who have had specialised rehabilitation, the transition from the highly structured world of the rehabilitation unit to 'real life' is very difficult without good local support (which will almost always be non-specialist).

Transitional Living

One method of easing the individual with TBI back into the community is by the supported independent living approach. Harrick et al. (1994) describe the results of a 3-year follow-up to such a community-based programme. This programme was provided at the Kingston Transitional Living Centre (in Ontario), which has both residential and non-residential placements. Placements last on average 6 months, with participation in memory/ orientation sessions, life and social skills programmes, therapy for substance abuse, behavioural programmes and recreational activities. Most subjects were involved in work trials and vocational training.

The outcome measures were separated into different categories of: productive activity; financial support; place of residence; level of supervision; and perceived problems. The programme appeared to breach the gap and help prepare individuals with TBI for a more independent lifestyle. This is shown by improvements in functional status, especially in productive activity, and also place of residence, and level of supervision, at 1-year follow-up, with improvements maintained at 3-year follow-up. However, the subjects reported more concern over loneliness and depression at 3-year follow-up — after finishing the programme — than when they started it. It may be that these residual emotional and social problems come to the fore once earlier concerns over employment and independent living are alleviated.

Community Living

For those who do not have access to specialised rehabilitation, the only help they may get will be that provided by local non-specialist services. However, all too often local services seem unaware of the individual with TBI, and even if contact is made, such services often lack knowledge and experience of managing head injury sequelae.

Some services with the potential to engage the individual with TBI, in order to achieve reintegration on a broad front, include:

- Non-specialist rehabilitation (local physiotherapy, occupational therapy, and counselling from a local psychologist).
- Practical help from family and friends.
- 'Special needs' courses in colleges.
- Careers advice.
- Housing agencies.
- Social Work services.
- Department of Employment vocational retraining.
- Day centres.
- Support/voluntary groups.
- Local employers providing simple work.
- Job coaching.

However, few individuals with TBI or their families have the knowledge, assertion and confidence to coordinate the various elements of help which would be appropriate. As such they do not receive what help there is available. So how do they obtain the help and services they need?

The Role of Case Management

It seems likely that access to appropriate rehabilitation-relevant services may be facilitated by a *case manager*, who has two related but distinct roles: *rehabilitation* and *support in the community*.

The role of *rehabilitation* may be provided by the case manager by utilising available services, some of which have been listed above. In one case, for example, a case manager was provided at the request of the solicitors to a young woman several years post-injury. She had achieved a good physical outcome, but had severe mental impairments, with virtually no functional communication. After rehabilitation she was living with her parents, but she had no structured activities and she would stay in bed for a good part of the day. Although known to the local National Health Service and Social Services, no active help was being provided.

The case manager was able to agree residential and occupational placements with local Social Work Department establishments by undertaking to appoint and train a carer to provide extra help. Voluntary work placement and enrolment in a special needs course in a local college were later incorporated into the programme. Such arrangements may seem obvious but a good deal of time, knowledge of resources and negotiating skill is required. The fact is that this sort of thing seldom happens and long-term follow-ups show the head injured living lives of high dependency and social isolation.

The case also provides an example of a further issue. After the period in which these various services are brought into play in order to improve the outcome, there will be a long-term need for some degree of ongoing support. In this case, the aim was that the client should have her own home with support by a non-residential carer, and probable occasional review by therapists. A modest need for overall supervision arises, with carers leaving and new ones recruited from time to time, and with carers being briefed and supported in learning to handle the various problems of the case. In other cases of more severe disability or with more complex problems, the degree of input will be higher with more extensive carer involvement, sometimes requiring a team of carers.

Such regimes of care may be long-term, but they will not run themselves and need to be carefully managed. The role of the case manager here, however, would not be as part of active rehabilitation but rather one of coordination and maintenance. Here the role is that of providing *support in the community*, organising the various services and sources of help needed for an individual with TBI to live in the community — in other words, providing a 'life support system'. This may consist of therapists, carers and home-helps in order to provide basic care; and sheltered or voluntary employment or attendance at day centres, clubs or societies to give structure, purpose and meaning to life.

In either role, the case manager should seek to make the best use of whatever is available, including specialised services and also planned and rational use of local (non-specialised) services from various sources. The case manager must assess the client's needs and then make referrals to appropriate agencies, negotiate so that the timing of various inputs can be complementary, and then reassess the outcome.

Who should be a case manager?

The primary processes of case management have been described by Dixon, Goll & Stanton (1988) as assessing, organising, coordinating, referring, negotiating, counselling and reassessing. To this might be added the principle of advocacy, which is particularly suggested by writers such as O'Hara & Harrell (1991). Individuals with TBI and families often lack the knowledge, confidence and assertiveness to coordinate the various agencies involved — something that even fit, articulate individuals without TBI would find daunting. O'Hara & Harrell also argue that the case manager needs a knowledge base in many areas including neuroanatomy, brain and behaviour relationships, TBI sequelae, community resources and financial and legal aspects.

The level of expertise required is something which will need clarification in the future. It is certainly fair to say that if very extensive expertise is required, the case managers are going to be extraordinarily hard to find. Our own view has been that it should be someone with a background in one of the health-related professions, such as the therapies, psychology, social work, nursing or in special education, and that the role of case manager should be one of coordinator, not therapist.

From this the question of what training is required also arises. It does not seem realistic to suppose that individuals with a very high level of expertise will be available in sufficient numbers and at an economic rate to act as case managers. It may therefore be that case management has to be provided by case managers who are not particularly expert in brain injury, but who have the kind of professional background mentioned above, and are briefed on the individual case and who belong to an organisation which provides ongoing training and supervision and support to them as necessary.

This in turn means that individual 'independent' case managers may be a less realistic option than groups (whether based around rehabilitation units, or other groupings of professionals, e.g. partnerships or consultancy companies) who can provide training and ongoing support for those case managers who lack extensive head injury experience. Indeed, even those with experience are likely to feel a lack of professional support in dealing with difficult cases if they are entirely independent. Groups also provide for better continuity of help to the person with traumatic brain injury, whereas in the situation of having an individual freestanding case manager, if that person were to retire or to move away, there might be difficulty in finding a suitable replacement.

At what point should case management commence?

A further issue of concern in the UK context is the precise point at which case management becomes most appropriate. A number of pilot projects, for example McMillan et al. (1988) and Greenwood et al. (1994), have taken case management to be a process of achieving relatively acute rehabilitation by encouraging and increasing the number of referrals made. On the other hand, case management could be viewed more as a matter of setting up and maintaining supported living with maximum involvement in the setting-up phase and relatively minimal involvement thereafter.

The need for case management initially came about as a result of a fragmented health care planning system where there was a vacancy for someone to take on overall responsibility for individual clients and provide continuity of care. The points at which intervention is needed may reflect the standard of local acute medical care, post-acute rehabilitation, outreach services and community support.

The effectiveness of case management

Where the case manager seeks to provide *rehabilitation* by encouraging and increasing the number of referrals made, the process could be assessed at an intermediate level by the number of referrals made in case-managed versus non-case-managed groups. It would be relevant to try to assess both the number of referrals and also the quality and duration of services which are delivered consequent to these referrals. The final outcome would be a matter of whether there was any advantage in terms of clinical status for case managed groups. As with the general trend in current rehabilitation studies, the accent would appropriately be on functional outcome and in particular on such things as return to productive activity and the degree of supervision required rather than on more traditional measures.

Greenwood et al. (1994) report on a controlled study of the effects of early case management after severe head injury. Their objectives were to examine the effects of early case management for patients with severe head injury on outcome, family function and provision of rehabilitation services. They had a subject group of 49 case-managed patients with a control group of 61 who received no case management and were left to the usual NHS provision.

The results show that case management significantly increased the number of patients in contact with formal rehabilitation in hospital and in the community. This effect was greatest for clinical psychology, social work and speech therapy (areas where referrals are otherwise rather rare). This increased referral did not, however, impact significantly on the later functioning of patients in terms of return to work, reduction of family stress, or need for supervision and care. A possible reason suggested by the authors is that the hours of treatment did not increase, only the number of referrals. This is seen as an important shortfall in this study. It would seem to the present authors that if local services are sparse and non-specialised, it is not necessarily surprising that they did not achieve improved outcomes. It may be that case management can only succeed in improving *rehabilitation* if a certain minimum level of service is available to be drawn upon. A viewpoint shared by others:

> It is also becoming clear that case management is often affected by the service context, so that, like other service components, it may work less well in poorly resourced areas, and better when it is an integral part of a well resourced network of services.   Huxley, 1993 (p. 368)

On the other hand, where the case manager's aim is to provide *support in the community*, then the criteria of success are entirely different. A clinical outcome measure would not be appropriate as no attempt would be being made to alter the clinical outcome. If the case manager is effective in this context, what will be achieved is a stable placement at a reasonable cost, and if the case manager is not effective, the placement will either break down and become unsustainable, or the costs will be uncompetitive compared with other possible forms of placement.

The following case is an example of such an approach. A young man received a severe head injury. He had previously had a promising career and had sporting interests. After injury he received no specialised rehabilitation and was discharged home. As a consequence of a medico-legal consultation, it was recommended that he attend a specialised unit which was paid for by an interim payment of compensation. He progressed well with substantial improvement in physical state, social skills, problem solving, and reduction of depressive elements.

However, on return home there was no on-going support from local services, even though they were aware of his situation. He followed the advice of the specialised rehabilitation unit by arranging activities to occupy himself, and buying a (suitably adapted) house. However, in the absence of ongoing services, some deterioration occurred and a case manager was recommended. The brief of the case manager was to make an assessment of the client's future needs and to arrange long-term management. The family tended to be over-protective and a key part of the case manager's job was to keep the family 'on side' while reducing this over-protective influence, which potentially would increase dependence. The case manager employed a rota of carers to provide appropriate help and more suitable activities were found to occupy the client. Inevitably, problems are inclined to arise between the client and certain carers, and a good deal of training and support in how to handle difficult behaviours is often required. The evaluation of such an approach rests, as noted above, not so much in clinical improvement as in whether or not it proves possible to maintain an acceptable quality of life at reasonable cost.

At present, in the rehabilitation context, case management of individuals with TBI remains unproven in the UK. It has however, received more coverage in other populations and countries. In the United States case management has been shown to confer advantages in the community for discharged psychiatric patients. For example, Mueller & Hopp (1983) carried out a study providing 20 discharged patients with case management and 20 matched controls without case management. Their results demonstrated that the case-managed subjects spent less time hospitalised, received better access to community resources, and the researchers noted that this was associated with a substantial reduction in cost for the case-managed group. In other studies authors have claimed an increase in the quality of life as well as an increase in service needs met (Bigelow & Young, 1991).

In the UK, successful results from case management have been reported in the frail elderly (Challis & Davies, 1985). In this study the case management process seemed especially useful in relation to the extremely dependent elderly and those who were relatively isolated. The success of case management has further been discussed as a tool for use in community care (Renshaw, 1987; Huxley, 1993).

No long-term management system is able to return individuals to the persons they were prior to their injuries. This is not to say that such care packages as are organised by a case manager do not have the potential to bring about and maintain substantial improvements in the quality of life of the individual whilst remaining cost-effective. Research studies will certainly be helpful in exploring aspects of long-term case management, but ultimately it will be a matter of whether sustainable and satisfactory living arrangements can be supported at an economic cost.

REFERENCES

Arcia, E. & Gualtieri, C. T. (1994). Neurobehavioural performance of adults with closed head injury, adults with attention deficit and controls. *Brain Injury*, **8**, 395–404.

Bigelow, D. A. & Young, J. A. (1991). Effectiveness of a case management program. *Community Mental Health Journal*, **27**, 115–123.

British Psychological Society (1989). *Psychology and Physical Disability in the NHS*. Report of the Professional Affairs Board of the BPS.

Brooks, D. N. Campsie, L., Beattie, A. & Bryden, J. S. (1986a). Head injury and the rehabilitation professions in the West of Scotland. *Scottish Health Bulletin*, **44** (ii), 110–117.

Brooks, D. N. Campsie, L., Symington, C., Beattie, A. & McKinlay, W. (1986b). The five-year outcome of severe blunt head injury: a relative's view. *Journal of Neurology, Neurosurgery and Psychiatry*, **49**, 764–770.

Brooks, D. N. McKinlay, W. W., Symington, C., Beattie, A. & Campsie, L. (1987). Return to work within the first seven years of severe head injury. *Brain Injury*, **1**, 5–19.

Brooks, N. (1984). Cognitive deficits after head injury. In *Closed Head Injury: Psychological, Social and Family Consequences* (Ed. D. N. Brooks). Oxford: Oxford University Press.

Challis, J. D. & Davies, B. (1985). Long-term care for the elderly: the Community Care scheme. *British Journal of Social Work*, **15**, 563–579.

Cornes, P. (1993). *Coping with Catastrophic Injury: a Follow-up Survey of Personal Injury Claimants who Received Awards of £150 000 or More in 1987 and 1988*. The Disability Management Research Group at the University of Edinburgh. Funded by the Association of British Insurers.

Cope, D. N., Cole, J. R., Hall, K. M. & Barkan, H. (1991a). Brain injury: analysis of outcome in a post-acute rehabilitation system. Part 1: General analysis. *Brain Injury*, **5**, 103–110.

Cope, D. N., Cole, J. R., Hall, K. M. & Barkan, H. (1991b). Brain injury: analysis of outcome in a post-acute rehabilitation system. Part two: Subanalysis. *Brain Injury*, **5**, 111–126.

Cope, D. N. (1995). The effectiveness of traumatic brain injury rehabilitation: a review. *Brain Injury*, **9**, 649–670.

Deutsch, P. M., Weed, R. O., Kitchen, J. A. & Sluis, A. (1989). *Life Care Planning for the Head Injured: A Step-by-Step Guide*. Athens: Ellitt & Fitzpatrick.

Dikmen, S., Machamaer, J. & Temkin, N. (1993). Psychosocial outcome in patients with moderate to severe head injury: 2-year follow-up. *Brain Injury*, **7**, 113–124.

Dixon, T. P., Goll, S. & Stanton, K. M. (1988). Case management issues and practices in head injury rehabilitation. *Rehabilitation Counselling Bulletin*, **31**, 325–43.

Eames, P. (1994). *What the UK Could Learn from the American Experience*. Presented at Headway, St George's Hospital Medical School, London.

Evans, C. D. (1987). Rehabilitation of head injury in a rural community. *Clinical Rehabilitation*, **1**, 133–137.

Gainotti, G. (1993). Emotional and psychosocial problems after brain injury. *Neuropsychological Rehabilitation*, **3**, 259–277.

Gloag, D. (1985). Services for people with head injury. *British Medical Journal*, **291**, 557–5.

Greenwood, R. J., McMillan, T. M., Brooks, D. N., Dunn, G., Brock, D., Dinsdale, S., Murphy, L. D. & Price, J. R. (1994). Effects of case management after severe head injury. *British Medical Journal*, **308**, 1199–1205.

Harrick, L., Krefting, L., Johnston, J., Carlson, P. & Minnes, P. (1994). Stability of functional outcomes following transitional living programme participation: 3-year follow-up. *Brain Injury*, **8**, 439–447.

Huxley, P. (1993). Case management and care management in Community Care. *British Journal of Social Work*, **23**, 365–381.

Jennett, B. & Bond, M. (1975). Assessment of outcome after severe brain damage. *Lancet*, **i**, 480–4.

Kreutzer, J. S., Gervasio, A. H. & Camplair, P. S. (1994a). Primary caregivers' psychological status and family functioning after traumatic brain injury. *Brain Injury*, **8**, 197–210.

Kreutzer, J. S., Gervasio, A. H. & Camplair, P. S. (1994b). Patient correlates of caregivers' distress and family functioning after traumatic brain injury. *Brain Injury*, **8**, 197–210.

Leach, L. R., Frank, R. G., Bouman, D. E. & Farmer, J. (1994). Family functioning, social support and depression after traumatic brain injury. *Brain Injury*, **8**(7), 599–606.

Lezak, M. D. (1978). Living with the characterologically altered brain-injured patient. *Journal of Clinical Psychiatry*, **39**, 592-598.

Lezak, M. D. (1988). Brain damage is a family affair. *Journal of Clinical and Experimental Neuropsychology*, **10**, 111–123.

Linn, R. T., Allen, K. & Willer, B. S. (1994). Affective symptoms in the chronic stage of traumatic brain injury: a study of married couples. *Brain Injury*, **8**, 135–148.

Livingston, M. G. (1986). Assessment of need for coordinated approach in families with victims of head injury. *British Medical Journal*, **293**, 742–44.

McKinlay W. W. & Brooks, D. N (1984). Methodological problems in assessing psychosocial recovery following severe head injury. *Journal of Clinical Neuropsychology*, **6**, 87–99.

McKinlay W. W., Brooks, D. N., Bond, M. R., Martinage, D. P. & Marshall M. M. (1981). The short-term outcome of severe blunt head injury as reported by relatives of the injured persons. *Journal of Neurology, Neurosurgery and Psychiatry*, **44**, 527–533.

McMillan, T. M., Greenwood, R. J., Morris, J. R., Brooks, D. N., Murphy, L. & Dunn, G. (1988). An introduction to the concept of head injury case management with respect to the need for service provision. *Clinical Rehabilitation*, **2**, 319–322.

McMordie, W. R., Rogers, K. F. & Barker, S. L. (1991). Consumer satisfaction with services provided to head-injured patients and their families. *Brain Injury*, **5**, 43–51.

Mauss-Clum, N. & Ryan, M. (1981). Brain injury and the family. *Journal of Neurosurgical Nursing*, **13**(4), 165–169.

Medical Disability Society (1988). *Report of a Working Party on the Management of Traumatic Brain Injury*. London: Development Trust for the Young Disabled.

Miller, D. & Jones, P. A. (1985). The work of a Regional Head Injury Service. *Lancet*, **1**, 1141–1144.

Mueller, J. & Hopp, M. (1983). A demonstration of the cost benefits of case management service for discharged mental patients. *Psychiatric Quarterly*, **55**, 17–24.

Murphy, L. D., McMillan T. M., Greenwood R. J., Brooks, D. N., Morris J. R. & Dunn, G. (1990). Services for severely head injured patients in north London and environs. *Brain Injury*, **4**, 95–100.

Oddy, M., Coughlan, T., Tyerman, A. & Jenkins, D. (1985). Social adjustment after closed head injury: a further follow-up seven years after injury. *Journal of Neurology, Neurosurgery and Psychiatry*, **48**, 564–568.

O'Hara, C. & Harrell, M. (1991). *Rehabilitation with Brain Injury Survivors*. Maryland: Aspen Publishers, Inc.

Renshaw, J. (1987). Care in the community: individual care planning and case management. *British Journal of Social Work*, **18**, 79–105.

Royal College of Physicians (1986). Physical disability in 1986 and beyond. A report of the Royal College of Physicians. *Journal of Royal College of Physicians, London*, **20**, 30–37.

Ruff, R. M., Marshall, L. F., Crouch, J., Klauber, M. R., Levin, H. S., Barth, J., Kreutzer, J., Blunt, B. A., Foulkes, M. A., Eisenberg, H. M., Jane, J. A. & Marmarou, A. (1993). Predictors of outcome following severe head trauma: follow-up data from the Traumatic Coma Data Bank. *Brain Injury*, **7**, 101–112.

Scherzer, B. P., Charbonneau, S., Solomon, C. R. & Lepore, F. (1993). Abstract thinking following severe traumatic brain injury. *Brain Injury*, **7**, 441–424.

Taylor, J.S., Harp, J.A. & Elliott, T. (1990). Traumatic brain injury: the silent epidemic. *Experts-At-Law*, **July–August**, 18–20.

Taylor, J.S. (1994). Personal injury litigation in the UK and the emerging field of neurolaw: commentary by an American trial lawyer. *Personal Injury Law and Medical Review*, **1**, 205–212.

Teasdale, G. & Jennett, B. (1974). Assessment of coma and impaired consciousness. *Lancet*, **ii**, 81–84.

Thomsen, I.V. (1974). The patient with severe head injury and his family. *Scandinavian Journal of Rehabilitation Medicine*, **6**, 180–183.

Thomsen, I.V. (1984). Late outcome of very severe blunt head trauma: a 10–15 year second follow-up. *Journal of Neurology Neurosurgery and Psychiatry*, **48**, 564–568.

Wade, D.T. (1991). Policies on the management of patients with head injury: the experience of Oxford Region. *Clinical Rehabilitation*, **5**, 141–155.

Yorkshire Regional Health Authority, Clinical Professions Group (1989). *Services Provided by the Clinical Professions to Patients with Acquired Brain Damage in Yorkshire Regional Health Authority*.

7

LEGAL CONSIDERATIONS

BILL BRAITHWAITE Q.C.

Exchange Chambers, Liverpool

INTRODUCTION

Teamwork by doctors and specialist lawyers from an early stage following a brain injury has the potential for significant effect on the eventual outcome of the individual case. This chapter sets out to explain to each profession how they can and should make the best use of the other, in order to maximise the patient's chances of achieving a good outcome.

As anyone practising in brain injury will know, there can be a vast difference in the facilities for rehabilitation and community support which are available to a patient, sometimes depending on whether there is, or is not, a good prospect of recovering financial compensation for injuries through the courts. The first object of both doctors and lawyers is to do their best to make sure that all patients with the chance of a legal claim investigate fully, in order to decide whether to make a claim. If a positive decision is made, the professionals should then do all they can to pursue it as quickly as possible, and to use the court procedures to maximum advantage, so that the inevitable psychosocial stress of the injury is not increased more than is necessary by the legal proceedings.

THE ACUTE STAGE

Obviously the first considerations are medical ones, to ensure survival and promote recovery, but the time comes when the attention of the family should focus on the circumstances of the accident. It may have been a road traffic accident, a mishap at work, alleged medical negligence, a leisure or domestic accident, or some less common problem. Whatever the circum-

Brain Injury and After: Towards Improved Outcome. Edited by F.D. Rose and D.A. Johnson.
© 1996 John Wiley & Sons Ltd.

stances, the family should undoubtedly make preliminary enquiries to see if there is any realistic chance of claiming compensation for the injured person: this should be done even if it seems unlikely that the accident was another person's fault. The hospital staff are often in an ideal position to advise the family how to go about this. For example, a recent case involved a lorry driver who was injured severely when he was overtaking a slow-moving vehicle: he collided head-on with an oncoming coach when he was on the wrong side of the road and the coach was on its correct side. Many people would say that the accident was entirely his own fault, but investigation showed that his employer had sent him out overloaded and with defective brakes. He recovered substantial compensation.

SELECTION OF SOLICITOR

Having decided to make the appropriate enquiries, the first major hurdle is to select an appropriate solicitor. It is important to choose a solicitor who specialises in brain injury litigation, but this is not always easy for a number of reasons. People are usually not prepared to quiz a solicitor in order to see whether he is a specialist, in much the same way as they do not question a doctor's expertise, and so they need help to find the right person. The hospital team may be able to suggest one or more specialist firms on the basis of their experience with other patients. In addition, there are various organisations which may be able to help, for example the Law Society, Action for Victims of Medical Accidents (AVMA) (in relation to alleged medical negligence), the Association of Personal Injury Lawyers (APIL) (Brain Injury Special Interest Group) and voluntary groups such as Headway and The Children's Head Injury Trust. Also, there are various organisations to which solicitors can belong which might tend to suggest a particular interest in this type of litigation, for example AVMA and APIL. The Law Society has created a Personal Injury Panel and is starting a Medical Negligence Panel, which solicitors can belong to only after they have satisfied the Law Society that they meet appropriate standards.

It is important to emphasise that the aim is not just to find a good solicitor, but to instruct one *who is experienced in brain injury litigation,* and can therefore make the very best presentation of the claim.

THE FIRST STEP

Once the appropriate solicitor has been chosen, he or she must be formally instructed: that simply means asking if he or she will represent the patient. In cases of severe brain injury, one would expect the solicitor to offer a free first interview, lasting as long as necessary to get a clear appreciation of the nature of the accident and the resulting injury and disability. Also that first interview, which may have to take place at hospital, should be arranged within a couple of weeks of the instruction, and ideally should include the family and a key member of the medical team. When it is finished, everybody should have a clear impression whether there is a realistic possibility of a successful claim, the next steps to be taken, and the timetable.

The timetable is not just the legal one. This is where teamwork becomes so important, because it can be essential to relate the legal proceedings to treatment, rehabilitation and recovery. For example, a patient who has to be discharged home from hospital in a wheelchair is likely to require extensive adaptations to his home, which may not be immediately forthcoming from the local social services. If he has a clear legal claim, the money for the adaptations should be obtained quickly by way of an interim payment (see below).

THE NEXT STEP

Because our system of litigation is based on fault, the victim of an accident cannot recover any compensation unless it can be shown that someone else was to blame, either wholly or partly. That is why it is so important to consider the circumstances of the accident with an expert as soon as possible. The issue of blame is called 'liability' by lawyers, and proving liability is crucial to obtaining financial compensation for the injuries sustained.

Obviously all cases are different, but it is possible in many of them to predict accurately what would happen if, when all the evidence has been obtained, a judge were to listen to it and make a decision. If the solicitor thinks that liability probably will be established, he is entitled to take advantage of a special system which allows this part of the claim to be dealt with quickly, called 'Summary Judgment' (otherwise known as 'Order 14').

SUMMARY JUDGMENT

Order 14 of the Rules of the Supreme Court provides a quick procedure for obtaining judgment (the final decision on fault) without proceeding to trial, and it should always be considered, unless it is obviously inappropriate, because it can make the claim far easier and quicker to manage. It is sometimes thought that if there are two or more defendants (people or organisations allegedly responsible) this procedure is not available, but that may be due to a misunderstanding. Similarly, insurance companies occasionally argue that, because they say that a plaintiff was partly to blame, he cannot recover summary judgment. Neither of those arguments is necessarily correct. For example, in one particular case the plaintiff had been the rear seat passenger in a car driven by a friend along a main urban road at night. That car was behind a taxi, travelling in the same direction. The taxi had to brake suddenly and sharply because another driver (who had consumed excess alcohol) pulled out from a side road on the nearside, and so drove right across the path of the taxi. The friend could not brake sufficiently to avoid the taxi, and so he pulled sharply to his right to overtake it. At that stage he was probably exceeding 70 mph (the speed limit being 30 mph) and he did not see the second car, because he crashed straight into it. The plaintiff sustained serious injury to his brain, and so rehabilitation had to be an early consideration: hence the need for summary judgment to obtain the necessary funding.

The defence insurers' reaction to the application for summary judgment was two-fold: first, they argued that the plaintiff could not obtain summary judgment because there were two defendants (and one might escape liability, there having been no conviction for careless driving): secondly, they sought to allege that the plaintiff had been to blame himself in failing to wear a seat-belt. The Judge rejected both arguments, saying that each driver was to blame, and putting off the seat-belt argument to another time. He therefore gave the plaintiff judgment for 75% of damages to be assessed.

INTERIM PAYMENTS

Once an action has been commenced for damages for personal injury and loss arising out of an accident, the plaintiff is entitled to ask the court to order the defendant to pay some of the damages in advance of the final award. The court's power is hedged about with limitations designed to make sure that a defendant is not prejudiced, but unfortunately the power seems to have become even more limited in practice. Interim payments can be the most important weapon in the plaintiff's solicitor's armoury, but they are also an area of the law in which there is bitter disappointment for many litigants.

The court is given the power by *Order 29 rule 11 of the Rules of the Supreme Court*. Some of the limitations are contained in the rules themselves, the most important ones being that:

1. The defendant must be insured, or a public authority, or able to afford to

make an interim payment.

2. It must be clear that the plaintiff will recover damages from the defendant: that is to say, it must be obvious that the accident was the fault of the defendant, either wholly or in part.
3. The court has a discretion whether or not to make an award.
4. The court must not award more than a reasonable proportion of the damages which are likely to be recovered.

Let me take a common example. A passenger in a car is injured severely when another car pulls out of a side road into the main road. The driver of that other car has excess alcohol in his blood. He tells the police that he did not see the oncoming car. On those facts, it seems to be obvious that the accident was caused by the driver of the other car, and so he is sued. In his defence, he says that the driver of the passenger's car was going far too fast, and was not looking where he was going. If the passenger was injured really badly, he is likely to need an advance payment of his damages, and so he applies to the court for an interim payment. He can apply against either or both drivers, although not everyone knows this. But, whoever he applies against, the argument will be raised that one cannot know, until trial, which of the two drivers was to blame. This is where some people lose heart and abandon their application, but they should not, because there is an answer. The driver who came out of the side road is bound to be blamed — not only did he drive into the main road without seeing the passenger's car, but also he was over the limit. Therefore the action against him is bound to succeed to some extent. In some cases, that driver might have a good argument against the driver on the main road, for failing to keep a proper look-out, but that does not concern the passenger: all he has to do is establish some element of negligence against the driver in the minor road. He can then recover the full amount of his damages against that driver, and can leave the drivers to fight it out between themselves. That being so, the passenger can obtain an interim payment. It is only where one cannot decide which of two or more defendants is to blame, *in circumstances in which one might escape altogether*, that one has to wait for the final trial.

The same principles apply to cases in which the defendant seeks to lay some of the blame on the plaintiff, and in other types of claim. However, I do have to sound a note of caution, because it is not quite so easy in factory accidents and leisure disasters to predict whether the plaintiff will be blamed and, if so, to what extent. Therefore, one cannot always say to the judge that the plaintiff will inevitably recover, say, 75% in the end, and so should obtain some of that money now. Nevertheless, the possibility is there, and should be considered.

There is no requirement for the plaintiff to show that he needs the interim payment for any particular purpose (Stringman v. McCardle 1994 P.I.Q.R. P230), and he can apply more than once if necessary. However, there is a growing feeling that, if plaintiffs want to encourage insurers to take a moderate view about interim payments, they must be prepared to meet them half-way, which means that it may well help to explain why the money is needed. Insurers are likely to be more obliging if they know that the litigation is being conducted responsibly and that the money is not being frittered away.

QUANTUM

'Quantum' is lawyers' shorthand to describe the process of calculating the amount of compensation. Let us assume that liability has been established, and that the patient is going to recover compensation in full. The object of our system is that he should be put into the position he would have been in had the accident not happened. This is a rather meaningless concept in the case of brain injury, and it is easier to say instead that compensation will be awarded for the injury, and for all the loss caused and reasonable expense incurred, both past and future. In order to calculate these amounts it is necessary to look at all the components of a claim. There is some concern that the present system of law does not provide sufficient compensation for the injuries, loss and expense caused by brain injury. One of the reasons traditionally given for this is that, because money can never replace what has been lost, therefore it is justifiable to keep the awards of compensation at a modest level. Whilst it would not be in anyone's interest to increase awards to ridiculous levels, the existing system certainly could be improved. One unfortunate aspect of large personal injury awards is that they are often given inappropriate publicity in the media, who make it sound as though the award is huge, and almost a privilege.

THE COMPONENTS OF A PERSONAL INJURY CLAIM

Putting together a claim for a person who has suffered a brain injury is a highly specialised technique, and plaintiffs and their professional advisers should make quite sure that everything possible is done to claim for every loss and expense. The object of the law is to pay the injured person fully for all financial loss, and to do its best, by a money award, to compensate him for the pain, suffering and loss of amenity caused by the injury. The claim is divided into those two basic parts: first, pain, suffering and loss of amenity, and, second, damages for financial loss.

Pain, Suffering and Loss of Amenity

This is an award made by the judge on the basis of his experience of personal injury actions, helped by reference to previous cases in which similar injuries have been considered. The maximum award, at today's value, is in the region of £140 000, although much depends on life expectancy (if it is reduced, damages will be less) and the nature and extent of associated disabilities and handicap.

Loss of Earnings

If the claimant has lost earnings, the amount lost can often be calculated fairly easily. The final figure will depend on the size of the annual loss, and the period for which it is lost. For example, a person who earns £10 000 a year net (net earnings are always used, not gross) would receive £50 000 if his case took 5 years from accident to trial. However, the sums are not quite so straightforward in relation to future loss. Someone aged 25 who is injured so badly that he will never work again has lost 40 years of earnings: if he was earning £10 000 a year net at the time of the accident it would seem that he should receive £400 000 (£10 000 × 40), but he will not. When there is a stream of loss stretching into the future, the courts adopt the actuarial technique of discounting for accelerated receipt of the money and for mortality risks, and so they use a 'multiplier' (i.e. the figure by which the annual loss is multiplied). There is currently an argument amongst lawyers as to the method by which that multiplier should be selected (this is a complicated and controversial topic, which was dealt with most recently in Quantum 24/11/94 and 13/7/95), but for the purpose of this chapter it is enough to say that the traditional multiplier for someone aged 25 will be 16 in relation to loss of earnings. Another complication is where the claimant's earnings at the time of the accident are not representative of all his future earnings, for example if he had been expecting promotion: this can be covered in the calculation provided that the lawyers and accountants recognise the possibility. This award for loss of earnings can be very substantial, amounting to hundreds of thousands of pounds if carefully prepared.

Care

Those with severe brain injury will often need some form of specialist care, either from relatives or from an outside source such as an agency. Even though no payment has actually been made to the relatives for care given, a claim can be made for the services provided by them. Again, the claim is for loss to the date of trial and for any future loss. The same method of calculation (i.e. the use of a multiplier) is used as described above, but if the need for care will last beyond the normal age of retirement from work (now 65) then the multiplier for a young person is likely to be 18 to reflect the additional years during which the care will be required beyond the age of retirement. This is very often the largest element of a claim arising out of severe brain injury.

Accommodation

Serious injury often causes a requirement for adapted housing, either by alteration of the existing home, or by moving to somewhere more suitable. The actual cost is easy to itemise if it has been spent, or to estimate if not, although the actual calculation is slightly complicated, and the courts use a method commonly called after a case in which the point was argued — Roberts v. Johnstone [1989] Q.B. 878. The result is that a plaintiff will recover only a small part of the actual cost of special accommodation. It is often important to pursue an early interim payment in order to obtain suitable accommodation, as this may be essential to the implementation of any therapy or rehabilitation programme, including appropriate space for therapy indoors and out, and accommodation for carers.

Aids and Equipment

Wheelchairs are the most obvious example, although many severely brain-injured people may not be wheelchair-dependent. There are many other items of equipment which may be of use to the brain-injured person, including computers, exercise equipment, domestic appliances and specialist educational and therapeutic aids. If equipment is expected to wear out within the lifetime of the injured person, as is usually the case, the costings must include replacements. It is also important that the costs of any necessary instruction should be included. For example, it is not sufficient simply to supply a personal computer to a brain-injured person, who may have difficulties in learning new information: rather, the choice of hardware and programmes should be guided by the appropriate technical expert, and determined by the individual's specific needs.

Transport

This may be an adapted car, or it can include a specialist vehicle to permit easier transfers. Special transport may be important for people who are not dependent on a wheelchair, due to physical or mental problems in using public transport, or to permit easier access to social and leisure facilities. Any other expenses, such as taxis or use of relatives' cars, can also be recovered.

Therapies

The National Health Service does not always seem to be able to provide appropriate therapies, or in sufficient quantity, for the longer-term care of the brain-injured. In many cases, therefore, an independent assessment of the need for treatment and rehabilitation may be required.

Financial Management of the Award

If the injured person is incapable of managing and administering his property and affairs by reason of mental disorder (defined by section 1(2) of the Mental Health Act 1983 as 'mental illness, arrested or incomplete development of mind, psychopathic disorder, and any other disorder or disability of the mind'), his compensation will be managed by the Court of Protection (see below), but otherwise the courts tend not to award compensation for the cost of managing the award of damages, although that is not an inflexible rule.

Case Management

This appears to be an increasingly important area. It relates to the management of the medical and therapeutic aspects of the case, as distinct from either the legal or financial sides. The first award to allow for lifetime case management has been made recently (Tricker v. Hoban 15th February 1994). This type of award may be justified in many cases, where injured people or their families cannot be expected to make all the arrangements for specialist care. However, judges are often reluctant to make such an award, and so medical evidence is required to show that ongoing case management is necessary.

Court of Protection

If it is necessary for the Court of Protection to be involved in the management of a patient's money, because he is not capable of managing and administering his own property and affairs, the costs of doing so are recoverable.

General

Financial losses incurred up to the date of the trial are called Special Damages: financial losses from trial onwards, and also damages for pain, suffering and loss of amenity, are called General Damages. Special Damages carry interest.

Generally, plaintiffs are not compensated for the time they spend on managing the claim. dealing with all the numerous questions which arise, and making sure that it is presented to its best advantage. If they were working before the accident, then the claim for loss of earnings might well cover the time which is now being spent on the claim. However, if the person was not working before the accident, and so is now performing tasks which he was not previously, compensation *might* be recoverable.

VALUATION OF THE CLAIM

In order to assess the full nature of the losses and expenses, it is usually helpful to try to establish with the patient and his family a comprehensive plan for the rest of his life ('a plan for life'). Many people imagine that it is impossible to do that, but in fact it can be quite easy, providing the lawyers know what is, and is not, realistic within the legal framework. Generally, someone who is injured severely will need purpose-built or adapted accommodation, care from the family and from outside sources, in addition to transport, aids and equipment. The preparation of this part of the claim may require the services of an accountant, who should also specialise in this type of claim. The best way to agree on a plan for life is to assemble together the plaintiff and his family, the solicitor, the barrister and some of the experts who have been instructed, so that all the possibilities and problems can be discussed between all those present. The alternative is to try to perform the same process in a more piecemeal way, by getting the plaintiff's views first, and then asking each expert to comment: what sometimes happens is that the experts do not agree that what has been suggested is practical or appropriate. It is very important that the team should be created from the outset, with as many of the key members involved as early as is possible. Of course the traditionalist can foresee all sorts of difficulties in this notion: legal aid, costs, insurers balking and so on, but I have had the advantage of seeing the system working, and sometimes also of having to cope with the alternative. There is probably nothing more frustrating than being instructed in an important case, when it is listed for trial in a week or two, or even a month or two, and wishing that you had been given the opportunity to discuss experts, tactics, presentation and all the other indefinable elements which contribute to a successful result. An early consultation can be justified in cost terms, both for plaintiffs and defendants, by the gathering together of all the strands so that there is minimum duplication by the experts.

It is most important for lawyers to make quite sure that they are really listening to what their clients are telling them. Families often know best, and the guiding principle is that the claim should be fitted to the patient and his family, rather than them being forced to accept solutions which they do not want and will not use. It is also vital that lawyers should stress to their clients and experts that the claim should be presented realistically, based on the client's genuine needs and losses: far too much time is wasted, and too much antagonism caused, by the inevitable confrontation between plaintiffs' and defendants' lawyers when claims are either presented unreasonably or defended unhelpfully and unrealistically.

THE COURT SYSTEM

The process of commencing and pursuing a claim for severe personal injuries is set out in The Rules of the Supreme Court.

If the claim is likely to be for over £50 000, as all severe brain injury claims are, it is commenced in the High Court (as distinct from the County Court, which generally deals with smaller claims). There is a 3-year time limit, although it should never be assumed that a claim is hopeless simply because it is over 3 years since the accident, as there are exceptions to the general rule. For example, the effect of the brain injury may have been to render the patient incapable of managing and administering his property and affairs, in which case the lapse of time will not be held against him. The claim has to be set out in writing (the Statement of Claim), and the person(s) or organisa-tion(s) allegedly responsible have to respond in writing (the Defence) within a set period. When that has been done, and any ambiguities cleared up, there is a process, called Discovery and Inspection, by which each party to the action reveals to the other all relevant documentation in his possession. Whilst this is going on, or after it has been done, the parties should be preparing their evidence, which involves enquiries into all the components set out above, and the instruction of experts, such as engineers of all sorts, road accident reconstruction specialists, doctors, architects, nurses, therapists and techno-logical and equipment specialists. When each party's evidence is ready, it is exchanged with the other side.

At about this stage, the plaintiff's financial claim is set out in a schedule of past and future loss and expense, so that the defendant can see how it is put against him. This is often one of the most important documents in the entire case, and it should be drafted with great care. The defendant then has to respond by way of counter-schedule setting out his arguments against the plaintiff's claim.

Traditionally, the case is then ready for trial by a judge, and the court is asked for a date (the case is 'set down'). Most cases involving severe brain injury settle, that is to say the parties agree a solution without having to go before a judge.

THE CRIMINAL INJURIES COMPENSATION BOARD

Until 1964, victims of violent crime had no right to compensation other than the ordinary right to sue the person who caused the injury, which was usually a worthless right. In 1964 a scheme for compensating victims of violent crime was introduced, although it was not enacted by Parliament and all payments were made 'ex gratia'. In general, payments were calculated on the existing common law principles which had developed over the years to compensate accident victims. In 1988 the scheme was codified, with some amendments, and put into statutory form, but the relevant provisions were not to come into force until the Home Secretary so ordered. He did not make such an order: on the contrary, in 1992 he said that he was going to change the system by introducing a tariff scheme under which awards would be based on a flat-rate tariff according to the category of injury, with no account taken of the circumstances of a particular case. This caused an uproar from all those involved with this type of claim because it was obvious that someone who suffered a severe injury would receive too little compensation. The Home Secretary's decision was challenged successfully in the House of Lords.

REHABILITATION

The two questions most frequently asked by lawyers and insurers are:

1. Does rehabilitation work?
2. How do we know rehabilitation works?

These two questions raise an issue of great importance in litigation involving brain injury, namely whether in any particular case the plaintiff's lawyers are justified in advising or arranging specialist rehabilitation, which can be very costly and which sometimes lasts for many months or even years.

Cope & Nathan (1993) recently summarised the area. They divided the studies into various stages:

- Intensive care unit/acute neurosurgical setting.
- Acute in-patient hospital rehabilitation
- Post-acute rehabilitation (residential and out-patient).

In the first stage, a study (Morgan, Chapman & Tokarski, 1988) established that patients given early rehabilitation stayed in hospital a shorter time (25 against 45 days) and had a better functional outcome at discharge. More recently another team of experts (Mackey et al., 1992) compared matched groups of severely head-injured patients, and reported substantial benefits for those who received rehabilitation: for example, 94% were discharged home (rather than having to be sent to chronic care or a nursing facility) compared to only 57% of the patients who did not receive rehabilitation. This type of result is likely to be of particular significance to personal injury practitioners and insurers, because of the obvious possibility of reducing the need for lifetime care. Moving on to the second stage, an analysis of data in 1990–1991 (Hall & Wright, 1991) showed that the length of in-patient stay was an average of 28 days for early admissions and 60 days for late ones: also, on long-term follow-up the early-admitted patients were only mildly disabled, whereas the others were moderately disabled with substantially worse social functioning. Rehabilitation can be important for outcome, and more so if it is started early. Consequently it demonstrates the need to obtain an early interim payment to fund the rehabilitation.

An opportunity which is waiting to be explored fully is in relation to insurers taking an informed and active interest in rehabilitation. In America many of the rehabilitation centres are funded by insurers, and they have 'insurance case managers' who positively help to place an injured plaintiff in an appropriate unit, so that he has the best possible chance of maximum recovery. There is some sign that some enlightened British insurers are considering involvement in this process, which is a development to be encouraged by plaintiffs' lawyers and experts, *provided* that it is done in a genuine spirit of cooperation and help.

Home-based rehabilitation is an area which requires the further attention of legal and medical practitioners. The family are sometimes the best people to manage and undertake effective rehabilitation, although it may also be pursued effectively in conjunction with external agencies. This type of rehabilitation can be supervised by a case manager who would be responsible for selecting and coordinating the various therapists in an appropriate rehabilitation programme. It certainly should not be assumed that the rehabilitation provided by the National Health Service is inevitably the most appropriate, or that it is adequate in extent. Depending on the nature and extent of the injury to the brain, private rehabilitation in a specialised unit may be the only solution. The vital message is that the team should consider all the options, including the resources, expertise and success of both NHS and private units, and home-based programmes.

Another important point is that rehabilitation should not be judged solely by whether the plaintiff can return to work, nor even whether the care regime can be reduced. Rather, one must ask whether the plaintiff's quality of life can be enhanced.

STRUCTURED SETTLEMENTS

Structured settlements are a method by which damages can be paid by a defendant in a stream of future annual payments, rather than by the traditional lump sum award at trial. What usually happens is that the lawyers come to an agreement about the value of the claim in the usual way, and then start to investigate whether it suits both the plaintiff and the defendant for some or all of the money to be invested in an annuity so that there is a guaranteed income for the life of the plaintiff. Generally, some of the damages are used to buy accommodation and equipment, and the rest is needed for the future expenses of living, including additional care, therapies and normal household expenses. The system is quite flexible, in that the plaintiff can choose how much of his damages should be kept as capital (a contingency fund), and there are various ways in which the structured settlement can be tailored to the individual's needs. The great advantage for a plaintiff is that the income is guaranteed for life, however long that might be, subject to the financial stability of the insurance company which is used to provide the annuity, and it is usually linked to inflation. The main disadvantage seems to be that the plaintiff loses control of the money which goes into the annuity, so that, if something unforeseen happens which requires him to use part of his capital, it will not be possible. A structured settlement is not possible unless the insurance company consents: it cannot be ordered by the court in the absence of consent.

There is a good deal of controversy at the moment about whether structured settlements are, or are not, a good thing (see, for example, the Law Commission's Report on Structured Settlements [Law Com. No. 224] 1994). Each case should be considered on its own merits, because not all are appropriate for this type of disposal: it is important to get the best advice. The decisive consideration is often security for the plaintiff and his family: when life has collapsed around you, it must be some comfort to know that you will receive a guaranteed income for life, linked to inflation.

The Law Commission made several recommendations:

1. There should be no judicial power to impose structured settlements.
2. Life offices should be able to make payments under annuities bought by

defendants free of tax direct to the plaintiff.

3. There should be provision for statutory structured settlements.

4. The position of intermediaries acting for both parties should be considered by the relevant professional bodies.

SUGGESTIONS FOR THE FUTURE

A Listing System

'Listing' is the scheduling of a case which has been set down for hearing, so that it comes before a judge as soon as possible. It is important that large cases, sometimes with a dozen or more experts, and always with a worried plaintiff, should be listed so that they are heard at the earliest possible opportunity, without adjournment caused by lack of court time or many of the other reasons which arise.

In litigation relating to building disputes there is a fundamentally different system. The judge is selected for his experience in the specialist area, and he deals with all interlocutory (intermediate) matters in an interventionist way. The trial date is fixed either within a few weeks of the commencement of the action or half-way through, when experts have met (i.e. opposing experts of like specialisations) and reported (either separately or jointly), thus seeking to clarify the issues. This system could be considered for personal injury litigation, but the fundamental requirement is for the lawyers, including the judges, to be specialists.

An Experienced Sympathetic Judge

Given the development of specialist judges in building, commercial, family and criminal work, it is not unreasonable to suggest that personal injury actions, some involving hundreds of thousands, or millions, of pounds, should be allocated to a judge who has spent at least a substantial part of his working life practising in that type of work.

Efficiency

On balance, I think that the real drive forward will be aimed at *greater efficiency on all fronts*, so that one can realistically expect an action to come to trial within 5 years at the most, or possibly even only 3 years, from the date of the accident. Cornes (1993) reported data for 152 cases of serious brain and spine injuries: the average period between accident and settlement was 64 months, only 26 cases took 3 years or less to finish, and 6 took more than 10 years. There can be risks in concluding an action too quickly, but it is not often necessary to take delaying steps because the action has been made ready for trial too quickly.

Having urged speedier litigation, it is imperative that the action is *not* settled before the brain-injured person's outcome is clearly established, because the existing legal system does not generally permit plaintiffs to return to court after their case has been finalised, complaining that the outcome has been worse than they anticipated. This raises a particularly difficult problem, to which the law does not seem to have a solution, and which is especially worrying in relation to children who have suffered brain injury. Assuming that the action is made ready for trial within about 5 years of the accident or birth (alleged negligence at birth being a very common cause of brain injury in children), so that the child is still, say, under 10 years old, it is desirable to put off the final settlement until outcome can be assessed with some degree of accuracy. There is a system called 'Provisional Damages', by which a plaintiff can be awarded damages on the basis of his current condition but with the reservation that, if there is serious deterioration in his physical or mental condition in a specified way, he can return to the court when that deterioration occurs and ask for an increase in his damages. However. that system is not likely to apply when there is no serious deterioration, as distinct from expected and gradual development. What is required is not simply to await the development of limited or aberrant future behaviour, but for the appropriate experts to make reliable prognoses and suitable interventions (rehabilitation in the broadest sense), to be planned and implemented before the problems emerge in full scale. If litigation becomes more efficient, and cases become ready for trial much quicker, then this problem may become more common.

This difficulty of predicting outcome at a comparatively early stage is linked with another common problem, which is that lawyers and doctors are sometimes too optimistic about the eventual outcome, and fail to take sufficient account of the future. Severe brain injury has immense financial implications, and there can be a tendency to think that compensation of 1 or 2 million pounds will solve all problems, both present and future. This is simply not the case, and all those involved should realise the enormity of the cost of suitable housing, good and extensive care round the clock, and technology which moves ahead so fast that the computer on which I type this is obsolete within 2 years.

This whole question of the adequacy of personal injury compensation was considered by the Law Commission in their report 'Personal Injury

Compensation: How Much Is Enough?' (Law Com. No. 225) (17th October 1994). One of their most striking findings was that, although most victims experience satisfaction at the time of settlement when faced with what appears to be a substantial sum of money, this satisfaction drains away over time when the reality of long-term ill-effects and reduced capacity for work bite. The study found that 32% of recipients of compensation complained that interest rates were very low, 20% that their shares had fallen in value, and 15% that they had received poor financial advice. It is of significance to all concerned with personal injury litigation that, of those people who received awards over £100 000, 65% were either fairly dissatisfied or very dissatisfied with the size of their compensation.

The Adversarial System

If specialisation and efficiency are pursued as suggested, then many incidental results are likely to follow. The adversarial system may require some modification in order to render it more suitable for complex personal injury claims. An enormous amount of time and money can be spent on medical and other expert reports, sometimes on both sides, and this may potentially be avoided in part by better management by the lawyers of the experts.

There is an opportunity here for an attempt to be made to settle the claim without actually taking it all the way to court: if the parties wish, they can arrange a meeting of the lawyers, accountants and experts, depending who they consider necessary, well in advance of the trial, so that the various issues can be discussed and, ideally, some agreement reached. However, this is not an opportunity which is used sufficiently. One further possibility is a pre-trial consultation between the lawyers for each side, supervised by a judge (not the one who will eventually try the case, but a specialist nevertheless), at which the parties canvass the arguments on each side, with guidance from the judge as appropriate: the object would be to create an atmosphere of realism in which the strengths and weaknesses of each side can be perceived through sensible discussion, and a settlement reached. This is not possible under our present system.

Management of Experts

A possible solution to these problems would be to *instruct the expert jointly*, by agreed letter: either solicitor would then have the right, if he chose, to obtain another report if he was not satisfied with the independent one.

An incidental result of this approach might be that experts would gradually become more neutral. I must make it clear that I do not mean to say that, as a body of people, they are not fair, but unfortunately a few have a tendency to produce reports which seem to be one-sided. With nonspecialist judges, such experts do occasionally carry the day, but generally they are counter-productive, raising issues where truly there are none, offending both legal and medical practitioners (and plaintiffs), and delaying resolution of the action.

An alternative would be to adopt the system followed in building litigation, whereby the *experts of like specialty must meet* at a comparatively early stage in order to define the areas of agreement and disagreement, and the reasons for disagreement. This can be a very effective way of eliminating unnecessary argument. A problem that many solicitors would be bound to point out, however, is that one expert might be browbeaten or overborne by the other, and so fail to maintain the position which he so confidently asserted in consultation. That emphasises the importance of choosing the appropriate expert carefully.

Education of Non-lawyers

All non-lawyers involved in litigation arising out of injury to the brain should know something about the legal procedures and requirements. Similarly, lawyers must specialise, and obtain a good working knowledge of the mechanics of injury to the brain, of acute treatment, rehabilitation, outcome, and resettlement in a suitably bought or adapted house with a care regime and all necessary equipment. In the past, there has been a divide between the professions, but interprofessional communication is improving and each side is beginning to appreciate the benefits. Communication is essential, but there should also be an appreciation that non-lawyers have the right to question all aspects of the legal process, particularly because it has a major bearing on the outcome of the plaintiff's claim and future life.

SUMMARY

In summary, an efficient system of personal injury litigation, which would provide a first class service to those who have suffered severe brain injury, should incorporate the following:

1. Specialist lawyers, both solicitors and barristers, who have developed knowledge and experience of the difficult problems of injury to the brain.
2. Education of medical consultants and other experts involved with the

treatment and rehabilitation of the patient, so that they understand the essentials of the legal system of personal injury compensation, and the considerations which may apply in the case of a patient who has, or may have, a legal claim.
3. Effective communication and teamwork between all the above, coordinated actively by the lawyer.
4. Designation of specialist personal injury judges, who would then be allowed and encouraged to take an interventionist role in this type of action.
5. The efficient conduct of a court case, so that it proceeds without unnecessary delay, with the plaintiff and the experts all being kept in the picture as to its progress and timetable.
6. Modification of the adversarial system, so that more time is spent on trying to work together to achieve a just result for the plaintiff and the insurers, and less energy is wasted on tactical manoeuvring and unrealistic argument.

REFERENCES

Cope, D. & Nathan, M.D. (1993). The effectiveness of traumatic brain injury rehabilitation and how it can be evaluated. Presented to the International Brain Injury Forum, John Radcliffe Hospital, Oxford, England, 30th March.

Cornes, P. (1993). *Coping with Catastrophic Injury*. Edinburgh: Disability Management Research Group, Edinburgh University.

Hall. K., & Wright, J. (1991). Presented at the Traumatic Brain Injury Conference, Williamsburg, Virginia.

Mackey, L. E., Bernstein, B. A., Chapman, P. E., et al. (1992). Early intervention in severe head injury: long-term benefits of a formalized program. *Arch. Phys. Med. Rehabil.*, **73**, 635–41.

Morgan, A. S., Chapman, P. & Tokarski, L. (1988). Improved care of the traumatically brain injured. Presented at the Eastern Association for Surgery of Trauma — First Annual Conference, Longboat Key, Florida.

8

LEGISLATIVE AND POLICY FACTORS

MICHAEL BARNES

Centre for Rehabilitation and Engineering Studies, University of Newcastle upon Tyne

Legislation can reduce both the likelihood of head injury and the ensuing disability and handicap. This chapter will review present UK policy in this area, draw on some experience from abroad and make some suggestions for future direction.

PREVENTION: HOW CAN LEGISLATION REDUCE THE INCIDENCE OF HEAD INJURY?

Road Environment and Car Safety

If members of the public are asked about the most effective means of reducing head injuries most people would probably cite either drink–driving or seat-belt legislation. Whilst these are accurate perceptions the situation is more complicated. Transport policy has a significant role to play in overall accident prevention. A journey made by car is three times more likely to injure a pedestrian than a journey made by bus (Transport and Health Study Group, 1991). The removal of subsidies to public transport in London by the Greater London Council resulted in increased road casualties (Allsopp & Turner, 1986). A greater emphasis on public rather than private transport should reduce road traffic accidents.

There is also room for improvement with regard to road safety measures. An interesting scheme in The Netherlands demonstrated a 25% reduction in

Brain Injury and After: Towards Improved Outcome. Edited by F.D. Rose and D.A. Johnson.
© 1996 John Wiley & Sons Ltd.

injuries following the introduction of a package of road safety measures, involving the exclusion of local traffic from certain areas and speed limitations (Janssen, 1991). In Britain the Urban Safety Project studied measures to redistribute traffic and improve road design in a number of urban centres. There was an overall reduction of 13% in all types of injury following the introduction of the schemes. The most successful measures were right turn prevention, right turn bays and central road dividers (Mackie, Ward & Walker, 1990). Another effective measure is traffic calming. There is a clear relationship between the speed of vehicles and the proportion of fatalities. When pedestrians are hit by vehicles travelling at 20, 30 and 40 mph the proportion killed is 5, 45, and 85% respectively (Department of Transport, 1993). The introduction of 20 mph speed limit zones as opposed to the normal 30 mph in urban areas has been shown to reduce casualties by more than 50% (Carlisle, 1993).

The safety of car occupants has been significantly improved following the introduction of seat-belt legislation. In Germany, for example, a law concerning the wearing of safety belts was introduced in 1984 and following this legislation there was a significantly lower fatality and injury rate in those wearing seat-belts. Serious injuries to the skull and brain were reduced by 80% (Teiske et al., 1993). A study in Scotland demonstrated the relative head injury risk for children travelling unrestrained in a car was just over three times the risk of restrained children. The study estimated that 24% of all non-fatal injuries sustained by a child car passenger could be prevented if all children were restrained in a child safety seat or seat restraint and that 49.5% of head injuries could be prevented in this manner (Ruta, Beattie & Narayan, 1993). If the seat-belt statistics are analysed from the financial point of view then this form of government legislation will actually save money. Rutledge et al. (1993) demonstrated that seat-belt usage was associated with a significant decrease in mortality rate, hospital charges, length of stay, intensive care unit stay, and ventilator requirements. Seat-belts had saved around 7.2 million dollars during the 2-year period 1987–1989 in patients seen in seven trauma centres in North Carolina. The only disadvantage is an increased incidence of whiplash injuries to the neck and other seat-belt associated chest and abdominal trauma.

The safety of car transport could be improved even further by more rigorous legislative standards for car design and the introduction of other safety measures such as the compulsory use of air-bags. Zador & Ciccone (1993) concluded that air-bags reduced the total number of all driver fatalities in frontal crashes by 28% compared to cars fitted with only manual seat-belts. Presumably the proportion of drivers and passengers with severe head injuries could also be reduced in this way. The recent introduction of legislation requiring the wearing of rear seat restraints should reduce the incidence of brain injury in the UK (Bodiwella, Thomas & Otubushin, 1989) and evidence of this effect is awaited.

The wearing of safety helmets for motorcycle drivers has been compulsory in the UK for many years. There is good evidence that this has reduced the number of fatalities and severe injuries in motorcycle accidents (e.g. Evans & Frick, 1988). A number of countries have now broadened the compulsory wearing of safety helmets to include those on pedal cycles. The most widely cited study of the protective effect of cycle helmets was conducted in Seattle (Thompson, Rivara & Thompson, 1989). It was calculated that riders with helmets had an 85% reduction in risk of head injury. This is a similar figure to the more recent study by Thomas et al. (1994) which found that wearing a helmet reduced the risk of head injury by about 63%. There is currently no UK legislation enforcing the wearing of helmets for bicycle riders.

Personal behaviour in motor vehicles has been influenced by the introduction of drink–driving regulations. This has clearly been associated with a significant reduction in head injuries and fatalities and has resulted in a change in socially acceptable behaviour with regard to drinking and driving (Dunbar, Penttila & Pikkarainen, 1987).

Home Environment

Brain injury secondary to falls and other accidents occurs quite frequently in the home environment. It is known that common domestic accidents in children, including falls, occur when parental supervision is reduced rather than being primarily due to household hazards. Some would argue that tackling the underlying problem of deprivation with better support for families at risk would reduce domestic accidents. However, better home design and building regulations may have had some effect on accident reduction. Handrails on staircases are now compulsory in the UK and the steepness of stairs is limited. Opening distances of windows in high rise buildings is controlled. However, the effectiveness of such legislation in actually reducing the incidence of brain injury has not been robustly tested.

Leisure and Work Environment

There are now a rather complicated number of regulations throughout the European community regarding health and safety at work. Employers have to liaise with their employees to ensure that all staff have adequate health and safety training. Employers have a duty to ensure that risks are reduced to a minimum, that equipment is properly maintained and that protective equipment for the individual employee is both provided and used. In turn the employee has a duty to understand and comply with the regulations. There can be little doubt that such commonsense regulations have reduced work-related head injuries, although there is little published evidence.

Enforcement of the use of safety equipment in hazardous sports is more difficult, although many of the individual governing bodies have clear guidelines on the proper use of safety equipment, particularly head protection. Mountaineering and horse riding are primary areas of concern and could be appropriate targets for health education programmes (Condie, Rivara & Bergman, 1993).

Health Education

Can we influence dangerous and risk-taking behaviour? There is some limited evidence that safety campaigns have some effect, particularly if targeted to specific groups. In the USA the Willie Whistle campaign was designed to reduce road accidents in 3–8-year-old children (Preusser & Blomberg, 1984). A number of films, posters and television programmes were produced and distributed widely in three cities. Observations after the campaign showed that children did cross the roads more carefully and there was a 21% reduction in road accidents. Promotion of other initiatives such as children's traffic clubs, cycle training programmes, helmet-wearing campaigns and the well known drink–driving campaigns appear to have a modest effect on influencing behaviour, but whether such behavioural change is sustained is not known. Although such campaigns should be encouraged, it would be sensible to combine the campaign itself with associated research studies to assess the most effective method of delivery and sustainability. A useful review of the literature on the effectiveness of health promotion interventions has recently been produced by Towner, Dowswell & Jarvis (1993).

HEALTH CARE

Improved outcome for people with brain injury depends not only on proper management in the acute phase but will also depend on the provision of an appropriate range of rehabilitation services. In general the UK has a good quality range of acute services provided both in local hospitals and in more specialist regional centres. However, the standard of rehabilitation services has been sadly lacking and has not been viewed as a priority for health service investment. In recent years there has been a modest improvement in the range and extent of rehabilitation services. Rehabilitation is slowly achieving a higher priority for the allocation of health resources. We are seeing the growth of locally based rehabilitation teams as a result of the drift from acute hospital based care towards community care. We are also seeing the growth of specialist regional rehabilitation centres. People with brain injury will often need access to such specialist centres for the proper assessment and management of a complex range of physical, psychological and behavioural problems that are often associated with brain injury. There are generally agreed guidelines on the scope and range of services that should be provided in a specialist centre (Royal College of Physicians of London, 1986; Association of British Neurologists, 1993). However, such centres, whilst useful, are of limited value if there is not a locally based service to support the disabled person and family in the longer term. How can legislation and policy improve this situation?

The UK has recently seen major changes in the delivery of health care. A fundamental change has been to split the purchasing of health care from the provision of health care. Health authorities are now responsible for determining the health needs of their local population and for purchasing a full range of health services to meet those needs. In addition some elements of the service can be purchased by local general practitioners who hold their own funds. The main providers of both hospital- and community-based health services are now NHS Trusts whose income depends entirely on contracts placed with the various purchasing groups.

Does this system benefit people with brain injuries? In principle it gives greater opportunity for change. If a purchaser is making a proper assessment of the health needs of the local population then it should be apparent that people with longer term disabilities, including those with head injuries, have been disadvantaged by a system that has traditionally favoured acute hospital and high technology care. A number of reports in recent years have emphasised the inadequacy of health services for people with disabilities (Audit Commission, 1986; Royal College of Physicians of London, 1986; Beardshaw, 1988; Medical Disability Society, 1988). However, the degree to which purchasers are prepared to move contracts towards health care support for people with longer-term disabilities is open to question and will undoubtedly vary from area to area. The present system does in theory allow for more effective lobbying of local purchasers. People with disabilities, their families, support groups and the local providers can all make representations to the local purchaser to press for further investment in rehabilitative health care. There is not a shortage of guidance on the delivery of such services

(British Society of Rehabilitation Medicine, 1993; Association of British Neurologists, 1993).

At the national level the Department of Health can still influence purchasing decisions. The government initiative entitled 'The Health of the Nation' has set out clear targets that purchasers should seek to achieve within limited timescales. Although health care services for people with physical disabilities, including those with brain injury, were in the initial consultative document, these services did not feature in the final document. Considerable work has now been done on the establishment of appropriate national targets covering a wide range of disability problems and it is hoped that national indicators and targets for rehabilitation are established at some stage (McLellan, 1992).

SOCIAL AND COMMUNITY CARE

A major problem for people with brain injury in the UK is the artificial divide that is placed between health and social care. Health care is the responsibility of the National Health Service whilst responsibility for social care largely falls upon the social service department of the local authority. Other areas of responsibility fall to other local authority departments, particularly housing, and other Government departments such as Social Security and Employment. This situation often leads to a person with longer-term disabilities both failing to understand the system and failing to access the different services provided. These problems have been recognised for a long time (HMSO, 1981; Audit Commission, 1986). The first serious legislation to address the social needs of disabled people came with the Chronically Sick and Disabled Persons Act in 1970. This Act aims to ensure that all local authorities identify and as far as possible meet the needs of people with disabilities. Other sections of the Act cover housing, access, parking and provision to ensure that people with disabilities are represented on certain committees. The Act improved the situation for people with disabilities but did not have the major effect that was hoped for. The Act had less impact because it was a Private Members' Bill subject to the limitation that it could make no provision which would commit the government to large-scale expenditure. It is generally accepted that the Act, whilst a step forward, has failed to achieve significant improvements. In the early 1980s the needs and rights of people with disabilities were achieving a much higher profile. In 1986 this led to a further piece of legislation which established certain rights for disabled individuals. The Disabled Persons (Services, Consultation and Representation) Act, 1986 identified four key rights:

● The right to assessment and appeal.

- The right to information.
- The right to be consulted by the local authority on matters concerning individuals with disabilities.
- The right to appoint a representative.

The Act has specific provision for a proper assessment of children and young people leaving education. Prior to this services for school leavers with disabilities had been particularly chaotic with individuals leaving mainstream schools and special schools without any follow-up service and being lost to all caring agencies until a crisis occurred (Castree & Walker, 1981; Bax, Smyth & Thomas, 1988). Once again this Act is a step forward but a number of problems remain. Although a local authority is now obliged to assess a disabled individual it does not have to provide the necessary services and thus the purpose of the assessment remains open to question. The assessment tends to be conducted on the basis of services that are available. The remit of the Act is also rather narrow, being confined to welfare services, and does not cover wider issues such as access to buildings and transport. However, one innovative feature of the Act is to recognise the critical part played by carers in maintaining individuals in private households. Carers have the right to ask for an assessment of the needs of the disabled person for whom they are caring, and the right to have their own ability to continue in the caring role to be taken into account when assessing the needs of the disabled person. The Act also requires local authorities to give information to the disabled person regarding not only local authority services but also services provided by other agencies.

At the end of the 1980s the major change that occurred in the National Health Service was also reflected by significant changes in community care provision. These changes were enshrined in the National Health Service and Community Care Act, 1990. The fundamental purpose of the Act is to place firmly in the hands of the local authorities the remit to assess the needs of disabled people and design, organise and purchase all non-health care services for people with disabilities. It was recommended that this function should mainly be handled by a named care worker, which thus enshrined in legislation the concept of a care manager. A further requirement is that a person in need of ongoing care should not be discharged from hospital without a clear package of care devised and without being the responsibility of a named care worker. In theory this should reduce the likelihood of a disabled person falling into the divide between health and social care. The local authority has been given part of the social security budget for residential care. This has placed the responsibility on the local authority for making a proper assessment of whether a disabled person is able to live in the community or requires a residential option. This should enable an appropriate package of community care to be delivered and avoid the perverse situation where social security policy was working in a way directly opposing community care policy. Prior to this legislation the more residential the care the easier it was to obtain benefits and the greater the size of the payment (Audit Commission, 1986) Previous studies had indicated that around half the people in residential accommodation could actually have been supported in the community had the necessary sources been available (Audit Commission, 1985). However, the immediate problem of the Act is that funding may not match the identified need, thus raising expectation and awareness without the ability to deliver the services. The Act also has major implications for the education and training of individuals to act as effective care managers. At the moment most local authorities rely on social workers and/or occupational therapists, who are insufficiently trained for the complex role of assessor and organiser of the array of different services delivered through different providers. There are many models of case management, some of which are known to be effective for specific client groups. However, more research is clearly needed to establish the proper role and place of case management for people with brain injuries (Hunter, 1988). It is still too soon to assess the impact of these changes on the actual delivery of care for people with disabilities.

Overall, the last 20 years have seen significant improvements in policy and legislation. The government is now beginning to recognise the needs and aspirations of disabled people. However, some would argue against the philosophy behind legislation that still views local authorities as handing out specific services, constrained by financial resources. Many would prefer the type of legislation introduced in the USA, which has given the disabled person specific rights in society for equal access to all services on the same basis as able-bodied people. The initial demise of similar proposals in the UK is to be regretted but it is hoped that some form of equal opportunity legislation can be on the UK statute books before too long.

SOCIETY, LEGISLATION AND THE DISABLED PERSON

I have addressed the issues of health care and social care as currently provided within the National Health Service and by the local authority. However, the overall outcome for someone with brain injury and their family depends on much broader issues involving social legislation as a whole.

Finance

There is no doubt that being disabled is expensive. The most comprehensive survey of the financial circumstances of disabled adults was reported in 1988 by the Office of Population Censuses and Surveys (Martin & White, 1988). This survey of 10 000 people demonstrated that on average disabled people spent £6.10/week extra because of their disability (1988 prices). In addition disabled people have extra expenditure on capital items such as equipment and special furniture. Altogether around 60% of disabled adults said they had incurred regular expenditure in the past year on items required solely because of their disability. The most frequent expenditure was on chemist items, costs associated with visits to hospitals, prescriptions, and home services such as home-helps or private domestic help. Another type of additional expenditure was found to be items required by most people but on which disabled people need to spend more. This included fuel, clothing, bedding, travel, food, laundry, telephone calls and home maintenance; 71% of disabled adults said they had incurred this type of additional expenditure, over the previous 12 months. The survey clearly demonstrated, not surprisingly, a great deal of variation in expenditure from an average of £3.20/week in those in the mildest category to £11.70/week for those in the most severely disabled category. Another important point to note is that the total income to families with disabled people is less than that of the general population. As an example, the average income for disabled non-pensioners was £91.70/week compared with the average equivalent income of £136.50 for non-pensioners in the general population. If one then adds into this calculation that an average 8% of this income is spent on disability-related expenses then the amount of available income to be spent on 'normal' living is significantly less than the able-bodied population. These figures have been disputed. The Disablement Income Group published a rebuttal to the OPCS survey and produced their own figures which were dramatically higher. This group found an average weekly expenditure of £65.92 for disabled people compared with £9.50 in the OPCS survey (Thompson, Buckle & Lavery, 1988). They also claimed that 47% of the individual's total weekly income was spent on the extra costs of disability compared to the 8% OPCS figure. Whatever the actual figure, it is quite clear that disabled people are at a significant financial disadvantage compared to their able-bodied peers. There can be little doubt that increasing income to people with brain injury and their families would improve long-term outcome, not only in material terms but by producing psychological benefit by reducing serious concern, anxiety or depression regarding financial circumstances. Physical benefit may also follow with an increase in real disposable income and the ability to buy relevant equipment, aids and adaptations. The potential reduction of care input by the main carer and also the reduction in stress on the carers should not be underestimated. How then are people with brain injury recompensed at the present time?

Compensation

A significant number of people with brain injury have recourse to the legal system for compensation. Legal considerations have been covered in the previous chapter. However, it is worth emphasising that legal advice for the brain-injured person should be sought as soon as possible if there is any likelihood of claim. A specialist firm of solicitors would provide the best advice and maximise the chances of proper compensation. Involvement of a solicitor in the early stage should also serve to educate the rehabilitation team, who should be aware of the intricacies of the legal system and the ability to access interim payments for special items of equipment or care.

There are other special compensation schemes run by the government. The Industrial Injury Scheme aims to provide benefit for an employee who 'suffers personal injury, caused by accident arising out of and because of work'. Another scheme is available to provide a pension for disablement which is due to or made worse by service in the armed forces (War Disablement Pension). A compensation scheme that is being increasingly used is the Criminal Injuries Compensation. This allows some degree of compensation for a personal injury directly resulting from a crime of violence in Great Britain. If someone suffers a brain injury or other disability as a result of a traffic accident by an uninsured or untraced motorist then a Motor Insurer's Bureau has an agreement with the government to provide compensation. Finally, there is a scheme for people severely disabled as a result of vaccination against specific diseases. Many of these compensation schemes are complex and advice from a welfare rights agency or solicitor in the early stages is worthwhile.

However, it is still a matter of chance rather than comparative need which dictates the level of benefit to which a brain-injured individual is entitled. Someone severely injured in the course of work may be entitled to a range of benefits that can even exceed the national average earnings. However, another person equally disabled from birth and therefore never able to work may be entitled only to limited means-tested and non-contributory benefits worth, perhaps, less than half the national earnings (Social Security Advisory Committee, 1988; see also the Disability Rights Handbook, 1994.)

State Benefits

What then are the benefits payable by the State to a person with brain injury and his/her family? This is an extremely complicated area and it is not possible in this chapter to summarise all the benefits and their payment criteria. The reader is referred to the Disability Rights Handbook (1994) for a complete guide to the full range of benefits. There is an array of benefits, some dependent on the degree or type of disability, others means-tested and others not. There are well over 30 different benefits in different circumstances. It is quite clear that someone with a brain injury may not have the cognitive abilities to make the appropriate claims and will often need assistance. The take-up of benefits is patchy and even in the OPCS survey (Martin & White, 1988) it was found that only in the two most severe categories of disability were more than half of the population receiving any disability benefit. In the most severe disability category as many as 26% were not receiving attendance allowance to which they were almost certainly entitled. Non-uptake can be a personal choice but is more likely to be a lack of information about the system or misunderstanding of the claims procedures. Any person with a brain injury would be best advised to contact a welfare rights agency or the local social services office to obtain assistance in claiming the benefits to which they are entitled.

If the brain injured person is unable to work then the State assistance depends on previous work record and previous National Insurance contributions. Normally for up to 6 months off work either statutory sick pay or sickness benefit is payable, and from 6 months onwards invalidity benefit. If, however, the disabled person has been incapable of work for at least 28 weeks and did not have enough National Insurance contributions to qualify for sickness or invalidity benefit then they are only entitled to a severe disablement allowance. This would, for example, cover people with brain injury incurred prior to the normal working age. If the total resulting income falls below certain levels then a further addition from Income Support is possible. Basically, if the income is lower than the law says one needs to live on then the difference is payable as Income Support. However, many would claim that the cut-off levels are barely adequate as a living income, particularly when extra needs of disabled people are taken into account. If there are real social needs then discretionary payments from the Social Fund are possible. This can be in the form of a loan to cover a particular crisis or one-off payment. There are also amounts payable to help people move from institutions into the community or to help families cope with exceptional pressures.

Non-means-tested Disability Benefits

The main allowance for disabled people that recognises extra care and mobility needs is the Disability Living Allowance. This was introduced in 1992 and is tax free, non-means-tested and paid on top of other income, including social security benefits. It can be paid for life but there is an upper age limit of 65 years for making the first successful claim. The allowance is split into a care component payable at three different rates, each with a different disability test, and a mobility component payable at two different rates. For the older disabled person, an Attendance Allowance is payable to recognise assistance from another person either during the day and/or the night. It is important to recognise that the Disability Living Allowance acts as a gateway to certain other types of help as diverse as exemption from road tax, higher pension premiums, disabled child premiums and a Christmas bonus!

Independent Living Funds

In 1988 the government established an Independent Living Fund which was an independent trust that made payments to individuals with severe disabilities to enable them to live independently in the community. Unfortunately the fund closed down in 1992, although two new funds took its place. These were the Independent Living (Extension) Fund and the Independent Living (1993) Fund. The former was designed to continue making awards to over 21 000 people who had claimed help from the original scheme. The latter is still aimed at enabling severely disabled people to live in the community, but can only provide cash help as a top-up to services provided by the local authority to people in their own homes up to a specified ceiling. Unfortunately the new scheme does provide less cash and less choice over personal care arrangements and its criteria are more restrictive than the original fund. If a local authority social worker decides that a care package designed to keep a person at home costs up to £500 a week then the Trustees can make an award up to a maximum of £300 per week. Paradoxically, if the care package designed to keep someone at home is costed at more than £500 per week then the Independent Living (1993) Fund will make no contribution. The fund is only available for people between the age of 16 and 66 years and, whilst restricted, it can sometimes make the difference between living at home independently and going into institutional care.

Carers' Support

Support to the main carer is now available through the Invalid Care Allowance. This was a recent and welcome addition that recognised the fact that most caring is performed by family members and not by statutory agencies. Invalid Care Allowance is payable to people of working age who regularly spend at least 35 hours/week caring for a severely disabled person.

This section can only be a very brief overview of the complex array of disability benefits. Some other benefits are payable which are discussed below under the relevant sections. Overall the benefit system has been significantly improved in recent years. However, the system is undoubtedly complex and still provides many anomalies according to the causation of the disability. Many disability groups now argue that there should be a single disability benefit that provides sufficient income to the disabled person to allow them to buy their own equipment and adaptations and to buy in the range of health and social care services required. Recent changes in community care legislation now make this scenario easier to achieve but very few parts of the country are going along this route. Such a system would enable the disabled person and his/her family to determine his/her own needs and provide independence of choice, which is sadly lacking in many aspects of the present system.

Housing

The independence of a brain-injured person depends not only on his/her individual physical and psychological outcome and the amount of care that is required but also depends on his/her physical environment. There are many people with brain injury who are unnecessarily handicapped by the fact that their housing is totally unsuitable for their needs. Many houses do not lend themselves readily to internal or external conversion. The disabled person is often faced with a stark choice of remaining in very unsatisfactory and handicapping conditions in his/her own home or moving into institutional care. Many housing adaptations are simple and would make life much easier for able-bodied people, particularly those with frail, elderly relatives or young children. Wider doors and corridors, more accessible bathrooms and toilets and a variety of labour-saving kitchen designs and equipment could lead to easier home circumstances for everyone. However, there has been no housing policy for minority groups. Official guidelines for disabled people did not appear until 1974 (Department of the Environment, 1974) and then a preference was seen for adaptation of ordinary dwellings rather than a more coherent and integrated policy. However, the 1974 circular did make available a small subsidy for each unit that was made suitable for disabled occupants and this did produce an increase, at least in the local authority sector, in the number of suitable dwellings. However, this modest progress was halted in 1980 with the advent of the Housing Act which allowed local authorities to sell property. Local authority stock has been significantly depleted.

The provision of adapted housing in the private sector is generally very unsatisfactory. A few countries, particularly in Scandinavia, have basic mobility standard regulations for builders and some even require private developers to build a certain proportion of fully adapted housing in any new housing scheme. No such regulation applies in the UK. There are some exceptions. The Habinteg Housing Association builds family homes to mobility standard with 25% of the dwellings built to wheelchair standards and dispersed throughout the scheme (Habinteg Housing Association, 1988).

There should be greater choice between the two extremes of an adapted house and institutional care. A variety of transitional living schemes should be available. There is no clear government policy or legislation on these issues and such limited transitional housing choice that does exist is largely provided by specialist housing associations or the voluntary or charitable sector (Fiedler, 1988). For example, Headway (National Head Injuries Association) is one of the few organisations which provides specific transitional housing (Headway houses) that gives support to people with brain injuries in the community and offer an environment in which training for independent living can be carried out.

Housing Adaptations and Benefit

A new system for grants to renovate, repair, improve and adapt houses in England and Wales was introduced in 1990. For those in receipt of means-tested benefits minor works are carried out by straightforward grants. Larger scale renovation is subject to more complicated grant arrangements and is often means-tested. Responsibility for this system rests with the local authority.

Some financial assistance can be obtained from housing benefit. This is a means-tested benefit which gives help with claiming rent to people on low income. Various schemes can assist with the reduction of council tax bills (see Disability Rights Handbook, 1994).

Employment

A major positive outcome for the younger person with brain injury would be the return to some form of useful employment. The OPCS survey (Martin, White & Meltzer, 1989) clearly demonstrated a significant employment disadvantage suffered by people with disabilities. Despite the fact that the survey incorporated people with very mild as well as severe disabilities, only 31% of the disabled adult population were working. Thirty four % were permanently unable to work and 5% retired. Only about 8% were not working and looking for work. Obviously, the more severe the disability the less likely is employment. People with head injuries are at a particular disadvantage in the employment market. The more subtle psychological and cognitive difficulties such as problems with social skills, memory and short temper all mitigate against successful employment placement and, just as importantly, retention of the job once found (Brooks et al., 1987; Rao et al., 1990). In times of economic recession, when the unemployment rate for able-bodied people is high, people with brain injury and other disabilities are further disadvantaged. Most government policy and legislation is directed towards the reduction of the crude unemployment rate and not specifically the unemployment rate for disabled people. However, there have been improvements in both policy and legislation which are now beginning to have an impact on employment rehabilitation and return to work. A number of special schemes have been introduced and the number of benefit-related perverse disincentives to employment have been reduced. There are now specific teams — Placement Assessment and Counselling Teams (PACT) — with disability employment advisors to help disabled people find employment. In the USA vocational counsellors are more normally part of the health rehabilitation team. A number of authors (e.g. Wehman et al., 1990) found considerable success by means of gradual reintroduction into employment, with the disabled person supported for a time by a 'job coach' — a trained vocational counsellor who can help and advise the disabled person, work colleagues and employers and assist in the successful reintroduction of the disabled person back into work.

A useful new venture is employment assessment carried out by mobile teams rather than the previous method whereby disabled people travelled to fixed centres. Employment assessment for the most severely disabled persons is now sometimes contracted out to specialist providers, including health service rehabilitation units. Hopefully this will allow for a more comprehensive and detailed assessment of physical and cognitive abilities and the potential for employment. Whether these new plans reduce the unemployment rate, particularly for people with brain injury, has yet to be assessed.

The employment services are responsible for registering people as disabled. This carries some limited advantages in that employers with 20 or more employees must employ at least 3% of their workforce as registered disabled people. However, this regulation is not often legally enforced. Disability employment advisors based at job centres are responsible for job finding and advisory services for all disabled people and they can use a number of special schemes in order to facilitate return to work. A new Job Introduction Scheme offers employers a weekly grant towards the cost of employing certain people with disabilities for a trial period. The scheme is useful if the prospective employer has reservations about the person's ability to do the job. Employers are also offered a grant for adaptation to premises and equipment and the disabled employee is sometimes offered special aids to employment on long-term loan, as well as other financial incentives such as assistance with fares to work and personal reader services for people with visual impairment. Modern technology does now make it easier for people with disabilities to work from home and a new scheme provides computer equipment and other aids for home use. There is also support in the form of a grant to people with severe disabilities towards initial costs of setting up a business. However, some people with severe disabilities are unable to work in open employment and for many years there have been a number of sheltered employment schemes. There are still some sheltered workshops run by Remploy, voluntary bodies and local authorities. A scheme of interest is the Sheltered Placement Scheme, which is for people with disabilities with a work output of between 30 and 80% of that of an able-bodied worker. It allows the disabled person to work in open employment alongside able-bodied colleagues whilst being paid the equivalent wage to that of the able-bodied worker. The financial equivalent of the smaller output is reimbursed to the employer. Up-to-date information regarding new employment schemes for disabled people is always available from local offices of the Department of Employment.

Finally, a new benefit, Disability Working Allowance, was introduced in 1992 which is tax-free and paid on top of low wages to people with disabilities. The amount of payment depends on a complex array of regulations. The theory is that disabled people may only be able to return to work in a relatively low-paid job at no financial advantage given the loss that may occur from reduction of state benefits once in employment (Disability Rights Handbook, 1994). The new allowance helps to correct this anomaly.

Although there are a number of schemes to assist people with brain injuries to return to work, the main problem in the UK is the gap that occurs between health rehabilitation, social care and employment rehabilitation. There is often very little contact between these statutory agencies. In the UK an employment advisor is a very unusual member of a health rehabilitation team, whereas in the United States such individuals are often an integrated part of the team. The concept of a job coach who works with the disabled person and employer from the early stages of injury produces clear benefits in terms of higher return to work rates (Kreutzer et al., 1988). Such schemes are commonly funded by insurance companies who see clear advantages in reducing the level of subsequent compensation and damage claims. Government policy does not promote these links and the civil service system does not make it easy for different Government departments to liaise effectively. However, there would be clear advantages to the State if such artificial barriers could be broken down. If people could return to work then it would reduce the financial burden on the State by reduction in benefits.

Access and Transport

A major area that can promote better outcome for people with brain injuries and that can be clearly influenced by government policy and legislation is access and transport. Surveys and accounts of the needs of disabled people (e.g. Silburn, 1988) nearly always highlight the frustrations that are caused by the problems of access to buildings and public transport. In 1985 the government introduced building regulations covering access for disabled people to non-domestic buildings and in 1992 further regulations required all new non-domestic buildings to be accessible. Disabled groups have argued that such regulations do not go far enough quickly enough. Major adaptations would be required to some of the older public buildings. Slow but steady progress towards better access should be possible but will need constant governmental and legislative pressure to make sure that positive change occurs.

There are now a wide variety of adaptations to motor vehicles that allow people with even the most complex disabilities to access and drive a car. The problem is that there are very few driving assessment centres in the country that can offer unbiased advice. Many adaptations themselves are often expensive. The most severely disabled people will need expensive cars in the first place followed by expensive conversions. There is a government Motability Scheme that enables people to receive loans in exchange for redirection of their mobility benefit into the scheme. There is also a Mobility Equipment Fund that can give discretionary payments up to £10 000 for major car adaptations. However, support in this area is inadequate. Inability to drive a car often leaves people dependent on public transport very little of which is easily accessible. There are some local exceptions such as the Tyne and Wear Metro system, although equally there are some notoriously inaccessible systems such as the London underground. There have been some improvements resulting from local initiatives and thus patchily provided across the country. There are a number of 'dial-a-ride' schemes or other special bus schemes but with wide variations in availability. However, taxi transport is improving slowly and in London all new licensed taxis are now required to be wheelchair accessible. This is the case in over 60 other licensing authorities across the country. The statutory committee, the Disabled Person's Transport Committee (DTPAC), was established in 1985 and has produced a number of useful recommendations, including specifications for design features for buses to make it easier for disabled and elderly people to use them. In 1994 the Department of Transport provided funding to support two trials of low floor wheelchair-accessible buses in London and North Tyneside. The technology and design capabilities to make public transport more accessible is available and needs clearer direction enforced through regulations in order to ensure broader availability of accessible transport.

CONCLUSIONS

This chapter has not attempted to be comprehensive with regard to legislation that affects people with brain injuries. I have not, for example, touched upon legislation in the education sphere and have not attempted to provide more than a brief resume of the complicated benefit systems. However, I hope to have demonstrated that outcome for people with brain injury and their families can clearly be improved by government policy.

What would be the most important steps the government could take to improve outcome for brain-injured people? The first step I would like to see taken is a more coherent attempt to reduce the incidence of head injury. Whilst much head injury is unavoidable I believe there is much the government could achieve by stricter legislation regarding car safety design. The compulsory use of airbags is one such measure. The reduction of speed limits in urban areas to 20 mph would be useful and further cash to local authorities to introduce more traffic calming schemes in areas of high risk would also be invaluable.

I believe the single most important step the government could take in health and social care would be legislation that permits joint purchasing by health authorities and local authorities. Such legislation would allow the development of a coherent rehabilitation plan that is not artificially divided between health needs and social needs. If such legislation could be taken one step further to incorporate purchasing by the Department of Employment, then vocational rehabilitation could be properly introduced in this country. A joint disability team involving health professionals, social service professionals and vocational rehabilitation experts would allow a coordinated and coherent rehabilitation life plan to be developed. Any policy that enables people with brain injuries to move in a coordinated fashion between agencies, be kept informed of available services and benefits and have a simple, and preferably single, point of entry into the system should help to improve outcome.

On the broader front of social legislation as a whole, there is one important piece of legislation that is still missing from the statute book. That is an Equal Opportunities Act for disabled people. Such legislation would improve employment opportunities, improve access to leisure facilities and transport and most importantly help to improve the status of disabled people in the community as a whole. The government recently 'talked out' such legislation on the grounds that it would be too expensive to implement. Let us hope for a change of heart so that brain-injured and other disabled people can begin to be treated as equal citizens and not second-class citizens.

POSTSCRIPT

Since this chapter was written, the UK Government has introduced a Disability Discrimination Bill which should become law during 1995/6. This Bill introduces a wide range of anti-discrimination legislation and other measures which will provide for:

- A statutory right of non-discrimination against disabled people in the field of employment.
- A statutory right of access to goods and services including the moving of barriers and the provision of aids where reasonable and readily achievable.
- The elimination of any potential discrimination of financial services.
- The creation of a National Disability Council to advise the Government on issues and measures relating to elimination of discrimination.
- Strengthening of policy and programme guidance for local authorities and the Department of Transport.
- New guidance on access standards for schools and consolation on ways to encourage schools to make themselves more accessible to disabled pupils.

Although the Bill is likely to become a formal Act of Parliament by 1996, there are a number of detailed regulations that will be issued thereafter and which will slowly enact the legislation over a period of time as yet undetermined. This is an important step forward, although many groups will consider that the new Act does still not go far enough in reducing the discrimination against disabled people.

REFERENCES

Allsopp, R. & Turner, E. (1986). Road casualties and public transport fares in London. *Accident Analysis and Prevention*, **18**, 147—150.

Association of British Neurologists, NeuroConcern Group of Medical Charities and British Society of Rehabilitation Medicine (1993). *Neurorehabilitation in the United Kingdom. Report of a Working Party*. London: British Society of Rehabilitation Medicine.

Audit Commission (1985). *Managing Social Services for the Elderly More Effectively*. London: HMSO.

Audit Commission (1986). *Making a Reality of Community Care*. London: HMSO.

Bax, M., Smythe, D. & Thomas, A. (1988). Health care of physically handicapped young adults. *British Medical Journal*, **296**, 1153–1155.

Beardshaw, V. (1988). *Last on the List. Community Services for People with Physical Disabilities*. London: Kings Fund Institute.

Bodiwella, G. G., Thomas, P. D. & Otubushin, A. (1989). Protective effects of rear seat restraints during car collisions. *Lancet*, **1**, 369–371.

British Society of Rehabilitation Medicine (1993). *Advice to Purchasers. Setting NHS Contracts for Rehabilitation Medicine*. London: British Society of Rehabilitation Medicine.

Brooks, N., McKinlay, W., Symington, C., Beattie, A. & Campsie, L. (1987). Return to work within the first seven years of severe head injury. *Brain Injury*, **1**, 5–19.

Carlisle, K. (1993). Written answer. *Hansard* (Column 24), 19th April.

Castree, B. J. & Walker, J. H. (1981). The young adult with spina bifida. *British Medical Journal*, **283**, 1040–1042.

Condie, C., Rivara, F. P. & Bergman, A.B. (1993). Strategies of a successful campaign to promote the use of equestrian helmets. *Public Health Reports, Hyattsville*, **108**, 121–126.

Chronically Sick and Disabled Persons Act (1970). London: HMSO.

Department of the Environment (1974). *Housing for People who Are Physically Handicapped*. Circular 74/74. London: Department of the Environment.

Department of Transport (1993). *Killing Speed and Saving Lives*. London: Department of Transport.

Disabled Persons (Services. Consultation and Representation) Act (1986). London: HMSO.

Dunbar J. A., Penttila, A. & Pikkarainen, J. (1987). Drinking and driving. *British Medical Journal*, **295**, 101–103.

Evans, L. & Frick, M. C. (1988). Helmet effectiveness in preventing motorcycle driver and passenger fatalities. *Accident Analysis and Prevention*, **20**, 447–458.

Fiedler, B. (1988). *Living Options Lottery. Housing and Support Services for People With Severe Physical Disabilities*. London: Prince of Wales Advisory Group on Disability.

Habinteg Housing Association (1988). *Annual report 1987. Design guide 1987*. London: Habinteg Housing Association.

Her Majesty's Stationery Office (1981). *Care in Action: a Handbook of Policies and Priorities for the Health and Personal Social Services in England*. London: HMSO.

Housing Act (1980). London: HMSO.

Hunter, D. J. (1988). Bridging the gap: case management and advocacy for people with physical handicaps. London: *King Edward's Hospital Fund for London*.

Janssen, S. (1991). Road safety in urban districts: final results of accident studies in the Dutch demonstration projects of the 1970s. *Traffic Engineering and Control*, **292**.

Kreutzer, J. S., Wayman, P., Morton, M. V. & Stonnington, H. H. (1988). Supported employment and compensatory strategies for enhancing vocational outcome following traumatic brain injury. *Brain Injury*, **2**, 205–223.

Mackie, A. A., Ward, H. & Walker, R. (1990). *Urban Safety Project 3: Overall Evaluation of Area Wide Schemes*, London: Transport and Road Research Laboratory, Department of Transport.

Martin, J. & White, A. (1988). The financial circumstances of disabled adults living in private households. *OPCS Surveys of Disability in Great Britain, Report 2*. London: HMSO.

Martin, J., White, A. & Meltzer, H. (1989). Disabled adults: services, transport and employment. *OPCS Surveys of Disability in Great Britain, Report 4*. London: HMSO.

McLellan, D. L. (1992). The feasibility of indicators and targets for rehabilitation services. *Clinical Rehabilitation*, **6**, 55–66.

Medical Disability Society (1988). The management of traumatic brain injury. A report of a working party. London: The Development Trust for the Young Disabled.

National Health Service and Community Care Act (1990). London: HMSO.

Preusser, D. & Blomberg, R. (1984). Reducing child pedestrian accidents through public education. *Journal of Safety Research*, **15**, 47–50.

Royal College of Physicians of London (1986). *Physical Disability in 1986 and Beyond*. London: Royal College of Physicians of London.

Rao, N., Rosenthal, M., Cronin-Stubbs, D., Lambert, R., Barnes, P. & Swanson, B. (1990). Return to work after rehabilitation following traumatic brain injury. *Brain Injury*, **4**, 49–56.

Ruta, D., Beattie, T. & Narayan, V. (1993). A prospective study of non-fatal childhood road traffic accidents: what can seat restraint achieve? *Journal of Public Health Medicine*, **15**, 87–92.

Rutledge, R., Lalor, A., Oller, D., Hansen, A., Tamason, M., Meredith, W., Foil, M.B. & Baker, C. (1993). The cost of not wearing seat-belts. A comparison of outcome in 3 396 patients. *Annals of Surgery*, **217**, 122–127.

Silburn, R. (1988). *Disabled People: Their Needs and Priorities*. Nottingham: Benefits Research Unit.

Teiske, A., Degreif, J., Geist, M., Schild, H., Strung H. & Schang K. (1993). The safety belt: effects on injury patterns of automobile passengers. *Rofo. Fortschr. geb. Rontgenstr. Neuen Bildgeb. Verfahr.*, **159**, 278–283.

Thomas, S., Acton, C., Nlxon, J., Battistutta, D., Pitt, W.R, Clart R. (1994) Effectiveness of bicycle helmets in preventing head injury in children: A case controlled study, British Medical Journal, 308l 173- 176

Thompson, P., Buckle, J. & Lavery, M. (1988). The OPCS survey. Being disabled cost more than they said. London: Disablement Income Group.

Thompson, R., Rivara, F. & Thompson, D. (1989) A case controlled study of the effectiveness of bicycle safety helmets. *The New England Journal of Medicine*, **320**, 1361–1367.

Towner, E., Dowswell, T. & Jarvis, S. (1993). Reducing childhood accidents: the effectiveness of health promotion intervention: a literature review. London: Health Education Authority.

Transport and Health Study Group (1991). *Health on the Move. Policies for Health Promoting Transport*. London: Public Health Alliance, Transport and Road Research Laboratory.

Wehman, P., Kreutzer, J., West, M. et al. (1990). Return to work for the person with a traumatic brain injury: a supported employment approach. *Arch. Phys. Med. Rehab.*, **71**, 1047–1052.

Zador, P. L. & Ciccone, M. A. (1993). Automobile driver fatalities in frontal impacts: air-bags compared with manual belts. *American Journal of Public Health*, **83**, 661–666.

9

TOWARDS IMPROVED OUTCOME

DAVID JOHNSON AND DAVID ROSE*

*Department of Neuropsychology, Astley Ainslie Hospital, Edinburgh and *Department of Psychology, University of East London*

INTRODUCTION

It has been suggested that '... the safest statement that can be made about any individual with a brain injury is that every brain injury is unique and outcome is uncertain ...' (Deaton, 1993, p. 100). Whilst this point is well taken we believe that the uncertainty must not be accepted passively. We must attempt to predict, assess and maximise outcome after brain injury. As Deaton points out, a host of bodies, from the patient, his/her family and employer, the clinician, the lawyer and, of course the health service manager, all want to know the outcome of a case in order that they may make their respective plans and adjustments, determine hospital and community care needs, agree financial compensation, allocate educational or vocational resources, fill the job vacancy if the patient cannot resume his or her employment, and so on. The multiple demands for information on different aspects of outcome have made it difficult to arrive at an operational definition of outcome which is acceptable to all. In the preceding chapters much has been reviewed that moves us closer to this objective. In this final chapter we seek to consider particular themes and issues arising from earlier chapters as well as to emphasise yet again the importance of continued and increased collaboration between all those groups having an interest in traumatic brain injury (Rose & Johnson, 1992). There are two themes we consider to be of particular importance. The first is the need, wherever possible, to relate the assessment and rehabilitation of the consequences of brain injury to the underlying brain

Brain Injury and After: Towards Improved Outcome. Edited by F.D. Rose and D.A. Johnson.
© 1996 John Wiley & Sons Ltd.

pathology (e.g. Bach y Rita, 1989). The second and related theme is the need to take into account the patient's age in predicting outcome.

BRAIN STATE — THE CRUCIAL VARIABLE

The central theme of this volume is that outcome following traumatic brain injury is the concern of many different professional groups. Some of these (lawyers, health administrators, policy makers, etc.) are unlikely to have any familiarity with brain structure and function. However, it is vital that in discussing assessment and rehabilitation following brain injury we acknow-ledge that brain state is the crucial variable. Brain state sets the limits in terms of impairment which, in turn, determines disability and, in large measure, handicap (see Chapter 1). Nowhere is the importance of referring back to brain state more clearly illustrated than in considering the patient's age in predicting the consequences of injury to the brain. In his chapter on Acute Care (Chapter 2), Martin Smith notes that the patient's age is one of the main considerations in predicting outcome. However, that must not be taken to suggest that traumatic brain injury in the young is not very serious and its consequences very persistent. The inherent vulnerability of the brain is greatest during its 16 years or so of development, with the frontal lobes of the brain not maturing until late adolescence, and there is now increasing scientific evidence from animal studies that the younger the brain at injury, then the greater its vulnerability and the more limited its post traumatic development (e.g. Kolb & Wishaw, 1989). However, recent studies have suggested that not all professionals concerned with brain injury are aware of, or guided by, the available scientific information regarding age and vulnerability (Hart & Faust, 1988; Webb, Rose & Johnson, 1995; Johnson, Campbell & Wright, 1995). There appear to be two schools of thought: first, those who believe that trauma to the immature brain causes disruption to the normal process of neurological development, with lifelong consequences (e.g. English, 1904; Snow & Hooper, 1994); second, those who believe that the immaturity of the brain is associated with increased plasticity, which conveys some form of as yet unidentified adaptive response to trauma, such that a child with head injury will recover, if not completely, then certainly much better than his/her adult counterpart with comparable injury (e.g. Langfitt & Gennarelli, 1982; Mahoney et al., 1983). As Hart and Faust (1988) point out, mistaken beliefs about the probable degree of impairment and recovery following traumatic brain injury are likely to exert major influences on the appraisal of the brain-injured child. Moreover, because of the authority vested in medical opinion, the range of influence for a prognosis is readily extended to many other realms of activity, for example, social services provision for the patient and the size of compensation claim submitted by his or her legal advisers. Hence, current beliefs about just one aspect of the brain, age at injury, may significantly influence outcome in a variety of ways.

There is no doubt that traumatic brain injury is a leading cause of death and disability for children as well as adults (Snow & Hooper, 1994). With a reported incidence of approximately 250 per 100 000 population for children between birth and 14 years old, the implications of the conflicting beliefs on age and recovery are of paramount importance to the assessments of need and provision of resources in health, education and social services, and litigation. In purely financial terms the differing beliefs translate into very different figures. To take the extremes for the sake of illustration, if the proponents of vulnerability are correct then the long-term consequences for a 2-week-old child who sustains severe head injury will be very long-term indeed. Conversely, if the 'young is better' proponents are correct, then the only costs will be in acute medical care.

It is not just the severe end of the injury spectrum that concerns us here. There is generally a consistent dose–response relationship between severity of injury and its consequences (Ommaya & Gennarelli, 1974) with structural pathology arising after even mild head injury (Povlishock & Coburn, 1989). In children who sustain mild head injury with no immediate loss of consciousness, significant neurological consequences may include dural haemorrhage and delayed deterioration (Snoek, 1989; Hahn & McLone, 1993). The conflict between the two schools of thought regarding age and brain damage recovery is, if anything, more serious in the context of mild head injury. The scenario is suggested where an 8-year-old boy sustains a mild head injury whilst playing; he is treated in hospital by those of the 'young is better' school of thought who consequently fail to assess and monitor adequately for neurological impairments and thus allow the gradually evolving subdural haematoma to result in coning, near death and the need for urgent neurosurgical intervention in a distant hospital. Post-operatively the patient is regarded by the neurosurgeon to do well and expected to make a complete recovery. With regard to his longer-term outcome, however, it is the opposing school of thought who seem to be right when the boy increasingly fails to achieve at school because of cognitive impairments, and becomes progressively more withdrawn, depressed and isolated. When the case enters the legal arena with a claim for medical negligence, a protracted and head-on clash ensues, with the two schools of thought conveniently allocated to the Plaintiff and Defendant sides, each resolutely maintaining their position, and the Court, with equal resolution, deciding that it is not there to decide on such scientific matters as the plasticity of the child's brain. If the child has become brain-damaged as a result of the alleged mismanagement and his educational, occupational and social achievements will be significantly less, then the potential claim for financial compensation would be substantial. If the concept of vulnerability is judged to be irrelevant, however, not only does the child fail to receive financial compensation but a precedent is set which may influence subsequent cases of children with traumatic brain injury. Recent estimates put the annual costs of compensation for medical negligence (1990–91, 1600 cases) at approximately £50 million, with individual cases ranging from nil to over £1.5 million (Fenn, Herman & Dingwall, 1994). The law of damages is currently under review by the Law Commission (Weitzman, 1994), but the reports so far do not indicate that children have been afforded special consideration (e.g. Law Commission Consultation Paper No. 125, 1992; Law Commission Report No. 225, 1994). If the inherent vulnerability of the child's brain is not given sufficient consideration then it is likely that a less than optimal outcome can be achieved, with consequently higher economic and social costs than would otherwise have occurred.

ASSESSMENT

Taking due account of the precise nature and extent of the injury, and therefore the state of the brain is also crucial in considering assessment and rehabilitation. The complex and wide-ranging problems of assessment (Oddy & Alcott, Chapter 3) mirror the multitude of neurological complexities of the brain at various stages after injury. Appropriate and meaningful assessment is the *sine qua non* for effective rehabilitation and determining outcome after brain injury. Yet the lack of a common basis in neuroscience has meant the lack of a coherent theoretical basis for assessment and, therefore, rehabilitation. Different professional groups may pursue increasingly diverse assessments and therapies with apparently little reference to the neurological basis of the problem, or the changes they hope to effect. The shortage of rehabilitation strategies of clearly demonstrated efficacy (especially in the area of cognitive remediation) is surely due, in large measure, to a primary absence of appropriate and routine assessment of the structure and function of the damaged brain. As Oddy & Alcott (Chapter 3) suggest, assessment should have implications for treatment and prognosis: how can one hope to improve outcome by successful rehabilitation if the basis of impairment is not fully understood? Appropriate assessment provides information on the precise nature of the problem, the accurate reflection of current brain state. Yet all too often rehabilitation staff and students at all levels are keen to get on with treatment and forget about the assessment. Assessment may be regarded as a tiresome necessity, something to be avoided, 'screened', or passed down to junior staff who, without appropriate guidance, merely perpetuate the problem. Assessment is a unique vehicle in neurological rehabilitation, not only as a quantity survey but also as the most precise means of delineating the nature and extent of the problem, identifying the most likely avenues of approach for remediation in all therapeutic disciplines, and refining the predictive ability of measures.

Even where assessments are carried out there is often a failure to interpret and understand the results of the patient's performance in terms of the brain that has been surveyed. Despite the obvious limitations of numerical values in describing brain function (e.g. Zangwill, 1947; Lezak, 1988, 1995), clinical and expert witness reports and a not insignificant part of the rehabilitation literature show a persistent adherence to numbers, whether quotients or terms such as 'within normal limits'. Whether in clinical, research or litigation forums, such numerical values are used ultimately as part of the equation to determine outcome. Often the stated reason for the request or presence of numbers is that they can be understood by all, irrespective of professional discipline (Bell, 1992). As Lezak (1988) suggests, however, numerical values and global indices such as IQ obscure more information than they yield, and that reinforces misunderstanding between different professional groups concerned with brain injury, recovery and outcome. Numerical data have their place and we are not suggesting that they have no value. However, we would argue for balance. Reporting what are essentially esoteric data, which bear little or no resemblance to the questions of how and what brain functions have been compromised by the effects of injury, offers no guidance on designing effective interventions and is unlikely to be of any clinical utility to improving outcome. The questions asked in assessment, by any profession, should be in terms of 'What has been the effect of insult upon the brain's functions?'; 'How does that evidence relate to other clinical findings and the patient's present complaints?'; and 'What can be done to remedy the situation and improve outcome?'. If the consequent data are reported in terms reflecting a common taxonomy, then the combination of the contributing parts could result in far more effective and efficient use of scarce resources. Without an appropriate level of meta-analysis by the rehabilitation team, however, successful remediation of the problem is certain to be less than optimum.

The potential benefits of coordinated efforts in the use of appropriate assessments in rehabilitation after brain injury will be evident (Rose & Johnson, 1992; Ruff et al., 1993; Crawford, Johnson & Myalchiuv, 1994). Oddy & Alcott suggest that such collaborative effort should extend to the continuing development of outcome scales, such as the FIM-FAM, and their relation to other common indices, such as neuropsychological tests (e.g. McPherson, Berry & Pentland, 1995). There are, however, not inconsiderable difficulties in getting standard measures adopted. The creation of trauma data banks offers some solutions to these problems.

REHABILITATION – A CONTINUUM OF CARE

At each stage in recovery and rehabilitation it is important to understand the mechanisms involved, in order to facilitate progress and thereby improve outcome. However, a multiplicity of factors acting either singly or in various combinations may produce the changes that are often observed after injury, and the delineation of optimum conditions remains a major challenge (Long & Ross, 1992). As earlier chapters have suggested, interventions have to be appropriate to the stage of recovery and the age of the individual. They must also be designed to be effective, and delivered in a consistent, collaborative and planned way. As Chapters 1 and 4 point out, the brain does possess a unique quality of plasticity which, depending on injury characteristics, has the potential to be harnessed by appropriate rehabilitation (Bach y Rita, 1994), thereby facilitating neuro-developmental processes to limit impairment, improve recovery, restrict handicap and improve outcome. The fundamental requirement, however, is to accept the brain as the holder of both vulnerability and the potential for further growth (Bakker, 1984). In turn, that requires an awareness of the experimental data on recovery from brain damage and the various techniques which offer the potential for improving brain state and function. Yet there remains in clinical practice a reluctance to acknowledge the demonstrated value of tools, such as environmental enrichment, which offer the potential for reducing the human and economic costs of brain injury (Goldstein, 1990; Rosenberg & Rowland, 1990). In a recent review, Bach y Rita (1994) suggested that recovery of function following brain damage is an active research area that will probably advance rapidly in coming years. The important part of this advance will be determining the limits of plasticity and what factors lead to the uncovering of latent plasticity which, in the case of brain-damaged patients, is often not manifested in the absence of 'appropriate rehabilitation'. Appropriate rehabilitation may be conceived as creating internal and external environments which facilitate the brain-damaged person's optimum functioning. In turn those environments are determined by the different rehabilitation professionals accurate and meaningful assessments which identify the nature and extent of problems.

Cognitive and behavioural impairments constitute the rate-limiting step in rehabilitation (Wroblewski & Glenn, 1994) and outcome (Brooks et al., 1987; Crepeau & Scherzer, 1993), irrespective of therapeutic approach, because all aspects of rehabilitation and community reintegration require some degree of learning and adjustment to environmental change. Mapou (1988) suggested a framework of cognitive functioning, based upon Luria's three functional units (Luria, 1973), which sensibly predicts that functional integrity at lower levels of complexity of arousal and attention, for example, are necessary for the complete functioning at higher levels of complexity, such as memory and learning. As impairments of cerebral arousal-activation and attention are characteristic pathophysiological responses to head injury, it is reasonable that the first stage of intervention should be to address such fundamental disorder, thereby increasing the brain's ability to receive, process, store and act upon information in a reliable, efficient and error-free way. Optimum levels of arousal are necessary for an individual to function normally (e.g. Klove, 1987), with very high or very low levels of arousal interfering with basic cognitive functioning (Duffy, 1972; Taylor, 1989). Underlying the cognitive and behaviour disorders, post-traumatic changes in neurotransmitter activity may persist indefinitely, with significant implications for poor psychosocial adjustment and general outcome (Barry, 1991; Hayes, Jenkin & Lyeth, 1992; Johnson, Roethig-Johnston & Richards, 1993).

The post-traumatic internal environment of the brain could be altered by a rational pharmacotherapy based upon demonstrated deficits and responses to treatment, and could yield significant benefits to outcome generally (Ross, 1992; Cope, 1994). Drug treatments in routine neurological rehabilitation tend not to be the first choice in ameliorating the underlying pathological activity. Certainly attempts at psychopharmacological intervention have produced mixed results (e.g. Ross, 1992, Cardenas et al., 1994). However, part of the problem may lie in the lack of appropriate assessments prior to treatment. A rational pharmacotherapy could be developed by collaborative working between disciplines, which becomes a planned and integral part of appropriate rehabilitation after brain injury (McIntosh, 1993; Whyte, 1994).

Physical exercise may offer a more accessible route to improving cerebral arousal-activation and neurotransmitter activity. The effects of physical exercise upon various mental processes, including mood and fatigue, have been demonstrated for a variety of populations (Astrand and Rodal, 1977; Blackburn & Jacobs, 1988; Martinsen, 1990; Wagner et al., 1992; Seraganian, 1993). The most likely basis for these benefits is a change in central monoaminergic activity (Fordyce & Farrar, 1991; Neeper et al., 1995) which, if maintained by appropriate physical activity, offers the potential for long-term benefits to both the patient and the family. Studies with brain injury are few in this area and report mixed results (e.g. Jankowski & Sullivan, 1990; Wolman et al., 1994).

Inactivity and fatigue are common complaints after brain injury, which limit the individual's interaction with his/her environments and thus restrict recovery and outcome. There is general agreement that to increase levels of interaction between the head-injured and their environments is a vital part of any rehabilitation process (e.g. Tinson, 1989; Long & Ross, 1992). Extensive experimental work has demonstrated that, in laboratory rats, increased levels of environmental interaction result in a more highly developed and more efficient brain (Renner & Rosenzweig, 1987), including a higher cortical metabolic rate. Increased environmental interaction has also been shown to enhance behavioural and cognitive recovery following many types of brain damage in animals (Rose, 1988; Will & Kelche, 1992). A more hi-tech approach to increase engagement, virtual reality (VR) technology, provides a powerful means of controlling the individual's direct interaction with a specified environment, using either immersive or desk-top instruments (Kalawsky, 1993). The vital characteristic of VR is that it is interactive, with every response that the user makes having a consequence to which he/she must adapt in terms of mental processes and behaviour. Moreover, since interaction with the virtual environment can be made contingent upon whatever motor capacity the patient has, this technology is particularly well-suited to this therapeutic application. The application of VR to brain-damaged patients offers a unique and potentially powerful way of increasing the quantity and quality of physical activity by controlling environmental interaction (Rose & Johnson, 1994).

LITIGATION ISSUES

For those who suffer brain injury by assault, accident or negligence, a carefully conducted claim has the potential to influence outcome significantly. The process of litigation for personal injury compensation requires the same careful consideration and communication as all other aspects of care after brain injury. From choosing the right expert early (Aitken & Johnson, 1996), to requesting interim payments to help with rehabilitation, and ensuring that all potential areas of long-term need are assessed, the key is an appropriate assessment of need, in the general sense. As Braithwaite (Chapter 7) suggests, effective communication and a common basis of understanding is as important to the litigation process as it is to clinical rehabilitation.

The age of the patient is of particular importance in litigation as there appears to be no appropriate vehicle by which children who suffer traumatic brain injury may receive periodic assessments of need and commensurate awards over a long period. The current system of Provisional Damages appears to require a risk of clinical deterioration to be present, a situation not applicable to the vast majority of children. The Criminal Injuries Compensation Scheme was revised in 1991 (Duff, 1991), yet it appears that no specific consideration was given to the long-term needs of children. The Government's recent proposals to introduce a tariff system for compensating victims of crime is of major importance to the outcome of children. A contemporaneous case report (*The Times*, 14 February 1994) showed that the difference in an award was over five times greater under the existing system (£1.3 million) than would have been awarded under the new proposals (£250 000). In personal injury litigation consideration of the problems raised by damage to the immature brain offers considerable potential to improve the outcome of thousands of brain-injured children each year (Johnson, Pentland & Glasgow, 1996).

Whilst it may be argued that expert witness representation in the individual cases of traumatic brain injury is an effective way of informing the legal profession about the critical factors of age and recovery, experience has shown that this is not the case. For every case that reaches the High Court or Court of Session, there are many more which are settled beforehand. Braithwaite's suggestion (Chapter 7) that both sides (expert and lawyer) should know something about the other side of the coin is the most prudent step forward. Provision of information to fill in gaps in knowledge, correct misinformation and facilitate greater understanding and collaboration between disciplines will undoubtedly contribute to ensuring an improved outcome for all those with traumatic brain injury.

LEGISLATIVE ISSUES

Prevention will always be better than cure in the case of brain injury (e.g. Grimard, Nolan & Carlin, 1995). Barnes (Chapter 8) discusses some of the main approaches to injury prevention. Within the area of legislative considerations also it is necessary to take account of the relationship between age of the patient and the consequences of brain injury. Take, for example, the education of the brain-injured child. The persistence of cognitive disabilities caused by brain injury impedes the child's progress in education and, as time since injury lengthens and the level of education increases (e.g. primary school through to university), the demands placed upon the damaged brain will increase disproportionately to its residual capacity and abilities. Several investigators have documented the increased need for special educational programmes, the failure to return to school and the need to be placed a year below (Johnson & Furlonger, 1989). Jones & Johnson (1994) reported that, despite an early indication of a complete recovery, on their return to school many head-injured children required additional help, formal Statementing and Special Needs provision. A particular difficulty in the Statementing process, however, is the absence of an identified classification for children with traumatic brain injury. Snow & Hooper (1994) refer to recent legislative changes in the USA whereby traumatically brain-injured children have been allocated a new Exceptional Children classification. The absence of special provision for the head-injured child in education and rehabilitation may parallel a more general situation for long-term care (e.g. Report of the Health Service Commissioner, 1994) which appears to be characterised by 'ping-pong responsibility', whereby health, education or social services each believe it is the responsibility of the other to provide the appropriate care. Clearly, it would be advantageous for the various agencies concerned with provision of services to communicate and plan accordingly for long-term care.

COMMUNICATION AND COLLABORATION

In recovery and rehabilitation there is a very substantial excess of questions over answers about effective interventions and ways in which to improve outcome, and yet rehabilitation continues in the absence of any theoretical basis or framework. It will be self-evident that the complexity of issues arising from traumatic brain injury is such that there are limits to the advances that can be achieved by any one discipline alone. Effective intervention requires collaboration between and within disciplines, which demands effective communication at a professional, as well as a personal level. In turn, communication requires a common terminology and frame of reference — simply that we all talk about the same thing in the same terms. The 'neuro' of neurological rehabilitation is in danger of being neglected by those in daily contact with the brain-injured patient, confronted by the overt face of suffering not only in the individual patient but also in the spouse and children or parents and siblings.

A fundamental obstacle to effective multidisciplinary or interdisciplinary communication is awareness and respect for another's profession and the contribution that it can make to patient care. For much more is at stake than simply interprofessional or mutual admiration; to otherwise independent and perhaps initially conflicting or overlapping approaches and opinions is given the opportunity to interact, simply by the vehicle of a common-based communication. Interactive combinations can lead to intervariable influences and rearrangement, with the result of a new, perhaps improved variable, creating the opportunities for a significantly changed perspective and, dare one say, the challenge and excitement that come from working with a different perspective on an old problem.

We have previously suggested that a different perspective on neurological injury and recovery may yield a more effective communication system and facilitate greater interaction and collaboration (Rose & Johnson, 1992). Progress in this complex and challenging field has been impeded by the lack of understanding and misinformation. It is not unreasonable that a common denominator should be the brain and that, by adopting that basis, all those involved in neurological rehabilitation will develop a common terminology and basis of understanding. Is the nurse's use of the term 'concentration' the same as that of the occupational therapist or psychologist, for example, and are the terms 'recovery' and 'outcome' used to convey the same meaning or information to patients and relatives? The adoption of a common and agreed taxonomy will improve communication simply by clarifying what we are all talking about. Bach y Rita (1989) suggested that the rehabilitation process has been the weak link in the health care revolution, and that increased survival has not been accompanied by commensurate improvements in quality of life. Let us now take the opportunity to redress that situation and work together towards an improved outcome for all brain injury survivors and their families.

REFERENCES

Aitken, C. & Johnson, D. A. (1996). The expert witness. In *Head Injury and Litigation* (Eds. Johnson, D. A., Pentland, B. & Glasgow, E.). London: Sweet and Maxwell.

Astrand, P. & Rodal, C. K. (1977). *Textbook of Work Physiology — Physiological Basis of Exercise.* Singapore: McGraw Hill.

Bach y Rita, P. (1989). Theory-based neurorehabilitation. *Archives of Physical Medicine and Rehabilitation,* **70**, 162.

Bach y Rita, P. (1994). The brain beyond the synapse: a review. *Neuro Report,* **5**, 1553–1557.

Bakker, D. J. (1984). The brain as a dependent variable. *Journal of Clinical and Experimental Neuropsychology,* **6**(1), 1–16.

Barry, S. R. (1991) Clinical implications of basic neuroscience research, II: NMDA receptors and neurotrophic factors. *Archives of Physical Medicine and Rehabilitation,* **72**, 1095–1101.

Bell, D. S. (1992). *Medico-Legal Assessment of Head Injury.* Springfield, Illinois: Charles C. Thomas.

Blackburn, H. & Jacobs, D. R. (1988). Physical activity and the risk of coronary heart disease. *New England Journal of Medicine,* **319**, 1217-1219.

Brooks, N., Campsie, L., Symmington, C., Beattie, A. & McKinlay, W. (1987). Return to work within the first seven years after severe head injury. *Brain Injury,* **1**, 5–11.

Cardenas, D. D., McLean, A., Farrell-Roberts, L., Baker, L., Brooke, M. & Haselkarn, J. (1994) Oral physostigmine and impaired memory in adults with brain injury. *Brain Injury,* **8**(7), 579–588.

Cope, D. N. (1994). An integration of psychopharmacological and rehabilitation approaches to traumatic brain injury rehabilitation. *Journal of Head Trauma Rehabilitation*, **9**(3), 1–18.

Crawford, J. R., Johnson, D. A. & Myalchiuv, L. (1994). WAIS-R performance in closed-head injury. *Proceedings of the British Psychological Society*, **2**(2), 57.

Crepeau, F. & Scherzer, P. (1993). Predictors and indicators of work status after traumatic brain injury: a meta-analysis. *Neuropsychological Rehabilitation*, **3**(1), 5–35.

Deaton, A. V. (1993). Predicting outcomes: the slippery slope. *Brain Injury*, **7**(2), 99–100.

Duff, P. (1991) *Criminal Injuries Compensation*. London: Butterworths.

Duffy, E. (1972). Activation. In *Handbook of Psychophysiology* (Eds. Greenfield, N. S. & Sternbach, R. A.). New York: Holt Reinhart Wilson, Chapter 15.

English, T. C. (1904). The after-effects of head-injuries. *Lancet*, **February 20**, 485–489.

Fenn, P., Herman, D. & Dingwall, R. (1994). Estimating the cost of compensating victims of medical negligence. *British Medical Journal*, **309**, 389–391.

Fordyce, D. E. and Farrar, R. P. (1991). Physical activity effects on hippocampal and parietal cortical cholinergic function and spatial learning in F344 rats. *Behavioural Brain Research*, **43** 115–123.

Goldstein, M. (1990). The decade of the brain. *Neurology*, **40**, 321.

Grimard, G., Nolan, T. & Carlin, J. B. (1995). Head injury in helmeted child bicyclists. *Injury Prevention*, **1**, 21–25.

Hahn, Y. S. & McLone, D. G. (1993). Risk factors in the outcome of children with minor head injury. *Paediatric Neurosurgery*, **19**, 135–142.

Hart, K. & Faust, D. (1988). Prediction of the effects of mild head injury: a message about the Kennard Principle. *Journal of Clinical Psychology*, **44**(5), 780–782.

Hayes, R. L., Jenkin, L. W. & Lyeth, B. G. (1992) Neurotransmitter-mediated mechanisms of traumatic brain injury: acetylcholine and excitatory amino acids. *Journal of Neurotrauma*, **9** (Suppl. 1), S173–S187.

Jankowski, L. W. & Sullivan, S. J. (1990). Aerobic and neuromuscular training: effect on the capacity, efficiency and fatigability of patients with traumatic brain injuries. *Archives of Physical Medicine and Rehabilitation*, **71**, 500–504.

Johnson, D. A., Roethig-Johnston, K. & Richards, D. (1993). Biochemical parameters of recovery in acute severe head injury. *British Journal of Neurosurgery*, **7**, 53–60.

Johnson, D. A., Campbell, C. & Wright, P. Age and recovery: beliefs of medical school practitioners (in preparation).

Johnson, D. A., Pentland, B. & Glasgow, E. (1996). *Head Injury and Litigation*. London: Sweet and Maxwell.

Johnson, D. A. & Furlonger, R. (1989). Return to school. In *Children's Head Injury: Who Cares?* (Eds. Johnson, D. A., Uttley, D. & Wyke, M. A.). Hove: Lawrence Erlbaum Associates, Chapter 12, pp. 147–162.

Jones, A. & Johnson, D. A. (1994). A study of the educational provision for head injured children. *British Journal of Special Education*, **21**(3), 113–117.

Kalawsky, R. S. (1990). *The Science of Virtual Reality and Virtual Environments*. Wokingham: Addison-Wesley.

Klove, H. (1987). Arousal, activation and effort in neuropsychological rehabilitation. *Journal of Clinical and Experimental Neuropsychology*, **9**, 297–309.

Kolb, B. & Wishaw, I. Q. (1989). Plasticity in the neo-cortex: mechanisms underlying recovery from early brain change. *Progress in Neurobiology*, **32**, 235–276.

Law Commission Consultation Paper No. 125 (1992). *Structured Settlements and Interim and Provisional Damages*. London: HMSO.

Law Commission Report No. 225 (1994). *Personal Injury Compensation: How Much is*

Enough? London: HMSO.

Langfitt, T. W. & Gennarelli, T. A. (1982). Can the outcome from head injury be improved? *Journal of Neurosurgery*, **96**, 19–25.

Lezak, M. D. (1988). IQ: RIP. *Journal of Clinical and Experimental Neuropsychology*, **10**(3), 351–361.

Lezak, M. D. (1995). *Neuropsychological Assessment*. New York: Oxford University Press, 3rd edn.

Long, C. J. & Ross, L. K. (1992). *Handbook of Head Trauma: Acute Care to Recovery*. New York: Plenum Press.

Luria, A. R. (1973). *The Working Brain*. Harmondsworth: Penguin.

Mahoney, W. J., D'Souza, B. J., Haller, A., Rogers, M. C,. Epstein, M. H. & Freeman, J. M. (1983). Long term outcome of children with severe head trauma and prolonged coma. *Paediatrics*, **71**(5), 756–762.

Martinsen, E. W. (1990). Benefits of exercise in the treatment of depression. *Sports Medicine*, **9**, 380–389.

McPherson, K., Berry, A. & Pentland, B. (submitted). Relationships between cognitive impairments and functional performance after brain injury, as measured by the Functional Assessment Measure (FIM and FAM).

Mapou, R. L. (1988). An integrated approach to the neuropsychological assessment of cognitive function. In *Cognitive Approaches to Neuropsychology* (Eds. Williams, J. M. & Long, C. L.). New York: Plenum Press, pp. 101–122.

McIntosh, T. K. (1993). Novel pharmacological therapies in the treatment of experimental traumatic brain injury: a review. *Journal of Neurotrauma*, **10**(3), 215–261.

Neeper, S. A., Gomez-Pinilla, F., Choi, J. & Cotman, C. (1995). Exercise and neurotrophins. *Nature*, **373**, 109.

Ommaya, A. K. & Gennarelli, T. A. (1974). Cerebral concussion and traumatic unconsciousness: correlations of experimental and clinical observations on blunt head injuries. *Brain*, **97**, 633–654.

Povlishock, J. T. & Coburn, T. H. (1989). Morphological change associated with mild head injury. In *Mild Head Injury* (Eds. Levin, H. S., Eisenberg, H. M. & Benton, A. L.). New York: Oxford University Press, Chapter 4, pp. 37–53.

Renner, M. J. & Rosenzweig, M. R. (1987). Enriched and Impoverished Environments: Effects on Brain and Behaviour. New York: Springer Verlag.

Report of the Health Service Commissioner (1994). *Failure to Provide Long-term NHS Care for a Brain Damaged Patient*. London: HMSO.

Rose, F. D. (1988). Environmental enrichment and recovery of function following brain damage in the rat. *Medical Science Research*, **16**, 257–263.

Rose, F. D. & Johnson, D. A. (Eds) (1992). *Recovery From Brain Damage: Reflections and Directions*. New York: Plenum Press.

Rose, F. D. & Johnson, D. A. (1994). Virtual reality in brain damage rehabilitation. *Medical Science Research*, **22**(2), 82.

Rosenberg, R. N. & Rowland, L. P. (1990). The 1990s — Decade of the Brain and the need for a national priority. *Neurology*, **40**, 322.

Ross, L. K. (1992). The use of pharmacology in the treatment of head injured patients. In *Handbook of Head Trauma: Acute Care to Recovery* (Eds. Long, C. J. & Ross, L. K.). New York: Plenum Press, pp. 139–164.

Ruff, R. M., Marshall, L. F., Crouch, J., Klauber, M. R., Levin, H. S., Borth, J., Kreutzer, J., Blunt, B. A., Foulkes, M. A., Eisenberg, H. M., Jane, J. A. & Marmarou, A. (1993). Predictors of outcome following severe head trauma: follow-up data from the Traumatic Coma Data Bank. *Brain Injury*, **7**(2), 101–112.

Seraganian, P. (Ed.) (1993). *Exercise Psychology: the Influence of Physical Exercise on Psychological Processes.* New York: John Wiley.

Snoek, J. W. (1989). Mild head injury in children. In *Mild Head Injury* (Eds. Levin, H. S., Eisenberg, H. M. & Benton, A. L.). New York: Oxford University Press, pp. 102–131.

Snow, J. H. & Hooper, S. R. (1994). *Paediatric Traumatic Brain Injury.* Thousand Oaks, California: Sage.

Taylor, E. (1989). Disorders of self-regulation in head injured children. In *Children's Head Injury: Who Cares?* (Eds. Johnson, D. A., Uttley, D. & Wyke, M. A.). Hove: Lawrence Erlbaum Associates, Chapter 9, pp. 111–120.

Tinson, D. (1989). How stroke patients spend their days. *International Disability Studies,* **11**, 45–49.

Wagner, E. H, LaCroix, A. Z., Buchner, D. M. & Larson, E. B. (1992). Effects of physical activity on health status in older adults. I: Observational studies. *Annual Review of Public Health,* **13**, 451–468.

Webb, C., Rose. F. D. & Johnson, D. A. (1995). Age and recovery from brain injury: clinical opinions and experimental evidence, *Brain Injury* (in press).

Weitzman, P. (1994). The compensation experiences of victims of personal injury. *Quantum,* **6**, 4–5.

Whyte, J. (1994). Toward rational psychopharmacological treatment: integrating research and clinical practice. *Journal of Head Trauma Rehabilitation,* **9**(3), 91–103.

Will, B. & Kelche, C. (1992). Environmental approaches to recovery of function from brain damage: a review of animal studies (1981–1991). In *Recovery From Brain Damage* (Eds. Rose, F. D. & Johnson, D. A.). New York: Plenum Press, pp. 79–104.

Wolman, R. L., Cornwall, C., Fulcher, K. & Greenwood, R. (1994). Aerobic training in brain injured patients. *Clinical Rehabilitation,* **8**, 253–257.

Wroblewski, B. A. & Glenn, M. B. (1994). Pharmacological treatment of arousal and cognitive deficits. *Journal of Head Trauma Rehabilitation,* **9**(3), 19–42.

Zangwill, O. L. (1947). Psychological aspects of rehabilitation in cases of brain injury. *British Journal of Psychology,* **37**, 60–69.

INDEX